MW00490080

JOURNEY AMONG BRAVE MEN

Also by Dana Adams Schmidt

Anatomy of a Satellite
Yemen: The Unknown War
Armageddon in the Middle East

JOURNEY AMONG BRAVE MEN

Dana Adams Schmidt

Grove Press
New York

Published simultaneously in Canada
Printed in the United States of America

First published in hardcover in 1964 by the Atlantic Monthly Press in association with Little, Brown and Company

First Grove Atlantic trade paperback edition: October 2018

The author wishes to thank the *New York Times* for permission to reprint here in greatly expanded form an account which was originally introduced in its pages.

Library of Congress Cataloguing-in-Publication data available for this title.

ISBN: 978-0-8021-2590-3
eISBN: 978-0-8021-4676-2

Grove Press
an imprint of Grove Atlantic
154 West 14th Street
New York, NY 10011

Distributed by Publishers Group West

groveatlantic.com

18 19 20 21   10 9 8 7 6 5 4 3 2 1

to Tania

CONTENTS

FOREWORD

"I went ahead with plans to cover what I considered
the greatest story in the Middle East, a story of violence
and heroism, of intrigue, of brave men fighting against
great odds, a story of great significance in the struggle
between East and West."

—Dana Adams Schmidt,
Journey Among Brave Men

Dana Adams Schmidt was that rare phenomenon among
foreign correspondents, someone who loved the people he
covered and was loved in return. His affection for the Kurdish people shines from every page of this book. Subsequent
Kurdophile writers—among them the indefatigable Jonathan
Randal, Gwynne Roberts, Christopher Hitchens, Gérard Chal-
iand, John Bulloch, Harvey Morris, Edward Mortimer, Chris
Kutshera, David McDowall, Jim Hoagland and myself—are
in his debt. His travels among the Kurds, though treading in
the intrepid footprints of Victorian adventurers, was the first
in the post-colonial era to bring Kurdish life to the attention
of the world outside their forlorn mountains in Turkey, Iran,
Iraq and Syria.

This classic of travel, political reportage and exploration
invites the reader to double admiration: of the Kurds and of
the man who wrote about them. It was no easy feat for anyone
in 1964 to smuggle himself into General Abdel Karim Kassem's
revolutionary Iraq and risk his life beside mountain warriors
under bombardment from the Iraqi air force. In his review of
the first edition of the book in 1964, James, later Jan, Morris
wrote, "It is not often nowadays that eminent foreign correspondents steal away on borrowed mules into forbidden territories,

leaving no forwarding address and revealing no details of their route." Schmidt disappeared from Beirut on 4 July 1962 and returned on 1 September, a fifty-nine-day disappearance that few editors would tolerate. For Schmidt and his newspaper, the *New York Times*, the story justified the time invested: his reporting won him the George Polk Award for the "best reporting requiring exceptional courage and enterprise abroad."

Journalists in 1960s Beirut congregated in the bar of the seaside Hôtel Saint Georges. A few reported to Langley as often as they did to their newspapers, and most showed no interest in a minor war in a backwater of the Iraqi hinterland. Schmidt received a call from the Kurds and held his first meeting with them at the Saint Georges. Their offer of a trip to Iraqi Kurdistan attracted him, but the US Embassy countered with official advice: "Don't do it. It would embarrass the American government if you got into trouble. It would embarrass the government even if you got through without any trouble." That was enough for any enterprising correspondent to head straight there. Schmidt did.

Aged 47, he was not a youngster out to make his name. His coverage of World War II in North Africa, Sicily, and France, as well as of the post-war conflicts in Eastern Europe and Palestine, had secured him the coveted Beirut bureau chief posting. He had a wife and an eight-year-old son. The probability he would not return was high, but his curiosity about a story his colleagues ignored was strong. The injustice that the Kurds suffered in Turkey, Iran, and Iraq outraged him. He wrote,

> Although the Kurds, not only of Iraq, but of Turkey and Iran, and Syria had quite evidently been denied most human, cultural and political rights, the diplomats felt that United States treaty commitments to support Turkey and Iran prevented them from doing anything, even from saying anything to help or sympathize with the Kurds.

Schmidt's journey was a quest. Its goal was a Stanley-meets-Livingstone encounter with the dynamic and mercurial leader of the Kurdish rebellion, the turbaned Mulla Mustafa Barzani. This legendary figure, whose son Massoud became president of Iraq's autonomous Kurdistan Regional Government in 2005, had troubled both Iran and Iraq for decades. The ancient hostility between Persians and Arabs, as well as between Turks and Persians, abated only in relation to their shared determination to deprive the Kurds of self-government and cultural freedom. The US had good relations with Turkey and Iran and wanted better relations with the regime in Baghdad. Schmidt was hoping to open American eyes to the harm those governments were doing to the largest ethnic group on earth without a state of its own.

The elder Barzani was not an obvious choice to lead the struggle for Kurdish nationalism. Schmidt quoted William Eagleton, an American diplomat who fell under the Kurdish spell while living in Kirkuk in the mid-1950s and wrote on Kurdish rugs and the short-lived Kurdish Republic in Iran: "The Barzani tribe itself consisted in 1906—when Mulla Mustafa was an infant—of only 750 families, but was expanded soon thereafter from various additional tribes who looked to the Sheikh of Barzan as their religious guide and master."

The tiny village of Barzan in the Zagros Mountains in what until 1918 was the Ottoman Empire was too small for its leaders to disrupt the balance among larger Kurdish tribes like the Jaf and the Surchi. Thus did Mulla Mustafa take up the mantle of uniting many of the tribes into a nationalist movement in the colonial era, first against the British in Iraq and then against the Shah of Iran. In 1946, he crossed the border with loyal followers to become minister of defense in what became known as the Mehabad Republic. When the Shah, with American approval, crushed it out of existence, Mulla Mustafa had to take refuge in the only country that had supported his revolution, the Soviet Union. He returned to Iraq after twelve years of exile, when the army deposed the British-aligned monarchy. The new dictator, Abdel Karim Kassem, held out the hope of Kurdish autonomous existence that the British and the kings of Iraq had not permitted. Kassem failed to deliver, and Barzani took up arms in 1961.

Schmidt at six-feet, three-inches and with blue eyes, wearing a seersucker suit in the days when journalists wore suits, was a hard man for his Kurdish guides to disguise. They took him across the border and eventually found Kurdish clothes large enough for him. To avoid the notice of Baghdad's spies, they moved at night. Hospitality and fascinating conversation awaited him in every village, along with Kurdish flatbread and yoghurt. It would be wrong to pre-empt Schmidt's own account by telling more of the tale here, but I must yield to an impulse to mention that, following one missed rendezvous after another, Schmidt met the leader.

> Barzani appeared about nine o'clock in the morning, suddenly and unexpectedly, from behind the place where I was sitting, so that he was there and sitting down in the place selected for him even before I could scramble to my feet. He was unshaven and seemed to be preoccupied. He devoted the barest minimum of words to greeting us, a sharp and rather deflating change from the flowery greetings to which I had grown accustomed at every stage of my progress across the country.

The conversation went on for hours, then days. Barzani, master of diplomacy as of war, spoke in riddles and sagas that to Schmidt's ears had "a cryptic, delphic quality." When Schmidt called him *Mon Général*, the old man turned to an aide and said, "I am not a general. I am just Mustafa." That was true for the visiting journalist from a country Barzani was courting, but Schmidt noticed that his men called him *Mamusta*, an honorific meaning roughly "professor." Kurdish men usually call one another *Kak*, "brother."

The only false note in the book is the final sentence, "And yet, in Kurdistan in the spring of 1964, the really important thing is that there is a chance for peace." Sadly, that was no more true then than it is now. Ten years after Schmidt wrote, the US gave military aid to the Kurds in an effort to pressure the regime in Baghdad to cede to the Shah of Iran the borderline he wanted along the Shatt al-Arab waterway. Saddam Hussein made the concession in March 1975, which prompted the Shah to close his border to Iraq's Kurds and US Secretary of State Henry Kissinger to cut all aid to them. The inevitable massacres followed. Barzani's family had to beg the US to permit him into the country for medical treatment, and no American officials would meet him. It was a shameful episode in American policy, but worse was to come. When Saddam Hussein murdered Kurdish civilians with chemical weapons in the village of Hallabja in 1988, the US denied the event had taken place and later blamed Iran.

Then came 1991 and the defeat of the Iraqi Army in Kuwait. George Bush called on the people of Iraq "to take matters into their own hands, to force Saddam Hussein the dictator to step aside . . ." Trusting the US to deprive Saddam Hussein of the use of the skies, they rebelled north and south. The Kurds captured most of Iraqi Kurdistan, and the Shiites took the south. Both forces were converging on Baghdad by the middle of March. Suddenly, the US informed the Iraqi government it could use its helicopters. That brought the rebellion to an end, as Saddam's helicopters dropped barrel bombs that the Kurds feared were filled with chemical weapons and delivered troops to the rebellion's frontlines. Millions fled to Iran and Turkey. For Saddam, it was total victory. The country endured twelve years of crippling sanctions in which children died of malnutrition until the US invaded in 2003 when more deaths followed.

Despite the repeated betrayals, the Kurds in 2003 trusted the US as much as they had when Schmidt met Barzani in 1962. For once, their trust paid off. They created a semi-independent state in northern Iraq, but they face enemies in the form of the Islamic State that are as vicious and brutal as Saddam Hussein's regime was. And, once again, they ask why the US is depriving them of the equipment and weapons they need to defend themselves effectively. The reason is what it was in 1962: America's desire not to offend Turkey, which launched another war against its own Kurds and attacked the Kurds in Syria. The US looked the other way when, after an ill-conceived referendum supporting Kurdish independence from Iraq, the American-allied Baghdad government seized Kirkuk and took control of the Kurds' airports and borders. Schmidt would not have been surprised.

—Charles Glass, 2018

AUTHOR'S NOTE

I want to express my special gratitude for the help I received in writing this book:

To Ahmed Tofiq, who was at the beginning of it, who organized my expedition to Kurdistan, and was my guide as far as Mullah Mustafa Barzani's headquarters;

To Apo Jomart, who was my interpreter and companion, and gave me my first insight into Kurdish history;

To Father Thomas Bois, the remarkable Dominican Father who has devoted a lifetime to the study of Kurds, and who supplied me with a wealth of materials on the history of the Kurds and their folklore, and who read large parts of the manuscript. I have made extensive use of his works, including *Les Kurdes, Histoire, Sociologie, Littérature, Folklore;*

To Shawkat Akrawi, one of Mullah Mustafa's representatives in the negotiations with the Iraqi government in Baghdad, who later became one of his representatives abroad, and who provided valuable assistance in compiling the political parts of the book; and

To Jelal Talabani, who combines the qualities of fighting leader and diplomatic representative of the Kurdish cause, and who gave me valuable guidance.

Particular valuable reference works have been, on the ancient history of the Kurds, *Kurds and Kurdistan,* by Arshak Safrastian, London, The Harvill Press, Ltd., 1948; and the classic work of C. J. Edmonds, *Kurds, Turks and Arabs,* London, Oxford University Press, 1957; and William Eagleton, Jr.'s *The Kurdish Republic of 1946,* London, Oxford University Press, 1963, which lighted up a little known episode in the history of the Kurds.

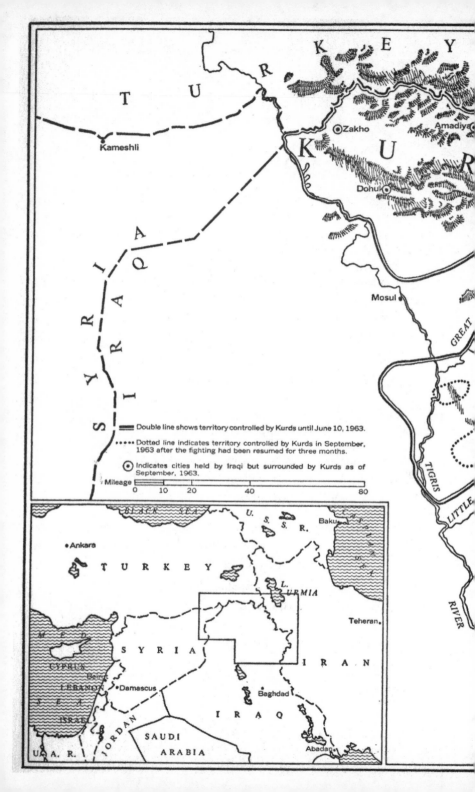

JOURNEY AMONG
BRAVE MEN

1

Phone Call from a Stranger

One balmy evening in May 1962, my wife Tania and I were leaving our home in Beirut, Lebanon, to go out to dinner, when the telephone rang. A man with an urgent manner announced that he had a message for me from General Mustafa Barzani, the leader of the Kurdish revolutionary forces in Iraq. The man wanted to see me.

Now the Kurds were—and are—a subject of mystery, romance and speculation. They are the inaccessible people of the mountains of northern Iraq, eastern Turkey and western Iran. For more than half a year General Barzani had been leading the Kurds of Iraq in rebellion against the Iraqi government. I, like every other correspondent in the Middle East, had written about it. But the truth was hard to come by. No reporter had ever seen the Kurdish forces; no reporter had visited the Kurdish people during this war; no reporter had been to see General Barzani. I felt a sense of shock, and elation. But I was also suspicious. Beirut is full of frauds, agents and *agents provocateurs*.

"Who are you?" I asked.

"I come from General Barzani's headquarters," he replied, evading a direct answer to my question. He spoke in thick but determined and understandable French, which made me even more suspicious. While French is commonly spoken in Lebanon and Syria, which were once ruled by France, English is more likely to be spoken by a Kurd of Iraq, where British influence has long predominated. Nonetheless, I made an appointment—out in the open—in the lobby of the St. George hotel. I wanted no tricks in shadowy corners. If the man was genuine let him show himself. General Barzani's representative hesitated, but agreed.

That was the beginning of an odyssey that was to take most of the rest of the summer. I met the man and two, three, sometimes four of his associates a dozen or more times—but not in hotel lobbies. I was soon convinced of their genuineness and of their need for obscurity.

They had met me in the St. George lobby, under the ever watchful eyes of a variety of observers, because they wanted very much to make the contact. But thereafter they urged more private meetings. They feared the agents of Premier Kassem, who would certainly have been prepared to kidnap or kill to head off this mission on behalf of General Barzani.

For this reason I did not insist on full identification from my Kurdish friends. Their leader once let me address him as "Murad" on an envelope of clippings I left him at a hotel desk. The others remained nameless and I did not ask unnecessary questions about identities, where they came from and how. I wanted to win their confidence just as they wanted to win mine.

They were very serious-faced, deeply tanned young men, each of them wearing a closely clipped, black mustache, and a very correct black suit. They were highly nervous, and sometimes, in the middle of our conversation, would suggest a move from one café to another, or from one parking place to another. They preferred the privacy of homes.

Barzani's message was that he wanted to invite Western newspapermen to visit him and his forces in the mountains of Iraqi Kurdistan. He would provide guides, guards, interpreters and transportation—everything. Clearly Barzani was anxious to present his cause to the Western world, with the ultimate hope of receiving American aid in his fight for political self-determination for the Kurds.

His message was addressed to the entire Western press, and several correspondents, particularly James Wilde of *Time* magazine, toyed with the idea. Our Kurdish friends tried to make it seem quite easy. They talked about an expedition of seven days. But as we probed for details it became evident that they did not know exactly where Barzani was. The trip might take seven days, or twenty-seven, or more.* We would ride horses or mules five, six, maybe more hours daily. We would probably be machine-gunned and bombed by the Iraqi air force. It would be dangerous.

One by one the other newsmen dropped out except for a Swiss named Richard Anderegg, of the Swiss Broadcasting Network, and a German, Hans Ferra, of the West German Television Network, and me. I had originally invited Anderegg to accompany me, with the thought that noncompetitive company would be more than welcome on such an expedition. But Anderegg, having obtained an assignment to do the script for television coverage in collaboration with Ferra, preferred to work independently. We parted company and they made their way into Kurdistan from a different country and by a shorter and quicker route. They left Barzani about a week before I got there.

Once I had made my personal decision my problem was to consult my home office in New York privately without tipping off my colleagues and a variety of Middle Eastern intelligence services who might wish to interfere.

I did so in a message through private channels to Nat Gerstenzang, the *New York Times* assistant foreign editor who was at the time filling in for Foreign Editor Emanuel Freedman in New York. In my message I said: "Someone will doubtless soon pick up this offer, and it might as well be me."

* In the end the trip took fifty-nine days from departure from Beirut on July 4 until my return on September 1. That included thirteen days getting from Beirut to the Iraqi border and later from the Iraqi border back to Beirut, thirty-six days on the move, mainly on mules and on horseback inside Kurdistan, and ten days at Barzani's headquarters. Because of my long absence from Beirut and reports published in the press that I had "disappeared in Kurdistan," the *New York Times* sent Mr. Richard Hunt, my predecessor as correspondent in the Middle East, out to look for me. He arrived in Beirut about a week before I reappeared and was planning trips to Damascus, Baghdad and Teheran for clues as to my fate.

Mr. Gerstenzang agreed to the trip with this caution: "I know you will take no inordinate risks that are not commensurate with the value of the story." A little later I also got approval from "Manny" Freedman personally. I met him in Istanbul, where he made a stopover during a tour of overseas posts.

Barzani's emissaries were young, eager and earnest, full of stories that bubbled through the barriers of their linguistic limitations. They spoke Kurdish among themselves, and most of the time worked through an Arabic interpreter, for, although their Arabic was limited, it was better than their English or French.

With infinite enthusiasm they told us how the Kurdish rebellion had started, why they fought and how. They told about petitions submitted in Baghdad, and rebuffed; of cultural rights promised, but not respected; of Kurdish schools shut down; of Kurdish officials, police, and soldiers transferred out of Kurdistan and replaced by Arabs from the South; of interference on the one hand, neglect on the other. They told how the government had stirred up some of the Kurds against others, how the Iraqi air force bombed Kurdish villages and how the army burned them. And they talked about their pride in what they believed to be their Indo-European ancestry, as distinguished from the Semitic ancestry of the Arabs against whom they were fighting. Although these young guerillas were hardly scholars, they spoke with pride about Kurdish princes and poets and the ancient reputation of the Kurds as warriors. All that they said was meant as an argument for Western journalists to come to Kurdistan and see for themselves.

Kurdish nationalism has grown slowly because the Kurds are geographically remote, lacking a seacoast, divided and compartmented by high mountains and narrow valleys, by fierce tribal loyalties and antagonisms. Their intellectual and cultural development has been delayed by geographical dispersion and lack of intercommunication which have given rise to several linguistic variants; by lack of a major urban focus; by centuries-long identification with the Ottoman Empire in the guise of Islamic solidarity; by systematic repression.

In spite of all this, Kurdish nationalism has shown itself

unsuppressible. Within the Ottoman and Persian Empires twenty-eight Kurdish principalities—successors to the ancient kingdoms of Gutium and of the Kassites—led a quasi-independent existence during the Middle Ages, and in a few cases until about a century ago.

In its modern form Kurdish nationalism appeared first in political clubs and periodicals in Constantinople after the Young Turk Revolution of 1908. Kurdish hopes of national resurgence rose to their highest point in the Treaty of Sèvres of 1920. They were dashed by the Treaty of Lausanne in 1923. And they were ground underfoot by the Turkish republic, which from 1925 to 1937 systematically destroyed the Kurdish tribal structure, deported, imprisoned and executed the Kurdish elite, and dispersed the Kurdish people. The treatment they received at the hands of the Turks during this period was for the Kurds an unmitigated national disaster.

But always the Kurds remained defiant; always they fought. In the 1930's a new fighting leader of the Kurds appeared. He was Mullah Mustafa Barzani, perhaps the most significant of all the Kurdish national leaders. He fought the Iraqi government and the British in the 1930's and '40's; he defended the Mehabad republic against the Persian army in 1946; and after twelve years of refuge in the Soviet Union returned to Iraq where, since September 1961, he has been leading his people in what may prove to be a climactic struggle.

Struggle for what? The struggle is for their right to live as Kurds, to speak their own language, have their own schools, wear their national costume, develop their own culture. This is the essential aim. Barzani does not ask for independence. Although in anger he sometimes uses the word "independence," and threatens to "separate" from the Iraqi republic, in quieter moments he recognizes that Iraqi Kurdistan could not live alone, that the Kurds of Iraq must live together with the Arabs of Iraq if both are to prosper. Barzani asks only for autonomy—states' rights—local self-government, as part of the Iraqi republic.

Although the Kurds of Turkey and Iran are obviously as dear to him as those of Iraq, Barzani does not speak for them now. He considers it best for his cause for them to keep quiet. He believes that if he can win Kurdish rights in Iraq the Kurds of Turkey and Iran will be able to settle their demands by peaceful political means.

I had little doubt that once inside Kurdish territory Barzani's men would be able to care for any visitor. But they could not do much toward solving the problem of how to get there. It was, after all, the screen set up around the Kurds by Arabs, Turks and Iranians that made them so mysterious. But for that screen they would already have had many visitors.

To solve this problem I set off on a series of reconnaissances to the four countries from which one might enter Iraqi Kurdistan—Turkey, Syria, Iran and the state of Iraq itself. I even made a trip to Rome to visit a man I thought might be helpful in breaking through this screen.

These reconnaissances gave me a lively appreciation of the Kurds' isolation. It is not just that Kurdistan has no ports and no airports, that the roads to Kurdistan are blocked by the Iraqi army and by determined border guards in Syria, Turkey and Iran. No one in any of these countries would help—except, of course, the Kurds themselves, who maintain an underground network of organizations and communications. Although I found individuals who admired and even felt affection for the Kurdish people, I could find no government official willing to help the Kurds or willing to help me reach them. Among governments in the area, it seemed, they have not a single friend.

Turkey and Iran, who have fought the Kurds for many generations, fear that the revolt in Kurdish Iraq will spread to the much larger Kurdish communities in their own territories. I would estimate that while there are probably somewhat less than 2,000,000 Kurds in Iraq, Iran has 3,000,000 or 4,000,000 and Turkey more than 5,000,000. Syria has along its northern border and eastern tip more than 300,000 while the Soviet Union is said to have a Kurdish community of 175,000. That would total more than 10,000,000.*

* The Kurds themselves usually claim 12,000,000 altogether. William Eagleton, Jr., the State Department official, in his recent *The Kurdish*

The British and the Americans in the Middle East were no more helpful than local officials. Because of their links to the Central Treaty Organization (CENTO) they feel obliged to avoid offending Turkey and Iran.

In the course of my travels I confidentially consulted several State Department officials about my proposed expedition to Kurdistan. Their official advice was: "Don't do it. It would embarrass the American government if you got into trouble. It would embarrass the government even if you got through without any trouble. We could do very little for you if you got caught by the Iraqis. Anyway, the story isn't worth it."

I realized that the officials had to take this line since they represented the United States government. They admitted that the United States was in any case uneasy about the Kurdish revolt. Although Americans like to think that their country stands for humanitarian principles, for democracy, for self-determination; although the Kurds, not only of Iraq, but of Turkey and Iran, and Syria had quite evidently been denied most human, cultural and political rights, the diplomats felt that United States treaty commitments to support Turkey and Iran prevented them from doing anything, even from saying anything to help or sympathize with the Kurds.

Still, I could not escape the feeling that privately my State Department friends hardly shared the State Department's official concern about being "embarrassed." I am glad to say that some of them seemed hugely intrigued by the possibility of such a trip to territories which they themselves could not possibly visit.

As I suspected at the time, my New York office had also consulted the State Department, had received much the same answer, and had come to conclusions identical with mine.

And so I replied to official cautions noncommittally. Secure in the knowledge that my own newspaper had approved, I went ahead with plans to cover what I considered the greatest story in the Middle East, a story of violence and heroism, of

---

Republic of 1946, offers estimates I consider very low: "5–6 million divided among Turkey (2–3 million), Iraq (1,200,000), Iran (1,500,000), Syria (200,000) and the U.S.S.R. (100,000)."

intrigue, of brave men fighting against great odds, a story of great significance in the struggle between East and West.

Apart from the Kurds, and Tania, I informed only two persons of my plans—my local assistant Ihsan Hijazi, who covered Beirut for me during my absence, and an American who, in case I got into trouble, would know at least exactly where and how I planned to go. To anyone who inquired about me Tania and Hijazi were to reply that I had gone to Libya to do a series of articles.

Tania was reconciled to a long absence of her husband, but, I thought, a little frightened. My son Dana, aged eight, sensed that something unusual was afoot. He clung anxiously as we said goodbye. "Bring me a present, Daddy," he said, and I replied, a little doubtfully, that I would try.

2

Into the Mountains of Kurdistan

On a scorching July evening in a certain town in a certain country I stood in a lighted window where I could be seen from the street. I had my suit coat on. This was a signal that I was ready to go. Then I went down to a street corner and waited for a man who, carrying a newspaper in his left hand, walked rapidly past and said, "*Bonjour.*" Next I returned to the hotel, got my baggage, consisting of a lightweight suitcase and an alpine pack, and sat in front of the hotel casually drinking beer out of a bottle. I watched for a car driven by the same man. After a few minutes he pulled up to the curb. I slipped in and we were off.

Shortly thereafter the cloak and dagger atmosphere of this beginning was complicated by a series of comic errors—which did not seem so funny at the time.

To begin with, we drove to a house where no one was home. We circled twice around the block. I could feel the driver's tenseness as he peered fixedly at the house, waiting for a light that did not appear. He did not speak but drove off again to another house, this one very old, built in the vaulted Arab style in one of the older parts of town. I followed him into a dimly lit, high-ceilinged room with many books piled on shelves. My contact man turned to me with an apologetic smile and spoke for the first time. "Stay here," he said in English and walked out quickly. A boy of four or five came and stared at me. An old man silently brought a cup of Turkish coffee and switched a radio to the news—in Russian. There I sat for half an hour on a ledge at one end of the room, growing more apprehensive by the second.

Then my contact man reappeared, and motioned me to follow. We walked to another car. "Get down low and out of sight," he said in a muffled voice. "I must not be seen with you." Later he explained that this was his father's house and he was of course known in the neighborhood, where questions might be asked about me. He had planned to change cars, to throw off anyone who might have observed my departure, but the second car would not start.

Hours later we stopped in the shadows of an unlighted farmhouse for dinner. The table had been laid in the garden, where it was shielded by the house from the street, and twelve or fifteen persons circulated around it, speaking in low voices. I was introduced to my host, a venerable gentleman and a distinguished leader among the Kurds of the region. At some risk to himself and, indeed, to us all, he had gathered together the Kurdish notables of the region to see me off in a manner they considered befitting the start of a great enterprise. One after another they shook my hand warmly and made little speeches assuring me that they and their people would ever be grateful to me, to my newspaper, and to my country for the trip I was undertaking, for the effort and the risk, to find out the truth about the Kurds. I tried to reply suitably that, on the contrary, it was I who felt privileged and honored by the trouble they had gone to on my behalf and on behalf of the *New York Times*.

Everyone was jumpy. At the sound of an unidentified footstep or a car we would fall silent. Once I heard a car pull up in front of the house and thought I heard the word "police," which seems to recur in many languages. My Kurdish friends heard it too and hustled me into a dark side room off the main corridor of the house. But it was a false alarm. The car pulled away again. And I never did find out why the word "police" was uttered.

Although I was far too nervous to do it justice, I tried to show that I appreciated the spread of succulent foods the

Kurds love so well. But I noticed the others were not eating with very much enthusiasm, either. My host lighted a dim kerosene lamp so we could help ourselves to the many dishes—chicken and mutton and rice; eggplant, grapes, dates, figs; milk, yoghurt, cheese and lots of sugary desserts. A fine spread and well meant—but not for us.

A young boy came in to say that the truck was ready and we had better get moving. At that moment, as I gathered together my belongings, I suddenly realized that my camera was missing. In vain we searched the car in which I had arrived. Obviously I had left it in the first car in which I had been picked up that night. My Kurdish friends were even more upset than I and one exclaimed: "The camera is after all the essential thing." He voiced a sentiment I often heard among the Kurds, that photographic proof of their existence, of their ways and deeds, was the surest evidence.

Much distressed, my Kurdish friends agreed to try to find the camera and to send it after us if possible. If they could not, they would buy another of a type that would be able to use the large supply of 120 film that I carried.

Then, with two young Kurds, I climbed into the cab of a big, much battered farm truck and we set off through the darkness toward Iraqi Kurdistan. The engine wheezed and roared. We lurched from side to side. I sat in the middle, well down in my seat, trying to be as inconspicuous as possible. Although someone had observed that there were Kurds who could match my height of six feet three inches and my blue eyes, I still was extremely conspicuous. For one thing, I was clean shaven, whereas every one of the Kurds wore a mustache. For another, I was wearing an American seersucker suit, whereas they wore a mixture of nondescript Western city clothes—leather jackets, sweaters, and occasional dark-colored business suits. They did not as a rule wear Kurdish national dress, partly because it is too heavy and woolly for the hot summer climate of this area, and partly because to identify oneself as a Kurd in any of the fringes of Kurdistan is asking for trouble. About my clothing there had been a misunderstanding. My contacts in Beirut had given me to understand that before I reached the border my guides would supply me with a Kurdish national costume. When I brought the matter up during dinner my friends said they had nothing to fit my height.

We talked about what we should say if we were to be stopped by police or by military checkpoints. I suggested that I might be visiting Kurdish friends quite innocently, to see what kind of life they led, but they shied away from any mention of their Kurdishness. They suggested that I might be up in this part of the country to investigate a story about a flood somewhere near the border. But why should we be traveling so late at night?

As we pondered this problem I noticed our driver muttering. "What?" I yelled. "Oh, never mind," he shouted above the noise of the engine, and then went on with a touch of bitterness in his voice: "After you've gone, you know, we are the ones who will have to deal with the police. But we've been taken in before. We've been beaten up before. That's what it's like being a Kurd."

I mention this remark because it was unusual. Expressions of bitterness and fear are rare among the Kurds.

I felt what an imposition my intrusion was, in a way. Still, these Kurds had wanted me, desperately wanted a newspaperman to come to see them. My reflections were interrupted by the violent jolting of the truck and I realized that we were off the main road and onto a very rough dirt track. We slowed down, and as my friends argued in Kurdish, apparently about the road, I realized that we were lost. We went a little farther and stopped outside a mud hut farmhouse. One of the men got out and began to bang on the door of the farmhouse.

I asked the driver, who spoke a good deal of English, whether it was not dangerous to waken people we did not know at such an hour of the night. I suggested that their suspicions might be aroused. The driver assured me there was nothing to fear since "All these people are Kurds and friends of ours." But he added that I should be quiet. It would be better if the peasant did not know there was a foreigner in the truck he directed. We started out again, but twice more that night we had to stop for directions. The second time, a grumbling peasant came out of his house pulling on his clothes and climbed onto the back of our truck to guide us through a sea of boulders to our destination—how, I could not tell, for I could see no road. But finally after another hour, we came to the right village and the right house. A man with a lantern stood smiling in the doorway of the mud hut. But it was too late to cross the border that night. No use starting, my friends explained, with the night more than half gone.

In a way I was glad, for I was already exhausted, and I fell asleep quickly, fully dressed, on a mat stretched out on the earthen floor.

In the middle of the night I had to deal with a problem that was to prove a source of constant embarrassment throughout the trip, namely, going to the toilet. Since it would never do for me to blunder around by myself in the dark, or even with a light, in places where I might be seen by unfriendly or uninformed persons, or attacked by the ubiquitous and very large watchdogs, someone had to precede me to find a safe place. Then, properly chaperoned (in Iraqi Kurdistan my chaperones always carried rifles) I could go forth and perform while my guardians stood discreetly at a distance with their backs turned.

Before dawn our host—the smiling man in the doorway—aroused us to move to another house which he thought safer. It seemed to me that my friends were subject to alternating waves of nervousness and lightheartedness. Once inside the new house they asked me to keep away from the window, and they drew the curtains and locked the door. But half an hour later everyone seemed inexplicably relaxed again. The door was opened and left open, so that children wandered in to stare at the strange foreigner.

We were in a room that is like tens of thousands of others throughout Kurdish territory, rectangular and low, with a floor of hard-beaten earth, and ceiling of split beams covered with boards and earth. The narrow windows on two sides of the room were set in earthen walls almost a yard thick, and always freshly whitewashed. Iron bars and a screen to keep out the flies covered the windows. In the walls were several openings to accommodate papers, books, chinaware or cutlery. Hand-embroidered cloths hung neatly over each of the two apertures. On the wall hung a picture of a young man in uniform.

As the weeks went by I grew accustomed to, and always looked for, the picture of the young man in uniform, and was rarely disappointed. Whether their young men served in Turkish, Iranian, Iraqi or Syrian uniforms, the Kurds always proudly displayed the young men's pictures. In this room as in many others there hung also some kind of diploma indicating that one member of the family at least had attained a degree of education meriting recognition by official document.

Although the room was very clean I saw a mouse pop out of its hole, and then scamper back again. From time to time chickens clucking around the house would start through the open door and someone would shoo them out. Once even a goat tried to get in.

The room contained no furniture of any kind. Only mats, rugs and bolsters. Everyone sat cross-legged on the floor, a position I found both uncomfortable and tiring. A boy about twelve years old came in with a bucket of water which he slopped on the dusty earth between the rugs. The men threw their cigarette butts onto this part of the floor. One even spit on it. The dirt floor is, after all, absorbent. The boy went out and returned with a large tray full of flat unleavened bread, cheese, bowls of yoghurt and a jug of skimmed milk called *doh*. He moved around the room pouring milk for each person in turn, in the same glass. A samovar was already steaming in the corner and one of the men poured tea into small glasses shaped like an hourglass. Into each he dumped three or four teaspoons of sugar, so that the tea became syrupy sweet.

Thus fortified, my friends stretched out on the floor and relaxed. How they seemed to enjoy this "being together" in an all-male circle bent on a common purpose. There was a sense of a camaraderie and of belonging. Young boys hung round the open door, not quite daring to enter the circle of men. Women scurried about the house, busy with their tasks, smiling and graceful, and unveiled.

The sound of an unidentified car pulling up in the village started a new wave of nervousness through our group. They pulled the flowered curtain tight and locked the door again. I listened to the slightly muffled sound of the chickens and ducks and twittering birds. Between the curtains I could just glimpse a distant field of wheat and notice a woman gliding quietly past in her colorful Kurdish costume, all sashes and swinging skirts, red and yellow and blue and green.

One of the group decided that we would be safer outside the village. A jeep drove us to the edge of some poplar trees about a hundred yards from a rushing stream. After the hot hut, the cool shadows of the trees felt delightful. We spread blankets and wandered down to the stream for a swim. Leaping into the shallow water I nearly sprained my ankle, and then found that I could hardly climb over the branches protruding from a muddy bank.

It occurred to me that perhaps it was a little irresponsible for a man with a slipped disk and a newly acquired back brace to be undertaking such a strenuous trip. My doctor had ordered the brace after I told him I positively could not accept his recommendation that I spend the next two weeks lying flat on my back.

Boys brought baskets of chicken, broiled and fried, flat bread, grapes and pears. In this idyllic setting I found it hard to realize that we were "illegal." Illegal, not because we had done anything wrong, but because we were preparing to cross the border secretly.

While I was in the bushes on a private mission one of the Kurds came after me to say I should stay there. A stranger had come through the woods and it was better that he should not see me. "Keep your head averted," he advised me. "You look too much like a foreigner. I wish you'd grow a mustache." I replied that if that would help, I would be glad to do so.

A group of women came down the hill behind us, and again I was told to keep my head turned away. I made a mental note to myself that I did not feel any sharp fear. My companions were men of a kind who inspire confidence. Strong men, men with great self-control, great restraint, good humor. I had felt apprehensive, mainly in anticipation, weeks before the journey began. Now that we had started qualms returned only occasionally, during the stillnesses of the night.

Some distance away a storm swept down from the mountains. You could see it approaching, like a huge cloud of dust. Great gusts of wind began to tear at the leaves of the trees. But only a few drops of rain reached us.

We were to cross the border that night, but since we had already been delayed a day by getting lost, it was decided that we should wait a few more hours. We hoped for some medical supplies, for my camera, and for a man who, if he came at all, would be my interpreter. They asked me to lie down in the next room, to get a few hours sleep until everything was set for the takeoff, sometime before dawn.

When I awoke it was dawn, and nothing was stirring. The wind had died down and the stillness was absolute, except for the sound of deep breathing and snoring.

I had a sudden sense of having been abandoned. Could they have gone on without me, decided that I was too great a liability? I sat tensely listening. I had visions of George Polk. (He was the Columbia Broadcasting System correspondent who was killed mysteriously in 1947 while attempting to travel from Salonica, Greece, into the Greek mountains, to visit Markos, the Greek Communist guerrilla leader. I remembered meeting Polk in Beirut just before he set out on his journey.)

Suppose the police closed in on this family and they had to choose between protecting me and their own safety. These were people who lived near the border and who had been in trouble before. They knew what it would mean to be caught harboring a foreigner clearly bent on crossing the border illegally.

Once again I heard a car in the distance, drawing closer. It stopped nearby. The door opened. Men spoke in low voices. I groped through the dimly lit room into the hallway. One of them turned to me. "Too late again," he apologized. It had taken longer than expected to get my interpreter. "We really must start early enough to get you out of danger before dawn." We would have to spend another day in hiding. The prospect was disturbing to us all. We must find another place, a safer location, away from the village. At last they decided on a little-frequented spot in a wheat field. "You will have to spend a few hot hours," someone said. "But you will be out of sight."

Again by jeep, another drive through improbably rough terrain, strewn with boulders. Then we went on foot through splendid fields of high, swaying wheat, full-eared and lush.

Apo Jomart, the old man who was to be my interpreter, was with us now, talking all the time. A little annoying, it seemed then. His knowledge of English was slight, but he spoke good French with a strong Istanbul accent. Excitedly he doubted whether he could keep up with my long legs. He fingered a short string of yellow beads. Somebody told him not to talk so loud. And so in a deliberately restrained voice he launched into a long story about the time that General Barzani spent in the Soviet Union, and about the history of the Kurds, and his own experiences fighting the Turks. His talk made me realize that this rebellion was just another episode in the evolution of Kurdish nationalism. Apo liked to connect the conscious nationalism that emerged around the turn of the century with the semiautonomous Kurdish principalities that existed during the Middle Ages and even later. Apo's family and friends were linked with the families that had ruled in some of the autonomous principalities inside the Ottoman Empire. He himself had helped to form Kurdish political societies in Istanbul around 1910. Everything about this man was intertwined with Kurdish nationalism and history.

I began to like this old man. His talk was incessant, but informed, and it was merry, always full of belly laughs and sly digs. Listening to him lessened my feeling of letdown after the two delays in our departure. But I was feeling weak and shaky. The combination of weariness, of heat, and strange, flyspecked foods was having its effect on my intestines, too. I dug out my medicine kit and took the first of a very long series of doses of sulfaguanadine.

As the sun rose, my Kurdish friends raised a strip of burlap on poles in the center of a great field of wheat. Some of us lay on blankets under the burlap, fighting a desultory and losing battle with the ants, while others wandered off to collect tomatoes, cucumbers and melons. All the fruits seemed unripe, but I ate nonetheless, against my better judgment. I hated to admit that I was already sick.

Lying there under the burlap and feeling worse every minute I could not help wondering what would happen if I were to get really sick. What would the Kurds do with me? To send me back now, for any reason, might give away our whole scheme and endanger all concerned. If we went ahead, would General Barzani's medics be able to take care of me? Would I in any case be able to travel?

My new interpreter distracted me from these depressing ruminations. He was a marvelous, unbelievable man, seventy-two years old, wise as an owl, and tougher than any of us. While I suffered he diverted me with his endless stories. He quoted the poet Hajar about a Kurdish mother crooning to her child whom she has swaddled tightly:

"I am sorry my child. I have bound you tightly because you are a Kurdish child, and one day your enemies, the Turks and the Persians and the Arabs, will take you and bind you. You must learn to suffer."

One of the local Kurds who accompanied us had a transistor radio tuned to Baghdad. He argued with another of the Kurds who was to accompany us across the border about the quality of Kurdish music as presented by Baghdad. Several other men whom I could not identify slept. One worked with the intensity of an artist on his identity papers. The heat was terrible. The burlap hardly shielded us. Strange children's voices alarmed us, but faded again.

The leader among the Kurds with me was Ahmed Tofiq, a young man of splendid qualities: courageous, tireless, good-natured, and, above all, intelligent. When a stranger came thrusting through the wheat field, Ahmed told me to keep down and keep my face averted. He went forward, and, with a sure tact which I soon learned to admire, diverted the stranger. More welcome was a large, beaming, motherly sort of woman who in the early afternoon came down to the field carrying food for us. She was accompanied by a small boy of seven, and Ahmed, who loves children, immediately engaged the child in conversation. "Are you a Kurdish boy?" he asked innocently. The boy eyed him quizzically and gave the right answer. "Yes," said he, "I am a Kurd."

"Who is the leader of the Kurds?" asked Ahmed. Again the boy answered correctly. "Mustafa Barzani," said he.

Ahmed hugged the boy and kissed him, and the boy, responding, kissed Ahmed on the hand. "Can you sing a Kurdish song?" asked Ahmed. And the boy responded with what I took to be a kind of anthem in which the name Barzani kept recurring.

Apo Jomart began declaiming a poem which I later made him translate. It went like this:

> *The lion has come*
> *The sun has risen*
> *The Kurdish sun has risen*
> *The lion has come into the land*
> *I give this glad tiding, that Barzani has come.*
>
> *The mountains of the Zagros were silent*
> *The gardens and vineyards were without color*
> *This battlefield was without battle.*
>
> *Now Suleimaniya is free*
> *Now it is the turn of Mush, and Van*
> *Mehabad, Suwah and Bavri.*
>
> *Glad tidings for the trees and rocks*
> *Glad tidings for the roses, the heather and the lilacs*
> *May the glad tidings enter our hearts and our minds.*

As the sun went down I began to feel better and Apo scolded me for lying under the burlap nearly naked. He said

I would catch cold, but I think he thought it was rather indelicate. In some ways the Kurds are quite prudish. Certainly they are very modest. It is their habit, and the mark of a Kurd, that when they are relieving themselves, they always squat and never stand. And when he swims in a mountain stream in the altogether, a Kurdish man will always hold his private parts with his left hand.

When the sun began to set we started out of our wheat field down to the riverside, where I refreshed my feet in the cold water. Then, by a circuitous route in the gathering twilight, we wound back to the village where we were to be picked up by cars.

At the edge of the village Ahmed suddenly thought better of it, and we skirted the habitations, through a field. Behind a clump of bushes he announced: "You'd better wait here," then went into a huddle with the other Kurds. Something was wrong, I knew not what. They did not always tell me everything. Ahmed came back to Apo and me waiting behind the clump of bushes and told us firmly to "keep quiet." Then we heard excited voices from the direction of the village. Ahmed and one of the others hurried forward to intercept whoever was approaching. I could hear the sound of argument. The word "Schmidt" recurred several times and then "Mr. Dana." Someone seemed angry. Then they quieted down and Ahmed returned. "Let's go," he said. Several new faces accompanied him, faces not quite so ready with smiles as the others.

Walking silently now, we came to several jeeps parked at the edge of the village, and climbed in. It was a beautiful night. A half-moon cast a brilliant light. We could see—and be seen—for miles. I wondered why they didn't wait until the moon was gone, but I was glad we were starting at last. About where we went and how we went I will say no more, lest I give a hint of our route.

3

Kurdistan at Last

Hours later, many, many hours later it seemed, we lay panting in the moonlight at the top of a vast hill of loose shale. Now there were left only Ahmed Tofiq, Apo Jomart, two guards and I. We had left the others at the foot of the hill, and they had gone back. Ahmed sent one of the guards ahead, over the hill to a Kurdish encampment, to get mules.

Apo complained how terrible it was to be old, yet he had made it up the hill as well as I had. Ahmed avidly unstoppered my water bottle, which he had filled with a potent brew of water and White Label Scotch whiskey. That last day while we were hiding under the strip of burlap he had insisted on ordering four fifths of Scotch whiskey. And the faithful members of the Kurdish Democratic Party had gone back to the nearest town and got it, along with other necessities.

Restored by the White Label, Ahmed and I lay on our backs gazing up at the stars, and began to ask the kind of intimate questions that only come out at such times: "What did you think of me when we first met? Why did you decide to come with us?" Apo grumbled and listened and would not touch the whiskey. Like many Kurds—but unlike Ahmed—he was a teetotaler. Meanwhile I answered Ahmed's searching questions as best I could.

At such times men seek less after truth than after reassurance. But I could tell him truthfully that I had admired his daring and his dedication from the first. As to why I had undertaken this mission, I reflected, my motives were mixed. I decided that there was an official *New York Times* motive as well as a private one. The official motive was that the *New York Times* believed in this sort of thing, that we had sent a man to cover Castro when he was fighting in the mountains of Cuba, and that we had sent a man to cover the Algerian partisans when the French still called them bandits. We believed in lighting up the dark corners of the earth. This was our service to the public. From us the public could expect the truth, which "officials" of one country or another would have preferred to suppress.

As for my private motive, it was simply this: that this was something I felt I had to do. I did not say it out loud but imagined to myself the French words, *je dois*.

We were bathed in perspiration, and as this dried on my skin and the temperature dropped in the early dawn I began to shiver. Ahmed helpfully dug my sweatshirt out of my alpine pack.

With dawn approaching we decided we had better start out without waiting any longer for mules, but just as we got going two men guiding the animals came over the top of the hill. The leader was a splendid fellow. I have not seen anybody like him since. "Right out of the movies," I thought. Perfectly attired in a gray and white Kurdish outfit, he seemed, in the half-light, clean and pressed, resplendent, particularly in contrast to the rest of us. His special headdress involved a kind of pleated duck tail in the back, and he possessed a dignity of manner that proclaimed to the world that leading a couple of mules for General Barzani's guests was indeed the most important and worthy work a man could do.

Smiling and efficient, he hoisted me onto a mule without stirrups. The wide pack saddle spread my legs in something like the splits and I wondered how my slipped disk was going to like it. Going uphill was easy enough but going down steep grades it was a bit hard to avoid sliding off the mule's head.

I was relieved and amazed when, on the other side of the hill, we saw a jeep winding across the plains toward us. So the Kurds even operated motor transport in their territory, I thought. But the impression was misleading, for I encountered Kurdish motor vehicles on only one other occasion. For the rest we moved on horses, on mules, and on foot. The practice was to commandeer mules or horses wherever we happened to be, to use them for a few days and to send them back home when we found suitable replacements.

A jeep, driven by the mayor of one of the villages, had been sent to meet us in response to word carried by the man we had sent ahead. We drove for perhaps an hour over fairly good mountain roads to our first Kurdish command post. There a handsome officer in a house overlooking a river ushered us into a long, low, fly-ridden and oppressively hot room with rugs and bolsters on the floor. He offered to let us sleep there. Exhausted though we were, the place seemed just too dreadful. "Couldn't they find a place outside, by the river, where we could sleep?" I asked. They could, and did. But not before I had been obliged to hold court in a way with which I soon became familiar. Certain formalities were always required. There were local notables who must be introduced, spoken to, and sat with. And I was expected to drink tea. If on top of that I would photograph them their joy would be complete. My Rolleiflex had happily been recovered and returned to me while we sheltered in the wheat field.

Meanwhile, our neat, quiet commander had ordered a shelter put up for us under the trees by the waterside. Like many of Barzani's men, this officer carried with him on a shoulder strap a transistor radio with a long aerial. Could this constant preoccupation with radios be some kind of psychological compensation for lack of a real military radio communications system? Or did the radio make the isolation of guerrilla life more bearable? Or was it the Kurds' love of music that made the radio so important? Perhaps all of these things.

It was hot down by the river, too, and toward dusk we went for a blessed swim. The water was muddy but marvelously cold. On the bank a hundred or so men and boys had gathered to hear a speech that Ahmed was to make. Rarely have I had such an audience for a swim.

I longed only to sleep, but it was necessary still to talk, first to those who seemed to me most interesting, then to those who thought I should talk to them, and then to those whom Ahmed thought I would be interested in.

One of the soldiers boasted that he had slept twelve months without removing his shoes or his cartridge belt. "Why did you join Barzani?" I asked. His reply revealed (if anybody doubted it) that motives for military service even in the Kurdish revolutionary army are mixed. "I am an ignorant man," he said, "but the leader knows. He says we are the oppressed Kurdish people. I am from the mountains. I have less than one hectare of tobacco [two and one-half acres]. I lived near Zakho. I abandoned my family. I decided it was better to die than to live like this."

"Could you go to see your family now?" I asked.

"I could go," he replied, "but I don't." And there the interview ended.

A man whom I took to be a junior officer tried to give an account of a battle near Zakho. He succeeded in painting a confused and nightmarish panorama of vicious soldiers, in this case Kurdish mercenaries employed by the Iraqi army as auxiliaries, going through the countryside burning villages and fields, while patriot Kurds watched with loathing from their mountain hideouts, awaiting the moment to strike.

He told about two groups of these auxiliaries (called *josh,* the Arabic word for little donkeys) who came to a village called Ase. They burned many of the houses and then after they left planes came over and dropped bombs. Of one hundred and eighty houses twelve were left. He said there were thirty other villages in the vicinity. Hardly anyone was left in them. Everyone had had to flee to the mountains.

Then he went on to tell of several hundred *josh* in a battalion of the Iraqi army who had been caught in a narrow pass near Zakho, and cut to pieces by the Kurds firing at point-blank range from the sides of the valley. I gathered that this was a truly murderous occasion. Survivors were few.

As we sat talking the local commander noted the holes in my socks and ordered one of his men to bring two pairs of new socks from his stores. He also noted that I had broken my watch strap, and immediately sent for a new one. Thus I was introduced in a small way to the Kurdish forces' remarkable ability to produce supplies when they wanted them.

Ten men came threading their way through the crowd. They were fully armed, and as tough looking, physically, as any I'd seen anywhere. Introducing them, one by one, the local commander said they were part of a guard of fifty men that had been sent to the frontier to meet us. The guard had waited five days and then given up, but these ten remained and were ready to accompany us to the headquarters of the Zakho region.

I longed for sleep, but the talking would not end. Ahmed, inexhaustible as always, had started delivering one of his political lectures to the men on the banks, about the great works of General Barzani, about what the future would hold for the Kurds if they followed Barzani, et cetera. I never could get him to give me a literal translation of what he told the soldiers. I think he was embarrassed after I had kidded him about his constant speechmaking. I named him our "Minister of Propaganda" and from then on we often called him "Mr. Minister." He was trying to imbue his listeners with his own fierce love of the Kurdish nation. This was his religion and his dream.

Before the next dawn we got in a few hours' sleep by the water's edge, and then Ahmed hurried us on. "The soldiers are ready," he announced urgently.

We walked in the dark around the outskirts of the village, and were then introduced to the leaders of a new group of soldiers in a truck—our second and last motor vehicle in Kurdistan. Apo and I sat in the front seat, and the man in the back passed up a cup of black tea so strong and bitter it nearly made me sick.

At the foot of the mountains, where the road petered out, the truck stopped and we started climbing on foot. We walked between walls of stones heaped up by many generations of peasants who were eternally attempting to clear the rocks from their fields. Here and there we passed a farmer working in the dark threshing his wheat. One of them said he had worked all night. He preferred to work only at night, he said, since one of Kassem's airplanes had machine-gunned his three donkeys.

By early morning we came to a handsome village of stone houses well up into the mountains. Disappointingly, it was not cool. It seemed as though we had climbed all those stony paths into, instead of out of, the heat. We lay down to rest on a roof, hoping to catch some breeze. A cradle with a baby in it, covered with a cloth, stood near us, and on the roof of the next house a man was praying. A village leader whom I took to be a member of the Kurdish Democratic Party brought Ahmed a Communist leaflet. Ahmed read and reread the leaflet. Obviously he did not like its contents. It seemed to trouble him, and he said he wanted to talk to me about it later.

In the leaflet the Communists purported to be supporting the Kurdish revolution. This was their new line after a long period of opposition to this revolutionary movement.

I remarked to the leader that his village seemed better built than most of those in the plains. He replied that here in the mountains most of the peasants owned their own land. "That is why they work harder and build better," said he.

Eager to try to explain their military maneuvers to me, some enthusiastic young Kurds got me to climb with them up the mountainside to a point where we had a grand view. But by the time we got to the top I was more interested in sitting in the shade! One of them demonstrated how Kurds could climb a sheer mountainside, and I took pictures of him. He went up the jagged rocks on the run, it seemed, carried from one perilous toehold to another by sheer momentum. These men know nothing about professional mountaineering equipment such as ropes and picks. I photographed also the pathetic caches of grain covered with branches and stowed away under rocky ledges along the mountain paths by peasants who had fled from bombed or burned villages. There was nothing new about the Kurds' ability to make the mountains their allies, nor anything new about the poor caches of grain along the mountain paths. For generations past the Kurdish mountaineers have successfully harassed and even defeated the regular armies of the surrounding Turks, Persians and Arabs. But always the regulars have returned to impose their authority on the disunited mountaineers and to take reprisals against their villages.

During the heat of the day we rested behind thick earthen walls in one of the village houses. Everyone was anxious to be hospitable. The temperature inside was hot, but tolerable. But the flies that swarmed in through the open door and the unscreened windows seemed to me insufferable. So I amazed my Kurdish hosts by producing an aerosol bomb from my baggage, spraying the room, closing it up for a few minutes, and then enjoying for a little while a room more or less free of flies.

This particular village had prospered by trading its grapes for the products of the valley—grain, meat, and so on. I was told they never made any kind of wine. But they did make a thick, concentrated grape juice syrup which was traditionally stored away for use during the winter. They brought me some, in a little dish, and I found it memorably delicious.

The village leaders told me that all the older people among them were illiterate. Although some of the younger ones had learned to read by going to distant schools, they said that, "We in this village built a school but could never get a teacher. We were told if we built a school a teacher would be sent, but he never came." They blamed Turkish rule yesterday and Arab rule today for their backwardness.

"If we had our own government," one of these old men began. And Ahmed interrupted, *"When* we have our own government then we will have our schools, and a clinic, and a pump, and a road."

And the old men, some of whom had indeed fought for these things and all of whom had dreamed of them for too many years, did not want to offend Ahmed's enthusiasm. They scuffed their feet, and smiled and said, "Yes, *when* we have our own government." Although Ahmed was no scholar and the old men had had no formal education at all, they were aware that there had been flashes of Kurdish independence and near independence in the distant as well as recent past.

That evening my Kurdish guides provided me with a little white horse which they had requisitioned in one of the villages for the next few days. On his back late that afternoon, I felt my strength redoubled as we climbed up and up and up.

At the top of the last breathless slope we emerged in the light of a setting sun onto a ridge surrounded by armed Kurds. There must have been one hundred of them, at least, all smiling, reaching out to shake hands. Barzani's guerrillas had turned out to greet me. I was glad they were on my side. For, even in their friendliest mood, they were a formidable sight—all lean, hard, deeply suntanned, armed with rifles or automatic weapons, with one or two cartridge belts around their waists or across their chests. Everyone wore the woolly, baggy Kurdish costume, but with variations—brown, gray, beige, some in solid colors, others broken by broad, vertical, light-colored stripes. Their dress and their turbans of gray, black, red and white and occasionally dark blue formed a natural camouflage. These were the late-summer colors of the rocky, dusty, sun-scorched mountainsides.

I dismounted and started to shake hands. My interpreter translated their little speeches: "We are grateful to you. . . . We thank the American people. . . . You who have come so far are welcome. . . ." I answered with alternating "Thank you's," "Greetings," "Hello," *"Bonjour,"* and sometimes a few more words in a cordial tone, such as "Wonderful of you to turn out to welcome me," and "Glad to see you."

At a word from Ahmed they all scrambled up a rocky hill to be photographed. Other groups of Barzani soldiers were gathered on the slope down the other side of the ridge. Ten here, thirty there, fifty another place, all anxious to pose for me.

I was told that the men who met me on this mountain were the fighting force which would bar an Iraqi army advance from Zakho toward the Turkish border. They said they could take Zakho any time they chose, "but we do not take towns without an order from the General. As a rule he considers it unwise for us to occupy towns."

The extent of their welcome alarmed me. "You must make it clear to these people," I said to Ahmed, "that I am a journalist, that I do not represent anything official at all, that I represent only the *New York Times*." But it was no use. Official or not, I was an American, the first who had ever visited them, and they were determined to make the most of it. To them I represented the United States.

As darkness closed in on the valley it was lighted here and there by campfires. At the mouths of caves, by the riverside, under the trees, thousands of refugee families from bombed or burned villages gathered here with their animals and whatever household goods they could save.

Some had taken refuge in caves or under heavy trees because their homes had been destroyed. Others had left their villages out of fear that their homes soon would be destroyed. Yet others continued to live in their villages, but before sunup every morning would leave and climb up to the relative safety of the forest mountain caves.

Under a dim oil lamp suspended from the trees we sat with the area commander and a leader of the Kurdish Democratic Party. At least fifty other men sat in concentric rings behind these two leaders. They were spaced out more or less in the manner of an Arab *majlis*, so that Apo and I sat at the top, our main hosts next to us and the others spaced out in an oblong formation more or less according to rank, the least among them sitting farthest away.

The party leader had with him his seven-year-old son, a quiet, large-eyed, observant child in an ankle-length striped, red and white shirt. The party leader said that the boy would stay with him for four days. This was the first of many young boys I saw with their fathers in the Kurdish forces. Fathers and teen-aged sons often went into battle together.

Unbelievably under the circumstances, these were smiling, cheerful men. Although they seemed formidable at first sight, when I saw them at close quarters, and when I heard them speak I discovered that they were a gentle people. There was nothing fearsome, rough or terrible about them.

A young man with shaky hands was pushed forward to

talk to me. A school teacher, he spoke English and had been writing a "history" of the war. I asked him to copy out what he considered some of the more interesting passages of his history, and later got them translated. But they turned out to be disappointingly stilted, wordy and propagandistic. At least, so they seemed when translated from the Arabic in which he wrote. Later this young man and another teacher who also knew some English sought me out privately and asked if there was some way I could help them go to the United States. They wanted to study. I had to tell them that until their war was over and they "returned to legality" their chances were extremely slight.

One of the peculiarities of the Kurds, which in a way underlines their tragedy, is that most of their literate men in these parts were literate only in Arabic. Except for a minority raised in the towns of Suleimaniya and Arbil and a few other places, only a very small number could read or write in their native Kurdish language.

The Kurdish cultural pattern is further complicated by the quite wide variations in dialect. Most of the Kurds of Turkey, for instance, speak a dialect called Kurmanj and most of those in Iran and some of those who inhabit Iraq speak a dialect known as Sorani. In addition the Zaza of northeastern Turkey have their own dialect. And the Lurs of southern Iran, whose identity as Kurds is disputed, speak in a fashion of their own. Quite often a Sorani-speaking Kurd finds it difficult to understand one speaking Kurmanj. The differences are about as great as, say, the difference between Swiss German and standard high German. While the Sorani used in the region of Suleimaniya has had more opportunities for literary expression, some students of Kurdish consider Kurmanj a purer and better developed language.

While educated Kurds from the Turkish area believe their language can be best written in a slightly modified Latin alphabet, those who have been brought up in the Iraqi and Iranian areas are accustomed to writing in Arabic script. They argue endlessly over which words from which dialect are best.

Also, which of the regional variations in musical styles is most beautiful.

I was intrigued that evening in a valley filled with Barzani's soldiers and refugees by a mullah who said he had given up his religious teaching in order to fight for Barzani. He was an elderly, rather seedy-looking man, armed with an even more elderly-looking rifle. Barzani's men were not overly impressed. Someone denounced the man as a Communist in disguise. My Kurdish friends suspected that he might also be a spy who would report on my movements to the Iraqi government authorities. Just to be on the safe side they arranged to have him placed under arrest for five days, until we would be well away!

There was so much to talk about. I could not bear to sleep, much though my body yearned for it. Barzani's men talked to me about their battles, their hopes and their arms, their clothes and their food, and their children until even Ahmed declared it was time for sleep. Somehow my Kurdish hosts had found two iron bedsteads which they set up under the trees for Apo and me. I did not realize then how unusual a thing is a Western bedstead in Kurdistan. Lying on the bed I could watch through the branches and almost reach out and touch the shadowy parade of the life around me—old men, young soldiers, women, children, goats, cows, sheep, donkeys. The moon shone down. A donkey brayed insanely, and I fell into an exhausted sleep.

In the morning we had a long session discussing the arms with which Barzani's guerrillas fought. They gathered together a collection of the different weapons for me to photograph, and they demonstrated the different kinds of automatic and semiautomatic weapons and displayed their marksmanship by knocking over cartridge cases set up at maximum range on the other side of the valley.

The Kurds also talked avidly about the costumes they wore. They were proud of their costumes, sentimentally attached to them. Kurdish dress was for them like a flag, better than any uniform.

Styles varied from tribe to tribe, the way of winding the turban, preferred patterns of material, the types of sash (a kind of cummerbund) to be wound around the waist and the manner of winding it, and so on. But the main characteristics, I learned, were these: to begin with, the turban is composed of one or two pieces of cloth very much like standard dish-cloths. The tribes in the western part of Iraqi Kurdistan usually folded one of the cloths into a triangle, rolled it tightly to its maximum length, then wound it tightly around the head over the base of a skullcap. Some men prefer one cloth; some wear two. Farther east, nearer the Iran border, the habit is to roll the cloths more loosely so that they hang down on the sides, often with a fringe (like that around the bottom of sofas) hanging down over their eyes and ears.

The Barzani tribe, whose warriors form an elite among the Kurdish revolutionaries, wore red-and-white-checked turbans as their special badge. The tradition is that he who wears the red and white check will never run away, even in mortal danger. Sometimes men long associated with General Barzani or his forces adopt the red and white check, and no one objects. But generally non-Barzanis who use a red-and-white-checked turban are supposed to turn the cloth inside out.

Most other tribes wear black and white, gray, or even all-black turbans.

Pants and jackets are made of a very rough wool, sometimes, I believe, a mixture of sheep's and goat's wool woven in the villages by the women. Often they use only natural wool colors instead of dyes. Preferred patterns are wide, vertical, brown and white stripes, gray and white stripes, solid gray, or solid brown.

The pants are about eighteen inches wide and can be worn flapping at the ankles in the manner of General Barzani, or tucked into socks at the ankle, or tucked into stockings below the knee in the manner of old-fashioned plus fours. A buttonless jacket is worn tucked into the pants and the whole thing held together by a scarf, usually flowered, and fifteen to twenty feet long, wound round and round the waist.

If he wants to go all the way in Kurdishness, the Kurd

wears under this outfit a very long-tailed shirt, with special
sleeves. The cuffs have attached to them extensions shaped
like oversized college pennants which, when unrolled, can
be used to dry the hands, wipe sweat from the brow, wipe the
nose, or perform any other service for which others might use
a handkerchief or even a towel.

On his feet the Kurd prefers to wear rope-soled shoes.
A few wear tennis shoes or other rubber-soled shoes. Boots
are rare. The rope soles are good for climbing. They are light
and flexible yet strong enough to protect the feet from sharp-
edged rock. The Kurds even make a special rock-climbing
shoe with a fuzzy kind of rope sole that is supposed to prevent
slipping. When rock climbing he is supposed to carry a third
shoe, in case one gets torn.

Much as I admired all of these appurtenances I was a
little glad that nothing to fit me had yet been found. For a
few more days I wore, alternately, my seersucker and a pair of
dark blue cotton pants. By day I was in shirtsleeves, at night I
wore a sweat shirt. I don't see how the Kurds can stand some
of the outfits they wear even during the hottest months of the
year, with yards of cloth wrapped around their stomachs, and
heavy goat's hair pants and jackets. Some also wear pressed
felt waistcoats under their cartridge belts, and top it all off
with wool caps as an alternative to the usual turban.

We left this valley in early afternoon on our third day in
Kurdistan and climbed up into a great natural amphitheater,
a place so remote as to be lost to ordinary men. But not to
the guerrillas, gathered there that day to hear Ahmed Tofiq,
our guide, discourse about their revolution. I estimated that
about three hundred men gathered in this place. They listened avidly, for their sources of information and their diver-
sions are few, and their sense of dedication overwhelming.

As we made our way away from the amphitheater down
a long, tortuous valley we heard someone chanting and wail-
ing. Apo and I dismounted and climbed around behind the
rocks to see what was going on. We found an old woman rock-
ing back and forth. She was a disheveled-looking creature,
with long hair streaming down her shoulders, and apparently

blind. She was crying out something like this, as it was translated to me: "There's an American from a newspaper in America in the valley, and he should know, he should see, what Kassem has done to us. He burned our house, he burned our house. Tell the American that Kassem burned our house."

In this area refugees have suffered long, for fighting began here nearly a year ago. So I asked a younger woman how long she thought she and other mothers could stand it, in flight from air attacks, living in caves, fearing always for her family's survival, its health, its food, its safety. She replied briefly: "We have already spent one winter in the caves," she said, "so we know we can do it. The children catch cold. We are uncomfortable. But we can manage, indefinitely."

She, like the others, had moved her entire household, including all the domestic animals, to the natural shelter of this cave. Her most valuable possessions and some stores of fodder and grain were put away in sheltered nooks farther up the valley. Down at the bottom of the valley her family's land remained unaffected. Whoever in the family could work went out from the caves, as they had previously from the village, to labor in the fields.

Moving on we passed a boy striding up the valley with a big basket of grapes on his head: "Help yourself," he told us with a grin. "I'm sorry they're not very good." But they were delicious.

As we moved on down the valley I grabbed a few black raspberries from the bushes we passed. We rode through groves of fig trees, which reached up to the edge of our path. The vineyards, tier upon tier, traveled down the mountainside and then up again the other side. The bottom of the valley glistened deeply green with rice fields. And next to them, tobacco plants were in flower. Farther on, where the mountain streams flow into the river in the plain, the waterside was bright with laurel blossoms.

"What marvelous country this is," I thought. Too stony and too steep to be called rich, but fertile enough, and infinitely varied. Enough to feed the Kurds and their animals, and leave a margin to sell to the towns in the south.

Farther up the mountain on the ridge we crossed yesterday, one might find wild apple trees, wild pear, wild grapes, and open slopes studded with oak trees. Thousands upon thousands of partridge race and flutter among the trees. They say that when a Kurd thinks of Kurdistan he thinks of oak trees and partridge. And if he is a hunter he thinks also of wild boar and bear and wolves and mountain goats prancing from ledge to ledge on the highest peaks.

4

Roots of a Nation

As the sun rose higher in a cloudless sky that day, we moved down out of the mountains into an oppressively hot plain. Out in the open, now, we watched alertly for aircraft of the Iraqi air force. All around in the plain and the foothills lay pathetic evidence of what an air force can do to mud hut villages and to pasture and farmlands when it has absolutely no opposition, except occasionally the fire of rifles and machine guns discharged with anger and futility into the air. Nine out of ten of the villages were completely gutted, and many of the fields around them blackened with fire. But the most thorough destruction, we noted, had been done not by the air force, but by the Iraqi army, particularly its *josh* auxiliaries.

The sun set, the moon rose, and the moon set, and still we plodded on—I was happily mounted still on my white horse—toward our destination in a village where a place for us to rest and eat had been arranged on the roof of a house inhabited by a Christian family. The Christians are Assyrians, some Orthodox, some Catholics, some members of the Chaldaean and Nestorian churches, fragments of the earliest Christian communities. They believe they are the remains of the people who built Nineveh and conquered a great portion of the Middle East until they, giving way to the parade of peoples, like all others before them, were conquered by their neighbors.

The British had used them in "Assyrian levies" to help

keep the Kurds in order. But the Iraqi government, once it became fully independent, dissolved the Assyrian levies and today the Assyrians make common cause with the Kurds. For the most part they inhabit the foothills, their way of life and their dress almost identical to that of the Kurds. Like the Kurds, they are good mountain fighters. And like the Kurds, they feel both oppressed and neglected.

Nowadays the religious difference hardly troubles either the Kurds or the Assyrians. The Kurds were rarely religious fanatics. And today nationalist motivation is more powerful than religious motivation.

Finding that dinner had not been prepared for us, in spite of a message sent ahead early in the day, we lay down fully dressed on the hot roof to rest. In a giant playpen-like structure on the roof three children slept soundly, one big boy and two little ones. Next to the playpen in a cradle a tightly swaddled baby began to howl, and its mother came to pick it up. I noticed that the child was tied down so that its penis would fit into a small pipe—the local solution, evidently, to the diaper problem.

When Ahmed came to wake us I felt like howling, too. Sleep had become a precious thing. But the moon was up and we must take advantage of its light so as to diminish the number of hours of daylight travel when we must contend with twin threats—the boiling sun and the Iraqi air force. In this open plain, travel by day was particularly risky. A glimpse of a group of armed men and mules might bring a MIG diving down, machine guns blazing. I was thankful for the cold water which a member of the household passed to each of us in turn, pouring from a pitcher into our hands, but was too sleepy to eat the heaping bowls of rice and *mast,* the local yoghurt, they had prepared while we slept.

By dawn we reached another Christian village where a man in a felt hat, the only one I ever saw in Kurdistan, ran alongside our animals in the half-light crying, "Hello, hello." His name, I soon learned, was Thomas, and he had been "boy" for a long succession of American air attachés in Baghdad. Now Thomas looked after us, not as "boy" but as host—and a very attentive host. He brought rugs, cushions and food, and did what he could to protect us from the scorching heat which must have reached 120 degrees that day. For me he arranged a cold bath in a huge tub set up in a ground floor storeroom. I sat on a little wooden trestle and poured huge pitchers of cold water over myself. It felt wonderful. But Apo shook his head. He predicted that I would never conquer my intestinal troubles if I kept shocking my system with cold baths and cold swims.

Later in the day Thomas agreed to share us with a young man who had studied to be a Chaldaean Catholic priest but had thought better of it. We moved to a second floor archway of the young man's house, savoring the local melons, listening to the whisper of a tiny breeze and the gentle sound of little children chanting "Ave Maria."

"Why did you give up the priesthood?" I asked the young man. He shrugged: "I think ours is a dying church."

Off and on during this trying day I had the company of a regional subcommander named Suleiman Hadji Bedri. Observing how miserable I felt, he sat by quietly most of the time. When I became more conversational, he informed me that he was one of seven brothers who shared some fertile property in one of the river valleys. Since there was no need for so many hands at home, he had joined the R.A.F. (Royal Air Force) levies and had risen to the rank of lieutenant. Now his knowledge of things military was at the service of General Barzani.

As we climbed again into the mountains that evening Suleiman loped easily alongside my mule (the lovely white horse had unfortunately been sent back to its owner). Suleiman tried to explain to me the course of the fighting in the hills through which we passed. "See, see," he kept exclaiming with gestures toward the blackened hillside. "Burned, all burned." He pointed to blood on a rock, "from the battle here ten days ago." At another point we examined hundreds of shell casings left by the Iraqi artillery. And in a corner of a burned field we examined the charred remains of an animal, apparently a goat.

At night while the moon was high, we came to a grassy clearing where a higher commander of the region awaited us. He was Isa Suwar, sometimes known as "The Tiger." Isa seemed so stiff and taciturn that at first it occurred to me he might disapprove of my mission. As we squatted on the grass in the moonlight I therefore devised a little speech to explain myself. I told him about the *New York Times* and its penchant for lighting up dark international corners, and I dwelt on the Kurds as "the unknown people," a people whose struggle, whose very existence was scarcely known to the world. If the Kurds were ever to achieve any of their ends, I said, they must make themselves known. This was the point, I said, where my mission and my interests coincided with Kurdish interests.

Isa said that he wanted to show me around the battlefields of the area in which he had recently fought. And although I would have preferred to hear his tale in the cool shadow of an oak tree I thought it best not to oppose him.

So we slept a few hours—blissfully under a blanket here, for we were gaining altitude again—and were off before dawn, inspecting bomb craters and scrambling over mountainsides while Isa explained how the Iraqi army and the *josh* had tried to penetrate these mountain fastnesses and had been harried back to the plains, with heavy losses in men and in equipment.

Approaching a regional headquarters until recently used by the Iraqi army and police, we boldly, or perhaps foolishly, marched during the late morning hours across a vast mountain face of bare rock. We moved rapidly, for we knew the risk that we might be caught by the Iraqi air force. But we were lucky. Just after we had at long last reached a grove of trees, and dismounted, the MIG's came roaring over, swooping low, evidently in search of military mule trains such as ours.

In the village in which this headquarters was located I found a splendid swimming hole—two large, concrete basins, through which the water flowed, fed by a spring. In happier days they were used by the inhabitants of the village for the ablutions which the Moslem religion requires before prayer.

My enthusiasm restored by this cold bath, I proposed to my dour commander, Isa Suwar, that he show me how the Kurds would make a charge. If they would stage a mock attack, I would endeavor to photograph it. This pleased him mightily and he gathered together a hundred or so men and put them through their paces in a mighty charge across a burned-out field. I had my doubts as to whether Kurdish guerrillas ever had or ever would indulge in such a Cossack-like charge. But I presumed that it would make a picture, and the exercise was enjoyed by all. I promised, as I always did, that I would try, someday, somehow, to send them the pictures.

Isa was now sufficiently relaxed to withdraw with me and an interpreter to a shady spot, and to talk about himself. He said he had joined Barzani when he was twenty years old, in 1943. "At that time I was pretty illiterate. But I could understand the situation of the poor Kurdish people, that we were oppressed, that we had no rights, that other nations had acquired rights but that we had neither education nor the means of developing our civilization. I felt I had to follow the great Kurdish leader, Barzani."

He had known about Barzani since 1932, when he was a boy of nine. Too young to join in the fighting then, he got his chance in 1943, when Barzani defied the Iraqi authorities who had "exiled" him to Suleimaniya, returned to Barzan, and raised the standard of revolt.

Late in 1945, Barzani moved into Iran to support the Kurdish rebel movement, and Isa Suwar went with him. The Barzanis remained in Iran more than a year to support the independent Kurdish government at Mehabad which was proclaimed at the beginning of 1946.

When Barzani fled to the Soviet Union early in 1947 Isa again went along. He recalled that after several years during which the Kurds were treated like soldiers, they were given a chance to go to school and get an education. They studied Russian and were taught trade or technical subjects according to their ability. He had been taught the textile business, he said, and had not quite finished his course when the opportunity came in 1958 to return to Iraq.

I asked whether the Russians had tried to convert the Kurds to Communism. "Oh, yes," he said, "they did try to influence us. But I don't think that for all that they made us into Communists."

Isa observed that the Kurdish national cause was in the tradition of his family. His father and grandfather gave their lives for it, fighting the Turks. His uncle Mohammad and his cousin Khalil Hoshewi were killed in battle with the Iraqi army, and their heads cut off and sent to Baghdad.

Isa mentioned that he had been married at the age of eighteen, and someone joked that the Kurds have to marry early, as the mortality rate is so high among their young males.

I was reminded of a Kurdish proverb according to which, "The male is born to be slaughtered."

And I remembered also an old man in one of the mountain villages who had told me that the Kurds could keep up the struggle for their national cause indefinitely. "Because," said he, "we are a people who would for this cause sacrifice the biological product of an entire year. For we know very well that our Kurdish women can make up the loss the next year."

It went through my mind that these Kurds do have their own special kind of frightfulness.

As we moved on, the forest cover on the mountainside began to grow somewhat thicker, and the air cooler. We were moving into high mountain country. The remote mountain villages, although fairly healthy places, showing signs of enterprise and industry, were totally illiterate. In every village we heard the same story, that even though the required schools were built, the government never sent the teachers promised.

In each of these poor places I found myself obliged to perform like a little king in the midst of a big group of anywhere from ten to seventy mixed villagers, officers and soldiers. Sometimes an advance courier went ahead to arrange for our meals and resting place. If we arrived unexpectedly carpets or mats could be laid out hastily. The best one was for me and Apo. Then ranging out from each end of our mat like the sides of a giant U, other rugs and mats were laid for the rest of our party and the elite of the area. Sometimes this gathering took place on a terrace, or in a courtyard, or around a fountain, but most often it was on a roof.

After many hours on my mule I was not always eager to squat cross-legged on my throne and observe etiquette. Ahmed and Apo, my guardians, did their best to save me from the more onerous formalities. Usually I was expected merely to remove my shoes, sit in the place of honor and accept a glass of tea. After that refreshment I was perfectly free to lean back and go to sleep. The others would go on, gabbling in Kurdish, smoking their home-rolled cigarettes in home-made cigarette holders of kavot wood. Gradually as the evening wore on the crowd would drift away.

If I wanted to ask questions, as I usually did, a public discussion ensued. It was almost impossible in these situations to speak to one person. Everyone listened in and everyone felt free to comment.

In this way I learned, and stored away in my notebooks, many things. I was told that most of the officers and other leaders I met were entitled to use the title "Agha," a hereditary distinction. But in the western sectors opposite the Turkish border the title was now hardly used at all. It was out of fashion. Too many of the titled "elite" had been "Arabized," and had become collaborators with the government, against the Kurdish nationalist movement.

Now that Barzani had prevailed in Kurdish territory these aghas were discredited. So were many of the mullahs (religious teachers) who had displayed a similar tendency to collaborate with the Iraqi government.

But in the eastern sectors along the Iranian border, I was told, the nationalist movement was older and stronger and was led by the aghas. In consequence, the main military leaders in the East were all aghas and did not hesitate to designate themselves as such.

I learned that although Barzani had succeeded in

defeating almost all his enemies among the tribes there were still places where the Barzanis met hostility. Not all the Rikanis or Zibaris could be trusted, I was told. The fact that Barzani's second wife was the daughter of the chief of the Zibaris, Mahmoud Agha, had not prevented the Zibaris from accepting Iraqi government arms and money. And Barzani had been obliged to invade his father-in-law's tribal area, to seize his men and burn his home.

One of the tribal leaders shook his head as he reflected on the errors of Premier Kassem of Iraq in attempting to divide the Kurds against one another, the way he had divided every other political, religious and ethnic group in Iraq. "But with us he made his big mistake," said the young man. "We Kurds were his best support. It was thanks to us that the government got the riots at Kirkuk in the summer of 1960 under control. And we might still be with him had he treated us fairly instead of intriguing against us."

Tucked away in a high, sheltered and pleasant valley I came upon a so-called hospital. Were it not for the cheerful spirits displayed by all, including patients, this institution would be little short of tragic. It had no M.D., no beds, and very little equipment of any kind. I found nineteen men stretched out on pallets next to a cliff under a canopy contrived of branches. A sparkling brook ran along the base of the cliff. It was cool and probably safe in that location from air attack.

The man in charge, a splendid fellow named Mouche, had got some medical training in hospitals of the Iraq Petroleum Company and the Royal Air Force. But I reflected that the beauties of nature and good cheer were surely no substitute for medical training. It seemed incredible that the Kurdish Democratic Party had not been able to recruit doctors of medicine for this struggle. I began to think about the rebellion's nature and origins, about the past of the people whom I saw fighting with so much courage.

In the weeks that followed, as we toiled up and down the Kurdish mountains, I used my interpreter, Apo, as a walking, or rather riding, history book. Most of the time riding his mule directly behind me, he discoursed loudly in French. From time to time he would whack the rear end of my mule to keep it going or to emphasize the points about the history of his people of which he felt so much a part. What he told me, combined with the reading I did before and since, was this:

The Kurds set great store by their belief that they are by origin Europeans, in contrast to the oriental Turks and Arabs. They acknowledge a kinship with the Persians, who are also believed to be of Indo-European origin. Most ethnologists believe that the ancestors of the Kurds in prehistoric times moved out of Europe through the Caucasus into northern Iraq and from there drifted gradually through the Zagros mountains westward into the Taurus mountains and into the rich valleys and plains of what is today northern Iraq and southeastern Turkey. These people are usually called the Medes, and it is generally accepted among educated Kurds that their ancestors were the Medes, though their earliest name was "Guti."

When Alexander the Great died at the age of thirty-two, his generals killed his Kurdish wife and their son and divided the empire among themselves. In the confused and chaotic centuries that followed, Kurdistan, the land of the Medes, and the kingdoms of Gutium and of the Kassites, a people closely related to the Guti from the hills of the Zagros mountains, were incorporated into the successive empires of the Seleucids (331 to 129 B.C.), the Parthians (247 B.C. to A.D. 226), the Persian Sassanians (226 to 636) and at last the Arab caliphs (638 to 1258). The warlike Kurds were enlisted as guardians of each of these empires.

Beginning A.D. 640 the Arabs, carried along with the zeal of a new religion, swept from their southern deserts into the mountains of Kurdistan and Persia. Kurds, Assyrians and Armenians backed their Persian ruler as "King of Kings" against the Arab invaders, but in vain. The armies of the caliphs of Islam imposed Islam on the Persian and Kurdish pagans by force. But the flourishing Christian communities they tolerated. The Kurdish princes, known as *derebeys,* meaning lords of the valleys, soon recovered, acknowledged the caliphate and reasserted their traditional powers.

Harsh though they were in many cases, the Arabs brought a great monotheistic religion to pagan peoples along with the language of their own great culture. Through Islam and the Arabic language many Kurds began in these times to emerge as men of learning; the Kurds were to be found in the highest administrative and military posts of the Arab Empire.

A far different type of invader were the Seljuks, a horde of Turkoman tribes who in the year 1160 began two centuries of destructive invasions, destroyed Byzantium and began the era of the Ottomans. But before the Ottoman Empire took shape there came other invaders, the Great Khan Mangu and his brother Hulaghu Khan leading the Mongol invaders, the Mongol Ilkhans and the murderous tribes of Tamerlane the Tartar in the thirteenth and fourteenth centuries. There are records of desperate resistance to these waves of invasion by Kurdish tribes and others.

At a time when the Seljuk invasions had just begun and the Christian Crusades to free the Holy Land were near their high-water mark, one of the greatest Kurds of all times appeared to lead the armies of the Arab caliphs. He was Yusuf Salaheddin, known to the world as Saladin, who was born A.D. 1137 in the fortress of Tekrit in northern Iraq where his father Ayub was governor. Invited by the Fatimid caliph to join his army in Cairo, Salaheddin replaced his masters and founded the Ayubite caliphate in the name of his father. Salaheddin united Syria and Iraq with Egypt, subdued the Arab-Kurdish and Seljuk princes from Arabia to the Tigris, and called out the entire East to resist the Crusaders. Part of his polyglot army commanded by a Kurdish tribal chief named Derbas captured the king of the Franks.

From the time of the collapse of the Sassanian dynasty under this impact of Arab invaders in the middle of the seventh century and the accession of Shah Ismail Safavid at the beginning of the sixteenth, Persia and Kurdistan, and indeed all of the Middle East, suffered nearly nine hundred years of utter laceration. As invasion followed invasion civilization suffered. It was a time nonetheless when the spread of Islam and of Arabic culture put a permanent stamp on the Middle East. It was a time also when the Kurdish warrior princes built stout castles in the mountains and laid a firm hold upon their domains and their hereditary rights and privileges.

Modern history begins for the Kurds with a battle in the plain of Chaldiran near the city of Kars, between Sultan Selim I and Shah Ismail Safavid of Persia in 1515. In this battle Sultan Selim scored a decisive victory as a result of which Turkey, rather than Persia, was able to dominate the Arab lands, Kurdistan and Armenia, that lay between the Euphrates and the Persian Empire. One of the reasons for the Sultan's success was that he had won the support of a great many of the Kurdish chieftains by proclaiming them *beylerbeys* (*derebeys*) of their respective domains, forever entitled to their hereditary rights and privileges, their castles, fortresses and lands. They were recognized as Kurdish *hukumats,* or governments liable only to an annual and nominal tribute and obligated to supply a fixed number of armed and mounted recruits in the event of a war. Under the supreme military command of the Ottoman commander in chief in Asia they constituted an *imperia in imperium.* This meant that, like the Greeks and Armenians under these early Ottoman sultans, they were accorded a large measure of civil and religious self-government. In the course of the next two centuries other Kurdish confederations and tribes were given similar rights.

Beyond doubt, the Kurds, like other peoples in the Ottoman Empire, did for a time derive advantages from these arrangements and from the self-government recognized by the sultans. Many of the remoter Kurdish *hukumats* were able for generations to avoid almost all contributions to the sultan in the forms of treasure and manpower. But as the Ottoman Empire fought war upon war in Europe and against Russia, and then against Persia, the sultan's agents became more exacting.

The liabilities of direct connections with the Ottoman Empire became more onerous. Many of the Kurdish tribes, whose young men enlisted eagerly in the sultan's armies, suffered a heavy toll. As tax collectors penetrated deeper and more persistently into the Kurdish strongholds, and as the sultan more and more disregarded the rights of self-government that had been agreed upon, it became evident that the Kurdish tribes were to pay a heavy price for having allied themselves with the sultans of Turkey. Little by little the system introduced during the reign of Selim I at the beginning of the sixteenth century broke down. For administrative convenience, and to reduce the power of the Kurdish tribes, the Ottoman authorities shifted the boundaries of the Kurdish *hukumats* and reduced the ranks of the Kurdish princes to that of mere Ottoman district governors. The real power was centralized in the hands of the three Ottoman pashas of Baghdad, of Diyarbekir, and of Erzerum. Conditions deteriorated in every respect: The pashas of Baghdad sold administrative posts to the highest bidder and broke down the system of tribal self-government at every opportunity; some tribes refused to pay tribute; as the Turkish authorities strove to impose their will, towns and villages were reduced to ruins, the countryside to desert.

During one of the incessant wars between the Ottomans and the Persian Empire Shah Abbas II, who reigned from 1585 to 1628, sought to win the support of some of the Kurdish tribes by reminding them of their ancient associations with Persia and by arousing their hereditary pride. He commissioned Prince Sharafeddin, a member of the Sharaf Khan dynasty, to write a history of the Kurdish tribes. The document Prince Sharafeddin produced in the Persian language is one of the classics of Kurdish history, an indispensable record of the life and times of the early Kurdish principalities.

A great Kurdish popular epic recounting the defense of Dim-Dim-Kala probably dates from this period. In this poem the chief of the Hartoshi confederation refuses to surrender the fortress at Dim-Dim-Kala to the shah's army. Men, women and children keep watch on the ramparts. For months the Persian assaults are repelled. At last food is exhausted. Messengers attempt desperately to slip through the besieging army to call for help. The Persians throw up great earthworks around the fortress to deliver their final assault. The exhausted and starving men and women of Dim-Dim-Kala fight to the last. Girls throw themselves from the ramparts to escape shame. And when the besiegers at last enter the fortress all are dead.

In their battles with the Turks and also the Persians during the seventeenth, eighteenth and even part of the nineteenth centuries, the Kurds were usually on the defensive, resisting attempts by the central authority to impose itself on tribes which had in varying degrees previously enjoyed autonomy. The Kurds resisted as individual tribes and occasionally in confederations of tribes but never during this period were they able to unite with anything like a national purpose.

In addition to their use of arms against their military opponents, the Turkish armies as a matter of routine dealt most ruthlessly with the Kurdish civil population. They burned villages, not just occasionally or in reprisal for some particular act, but as a matter of policy and in entire districts. Thousands of women and children lost their lives. The conduct of the Turkish armies recalled that of the Mongol invaders of earlier centuries.

During the last decade of the nineteenth century, the Turkish Porte decided to organize a Kurdish cavalry corps which would absorb many of the best young Kurdish fighting men and make it easier to turn them against their own people. They were drawn from the northern and historically younger Kurdish tribes—not from the older tribes which are located more to the south in territory where once existed the kingdoms of Gutium and of the Kassites. From these more southerly Kurdish tribes the sultan at this time recruited a good many young people to be educated in Constantinople. As in the case of the formation of the Turkish cavalry regiments, the object was to win the young men for service to the Ottoman Empire, and at the same time destroy the Kurdish national cause.

The Young Turk Revolution of 1908 provided the intellectual and political stimulus needed to launch a Kurdish national movement. But even before that the Kurds had begun to stir politically. A few families had been educated in Switzerland and France and had absorbed ideas of modern nationalism. The first Kurdish newspaper was launched in Cairo in 1892; the patriotic poems of Haji Qadir were stirring Kurdish minds and emotions.

In hopes of stemming the disintegration of the Turkish Empire and reconciling its people in harmonious cooperation under the Turkish flag, the Young Turks who had overthrown the sultan proclaimed freedom, equality and fraternity for all. In Constantinople a national school for Kurds was founded and young men from the eastern provinces flocked in to mingle with Arabs, Armenians, Bulgars, Serbs and all the other peoples of the Old Empire in an exciting exchange of mutual aspirations. In 1912 Turkish authorities issued a permit for the formation of a Kurdish League. It existed legally until 1920, enlisted 1700 members, published weekly or monthly newspapers and exerted vast influence on the future development of Kurdish nationalism.

The Proclamation of President Wilson's Fourteen Points further stimulated Kurdish aspirations, and in 1919, when the Turkish Empire seemed finally to be breaking up under the blows of the Western Allies, a Kurdish political party was formed at Diyarbekir, with branches spreading during the following year.

But meanwhile other forces were also at work. The Young Turks were quick to become suspicious of Kurdish and Armenian national movements. During their very first year in power, in 1908, the new rulers began military measures against Kurdish tribes that had enjoyed the favor of the former sultan. They struck out particularly against the Yezidi tribes, the Mihrani in the area of Diyarbekir, and the Barzanis in the mountains of Iraq. At Barzan a boy named Mullah Mustafa Barzani was then just about four years old.

Unfortunately not all the Young Turks believed in national reconciliation with the Kurds and Armenians any more than all the Kurds understood the advantages they might derive from realization of the Young Turks' ideas. While Young Turks, like the Old Turks, discovered the empire's need of recruits and taxes from the eastern provinces, some of the Kurdish tribal leaders denounced the new

regime as godless Freemasons. Lawlessness and highway rob-
bery spread in the eastern provinces. The prosperity that had
taken hold there since the fall of Abdul Hamid's corrupt
regime began to falter.

During the First World War from 1914 to 1918 the
Kurds suffered greatly. The deaths of a very large number
of Kurds in the Turkish army, particularly in the cavalry regiments recruited from the northern Kurdish tribes, represented only a small part of their losses. More serious was the
devastation of the eastern provinces which were occupied
and re-occupied, by Russians and Turks and finally in some
areas by the British.

But worst of all was the impact of the advance of the Russian armies into the provinces of Van, Bitlis and Erzerum in
1915 and 1916. Most of the Kurdish tribes fled, either of their
own accord or under pressure from the Turks. The tribes were
driven ahead of the retreating Turks through winter's snow
and summer's heat with their flocks and possessions south to
Diyarbekir and Mosul, west into the sandy malarial plains of
Anatolia. Prince Sureya Bedir-Khan has estimated that the
Turks in this fashion deported nearly 700,000 Kurds during
the First World War and that nearly half of them perished.
The disasters were compounded by the political and moral
effect of enlistment of large numbers of Kurds in the Turkish
forces, where they were taught that the Armenian "unbeliev-
ers" had risen against Caliph and Empire. In consequence
many Kurds, ignorant of the efforts made by Kurdish national
leaders to cooperate with the Armenians in a common struggle for independence, participated in the Armenian massacres then beginning.

While some Kurds were cooperating with the Turkish
government in Constantinople, others worked with the Western Allies. In Cairo Prince Sureya Bedir-Khan and his friends
set up a Committee for the Independence of Kurdistan, and
named General Sharif Pasha, a Kurdish leader from Dersim, who had been Turkish ambassador to Sweden, to present the Kurdish case at the Paris Peace Conference. Sharif
Pasha signed an agreement with the Armenian representative

Boghos Nubar Pasha to regulate the common pursuit of the two peoples' interests.

Thanks partly to the efforts of General Sharif Pasha, thanks also perhaps to British plans for breaking up the old Turkish Empire and to reports of the condition and aspirations of the Kurds by Major E. W. Noel, an able British officer who in 1919 made a thorough survey for the British government of the eastern provinces of Turkey, the Allies on August 10, 1920, signed the Treaty of Sèvres, which gave the Kurdish nationalists more reason to be hopeful than ever before.

British policy toward the Kurds in the closing days of the First World War and for some months thereafter must be regarded as an essential part of the background of this treaty. At the beginning of 1918, as they pressed the Turks back in northern Iraq, the British recognized Sheikh Mahmoud Barzindji as "Hukumdar" or ruler of the area between Sirwan and the Great Zab. Soon thereafter the British tried to restrict Sheikh Mahmoud to the smaller area of Suleimaniya, but this original recognition could never be forgotten. On May 23 of the following year Sheikh Mahmoud seized Suleimaniya and put the British out. The British quickly reasserted their authority and exiled the Sheikh to India. Yet in 1922 when they needed a symbol to consolidate Kurdish national feeling against the Turks, the British allowed Sheikh Mahmoud to return, and he proclaimed himself king of southern Kurdistan. British toying with Kurdish nationalism was, however, almost at an end and Sheikh Mahmoud was soon driven out of his capital.

The treaty recognized the right of the Kurdish people to constitute an autonomous Kurdistan and, if they should show that they wanted it, the right to independence. On the diplomatic front this treaty, signed by Britain, France and Italy, was the high-water mark of Kurdish nationalism. Although stillborn, the Treaty of Sèvres put the dream of an independent Kurdistan on record in an international document.

Mustafa Kemal, known as Ataturk, who had already pulled together the fragments of the collapsing Ottoman Empire and was on his way toward putting the war-weary

Allies out of Turkey, would not accept this treaty. While the Allies were debating, Ataturk was busy making it impossible for such a treaty to be executed. His agents, backed by a reorganized Turkish army, moved into Diyarbekir and other eastern towns and put the new Kurdish League out of business. Turkish agents put about the word that the Allies had taken the Caliph prisoner and in this manner succeeded in rallying many of the old aristocracy, aghas, beys and landowners, who had been resentful of the Young Turks' reforms. Little did they understand how much further the anti-religious reforms of Ataturk would go.

On July 23, 1923, the Allies signed the Treaty of Lausanne with a government headed by Mustafa Kemal. In this treaty there was no more talk about an independent Kurdistan or even of autonomy. But there were some clearly worded articles committing the Turkish government to protect and respect minorities.

The Treaty of Lausanne no longer dealt with the problem of the Kurds, only with the problem of Mosul. The old Ottoman *wilayat* had been largely occupied by the British, who claimed that it should become part of a new state of Iraq. For this they had good arguments, but their overriding motive was undoubtedly that in this *wilayat,* extending from the Syrian border at Zakho across to the Persian border east of Suleimaniya, were located rich oil deposits. But the Turks claimed the *wilayat* of Mosul as an integral part of Turkey. The League of Nations therefore named a neutral commission headed by Count Paul Teleki of Hungary to determine the rights and wrongs of this matter.

On December 16, 1925, the League decided, on the basis of its commission's report, that Mosul should become a part of Iraq under League of Nations mandate for twenty years. Furthermore, attention should be given to the desires expressed by the Kurds that officials of Kurdish race should be appointed for the administration of their country, dispensation of justice and teaching in the schools. Kurdish should be the official language of all these services.

Disappointment over the Allies' failure to carry out the

Treaty of Sèvres was felt bitterly among the Kurdish nationalists. They had no illusions about the protection of minorities.
They could expect little in the way of results from the Treaty
of Lausanne. Almost inevitably the Kurds turned to violence.
In 1924 three notable Kurds led a revolt from Beit el Shebab
quite close to the Iraqi border. They were Ihsan Nuri Pasha,
Taofik Jamil and Khurshid. Their action probably stirred the
Turks to action and hastened large-scale Turkish reprisals. In
any event it was after this rising that the officers of the Kurdish
League, which was still active at Erzerum, were arrested and
put on trial for sedition. The Turks knew that a certain Sheikh
Said had been working with the organization and summoned
him as a witness. This action touched off the revolt of 1925. It
began a period of almost continual revolts and bloody repression that continued until 1938.

Sheikh Said was at that time in the village of Khinis near
Erzerum. He made excuses for not responding to the sum-
mons to Erzerum and departed on a pilgrimage to the tombs
of his ancestors at Palu. As he moved through the countryside
many Kurds gathered around him, as is traditional on such a
pilgrimage. But on this occasion the traditional gathering was
far greater than usual and soon the Sheikh was surrounded
by an army of supporters.

When this excited crowd reached the town of Piran,
local Turkish authorities arrested some of them for some tri-
fling reason. In reprisal some of the Sheikh's men killed several gendarmes. And so the revolt started. The date was March
7, 1925. Sheikh Said was probably unaware that the outbreak
which he precipitated upset the timetable for a Kurdish revolt
that had been planned by a considerable network of Kurdish
leaders led by Colonel Khaled Bey, chief of the Djibran, for
March 26, 1925. Khaled Bey had not yet had time to deploy
his officers and arms and was not able to do much to support Sheikh Said's spontaneous and disorganized revolt. The
swarm of Kurds around the Sheikh divided into three col-
umns: one moved toward Erzerum, another toward el Aziz,
and a third toward Diyarbekir.

At first, taking the Turks unawares, they were victorious.

But as soon as the Turkish army rallied, the Sheikh's forces were scattered. In the next six months many of the remaining bands of rebellious Kurds were rounded up. Sheikh Said with his principal lieutenants and fifty-seven other leading Kurds were arrested. A three-month trial before a so-called "Tribunal of Independence" at Diyarbekir ensued. During this trial the president of the court made a statement which accurately summarized the whole problem of Kurdish nationalism and revolt at that time: "For some of you," he said, "the administrative abuses of the government have served as a pretext for revolt, others have claimed to defend the caliphate, but you are all united on one point: to create an independent Kurdistan. It is on the gallows that you shall pay the price of the ruined homes and of the blood spilled."

Meanwhile the Turkish campaign of repression was getting under way. Where they were not arrested, imprisoned or executed, Kurdish intellectuals and leaders were rounded up and deported to villages in the western part of the country to become lost in a non-Kurdish majority. In many places use of the Kurdish language and the wearing of Kurdish national dress was forbidden.

During Turkish repressive operations against the Kurds between 1925 and 1928, 206 Kurdish villages with 8758 houses were burned and 15,206 persons killed.* No less than one-half million Kurdish men, women and children were deported from the eastern to the western provinces during the same period.† Thousands died as they struggled along the roads leading westward through winter snows and summer heat.

In the spring of 1927 a secret conference of Kurdish leaders met somewhere in the mountains of Kurdistan. Representatives of patriotic organizations, tribes, town dwellers and refugees decided to dissolve all existing organizations, and to unite for a supreme struggle. On October 5, 1927, they founded the Kurdish National League called the Hoyboun (independence). They named Ihsan Nuri Pasha of Bitlis their

* Dr. Bletch Chirguh, *The Kurdish Question,* Cairo, 1930.
† L. Rambout, *Les Kurdes et le Droit,* Paris, 1947.

generalissimo and established a civil administration headed by Ibrahim Pasha Haski Tello. On October 28, 1927, they proclaimed the independence of Kurdistan, as laid down in the Treaty of Sèvres, and raised the Kurdish flag in the Agri Dagh (Ararat) mountains in the Jelali tribal area of the Van region.

During the next four years Ihsan Nuri Pasha, together with a remarkable tribal leader named Hasso Agha, held out in the high mountains against forces which are said to have involved a hundred thousand men of the Turkish army.

The first reaction of the Turkish central government to such unified Kurdish action was to propose negotiations. In September 1928 a meeting took place at Sheikli-Keupru some thirty kilometers from Bayazid between representatives of the government and Ihsan Nuri Pasha. The government representatives proposed a general amnesty and personal advantages for the Generalissimo. But the Kurds were in no mood to come to terms for any mean price.

In another area the tribal chief Alie Unis in the area of Sansun near Bohtan maintained the standard of revolt for a decade, from 1925 to 1935. The military operations usually designated as revolts during this period were more often really struggles against the deportation of entire villages and tribal areas.

On May 5, 1932, this policy of deportation of Kurds to the western provinces, where they were to be submerged in the Turkish majority, was systematized in a law dividing Turkey into four zones of habitation, three of them located in Kurdish territories. One area was to be entirely evacuated and prohibited "for sanitary, material, cultural, political, strategic and security reasons." The law was designed to destroy the traditional tribal structure of the Kurds. It did not "recognize the moral personality of the tribes," and all acquired rights and powers in these domains were to be abolished. The law went on to confiscate the property of the chiefs, beys, aghas and sheikhs. It specified that the minister of interior, by decision of the cabinet, had the power to transfer to zone number two all persons who had been chiefs, beys, aghas and sheikhs of tribes as well as persons "suspected of espionage near the frontiers and persons possessing a predominant position in the east."

The intention to scatter and destroy the Kurds as a nation was clearly indicated in the paragraph stating that persons speaking a mother tongue other than Turkish would be prohibited from founding any new villages or quarters or groupings and would be barred from making use of the whole of any village or quarter or from dominating any occupation or branch of work.

It would be difficult to reconcile such actions and such legislation with the Treaty of Lausanne.

In the summer of 1934 the Kurdish inhabitants of Bohtan struggled against an army corps backed by squadrons of bombers who moved in to deport them.

In May 1937 a similar operation began against the inhabitants of Dersim, a particularly remote mountain area that had long been almost completely isolated. A force of some 25,000 men penetrated into the mountains to the central village of Dersim, whose inhabitants were dispersed and whose leaders were hanged. All that happened in these mountain villages will never be known. But undoubtedly thousands were killed and tens of thousands uprooted from their homes.

While the Kurds of Turkey were engaged in this desperate struggle, modern Kurdish nationalism was also coming to the fore in Iraq. In the 1920's Sheikh Mahmoud enjoyed a brief reign at Suleimaniya, and in the 1930's Mullah Mustafa Barzani began leading the fighting tribe of Barzan and allied tribes against the Iraqi government and the British. Of this phase of Kurdish history I have written in greater detail in the chapter called "The Barzani Story."

5

The Kurdish Army and Its Enemies

We had talked so much about going to "headquarters" that I had gradually built up some kind of vague expectation. "Headquarters" must be an impressive place and the commander somehow a lofty personage. What we found at regional headquarters for the western Kurdish-controlled area was an aquiline-featured, slightly built, mild-mannered gentleman sitting on a blanket under a tree above a mountain torrent. This was Assad Hoshewi, commander of the northwestern sector and of about one third of the entire Kurdish force. Next to him on the blanket sat his aide, a young man named Mullah Hamdi, fair-skinned, blue-eyed and smiling, with a sheaf of papers in Arabic script in his hand. A few feet away sat four or five other men who were introduced as subcommanders. All had rifles or semiautomatic weapons. The commander's hung on a broken branch above his head. A canvas bag, apparently containing some papers, hung from another branch.

A rather grimy boy about six years old, the commander's nephew, played among the men. A dozen or so soldiers sat a short distance away, but close enough to overhear the conversation. And this was about all there was to the second or third most important headquarters, after that of General Barzani himself, in the entire Kurdish-controlled area. No telephones, no files, no clerks, no furniture, no uniforms, no vehicles. That epitomized the character, stripped down to essentials, of the Kurdish guerrilla army with which I was to get considerably better acquainted in the ensuing weeks.

Guerrilla fighting comes naturally to the Kurds. Kurdish boys grow up with rifles. They learn to use them and care for them with all the affection that many American boys bestow upon automobiles. Much as an American father may try to teach his son respect for the power and destructive force of a half-ton of metal whose progress is controlled with the tip of a toe, so a Kurdish father may seek to instill in his son a sense of respect and caution for the death-dealing explosions he can set off by touching the trigger of his weapon.

So it has been for many centuries in Kurdistan. A Kurd does not feel quite a man unless he carries a rifle.

When a Kurdish tribal chief calls together the men of his tribe he has a natural guerrilla force, suited by training, equipment, and temperament to fighting in the mountains of their homeland. General Barzani's army consists of a combination of such tribal forces as these, plus some units of mixed tribal origin, plus some volunteers of non-tribal origin from towns. These he has welded together into an army fiercely loyal to his leadership and his discipline.

The inevitable friction between traditional tribal elements and non-tribal elements recruited by the party mainly from the towns has been kept under control thus far by the universally acknowledged leadership of General Barzani and the predominance of tribal leaders among the commanders he has appointed. These include many natural leaders of commanding presence such as Abbas Mamand Agha, the six-foot five-inch chief of the Ako, largest of the tribes in the central command, and Sheikh Hossein Boskeni, chief of the Pijdar.

Also Mahmoud Kawani, a tribal leader from the region around Acre, who until killed in an air attack in August 1962, was counted the most brilliant tactician after General Barzani himself, although he could scarcely read or write. An important leader of political party background is Jelal Talabani, twenty-nine-year-old former editor of the Baghdad newspaper, *Kurdistan,* commander of the southern third of the

Kurdish area and the man Barzani selected to negotiate with the new regime after the coup of February 8, 1963.

My impression was that the northwestern command was efficiently organized under tribal leadership, the southern command under party leadership, and that the central area was evolving a combination of the two under General Barzani's personal guidance.

Barzani has given the army an overall system of organization and supply and has developed guerrilla tactics into a grand strategy. The combination adds up to one of the most effective guerrilla forces on earth: guerrillas, one should add, who readily adapt themselves to the needs of regular armies, and who are probably the best soldiers in the Middle East. Located on the flank of any possible Soviet advance to the Middle East, their military capabilities and their political attitudes are, as General Barzani quite frankly pointed out to me, of great significance to the United States and the Soviet Union.

I estimated that the Kurds of Iraq in the summer and the fall of 1962 had 15,000 to 20,000 men in action, or 30,000 to 40,000 if armed reserves are included. The Kurdish forces are composed of several elements. First comes a hard core of 4000 to 5000 permanent partisans who call themselves Pej Merga, meaning "the devoted ones," or "the ones ready to sacrifice themselves." "Pêches Melba" we used to say irreverently. The Pej Merga are composed very largely of men of the Barzani and associated tribes who fought in defense of the short-lived Mehabad republic in 1946 and some of whom accompanied General Barzani in flight into the Soviet Union at the beginning of 1947. A few had fought with Barzani in his first tribal fights way back in 1931!*

With so many years of experience behind them they operate with great self-confidence. While more successful than other forces they also suffer lighter losses than any other.

---

* By early 1964 the Kurdish forces were becoming more military and less tribal in organization. They had been augmented by several thousand men—and among them a high proportion of officers—who had deserted from the Iraqi army.

They know how to take care of themselves, to take cover under fire, to attack without exposing themselves unnecessarily.

These permanent partisans rarely take leave. The army is their life. They expect to be in continuous service until the revolution is over. Backing up the hard core is a rotating reserve of 5000 to 15,000 men who are called up by the central command for six months' service at a time. Scattered through the Kurdish territories are another 10,000 to 20,000 reserves who can be called up by local commanders for a few days' service in emergencies. These might be called home guards or territorials.

Although the Kurdish forces generally wear no uniforms other than their Kurdish costume and no insignia of rank, there are clear distinctions among them according to their responsibilities and the number of men under an individual's command. Thus, one may be a commander of a *dasta*, of ten men. A *pal*, of 50 men. A *surpal*, of 150 men. A *lek*, of 350 men or a *surlek*, of 1000 men. Within this hierarchy a distinction is also made between officers, noncommissioned officers and privates.*

The lack of distinctive uniforms has sometimes cost lives among the Kurds. I heard of instances in which one group of rebels mistook another for a unit of the *josh*. Leaders of the Kurdish Democratic Party have been trying to introduce a khaki-colored uniform with a visored cap. The material thus far was a cheap cotton imported from Communist China.

I would say, however, that even in the unlikely event that a continuing flow of this cotton material could be assured, the practical advantages offered by such an austere uniform would be easily outweighed by the sentimental value the Kurds attach to their colorful, traditional dress. A further point is that the traditional dress can be almost entirely made in the villages by the village women, who raise the sheep and goats, spin the yarn, weave the cloth and sew the clothes.

* In Jelal Talabani's southern command area, however, khaki uniforms, ranks and all the paraphernalia of regular military organization are gradually being introduced in 1964 in units composed largely of urban volunteers.

The Kurds are equipped mainly with rifles and semiautomatics, plus some machine guns and light mortars. They lack heavy guns, armored cars, tanks and aircraft.

Their favorite, for its long-range accuracy, is the Brno rifle (7.98 mm. caliber). Of these the Kurds may have about 10,000. Some were said to be part of a gift of 10,000 Brnos made by the Soviet Union to the Mehabad republic in 1946. Others, which have a crown stamped on the barrel, have been smuggled from Iran, mostly since the Iranian army gave up the Brno in favor of the American army carbine. And yet others are said to have come across the border from Turkey, sold, it seems, by Turkish soldiers. Because this weapon is not used by the Iraqi army, which is the Kurds' usual source of supply, ammunition is scarce. It costs up to 500 fils ($1.35–$1.40) per round.

Also favored by the Kurds is the British Lee-Enfield (.303 caliber), several thousand of which have fallen into the rebels' hands, thanks to large-scale police desertions. Somewhat less than 3000 Soviet Seminov semiautomatic rifles have also been taken from the army and the mobile police.

The Kurds also esteem highly the Soviet Glashinkov, a very light automatic weapon between a submachine gun and a light machine gun, which carries 30 rounds and is only 34 inches long. Its range is only 400 yards but it weighs just 7.7 pounds and is easy to handle.

The Degtyarov, an air-cooled light machine gun with a range of 500 to 1000 yards, has also been captured from the Iraqi army and the police in considerable numbers.

In addition there are Brno automatics, Stens, Sterlings and Vickers machine guns, 50 or 60 two-inch mortars, and about 12 three-inch mortars. For the latter there is almost no ammunition. The Kurds also carry a profusion of old Mausers, French, Spanish and czarist weapons, but ammunition is a problem here, too. Captured bazookas came into increasing use in 1963 and '64.

They have 50 to 60 wireless sets, including some transmitters which they use for urgent communications between Barzani and the three main commands. Probably for lack of qualified personnel, the Kurds I saw made no effort to use radios in action. They preferred to write little notes in Arabic script, roll them up into tight little bundles, sealed with Scotch tape, and send them flying off in all directions by courier.

The captured wireless sets have proven useful especially for monitoring Iraqi army and government communications. Former members of the Iraqi army signal corps break the Iraqi government and military codes to keep the Kurdish command intimately informed of the enemy's plans and problems. This monitoring provided the Kurds with an incredibly good intelligence system.

Logistics problems are kept at a minimum. Nonessentials must not be allowed to creep in—no soft drinks, no candy, no movies, no laundries, really, nothing but men with rifles.

But the army does have some supplies—sugar, cheese, grain and rice—tucked away in caves and scattered across the country. Peasants are supposed to set aside ten per cent of their produce for the rebel army. The army also makes some of its own clothes in tailoring shops set up in and around caves in the mountains. It has established the beginning of an arsenal in other caves where rifles and other weapons acquired from the Iraqi army are stored.

While the army does provide in some respects, the soldier is largely responsible for outfitting himself. He usually wears the clothes and carries the weapons he brought with him when he joined the rebels and looks to the army only for replacement and ammunition.

Most of the time the army lives off the land, paying for some food but receiving most of it as donations from villages.

I learned that Barzani's army operates with very little money, often with none at all. "Do you pay for the food your men eat?" I asked Suleiman Hadji Bedri, one of the first officers I met in Kurdistan. He replied that he had money to pay for food, "but the villagers will not take it. They are insulted at the very suggestion."

It was true that except to the extent to which he can smuggle produce out to towns like Suleimaniya, Kirkuk, Arbil and Mosul, the farmer was cut off from his market and from places where he could buy. So he might as well be patriotic and let the rebel forces have all the food they wanted.

The money economy only barely existed in the Kurdish-controlled area. Once while we were delayed for thirteen days in one village we contributed a few dinars (one dinar equals $2.80) toward purchase of flour, and for extra meat to be bought for us from another village. We also provided a small sum to purchase batteries for the only radio in the village where we stayed so long. (It required a full day's journey to get the batteries.) On another occasion we paid a few fils (1000 fils to the dinar) for eggs. Always these sums were for payment to a third party, because our host lacked what we needed. No peasant would dream of accepting money for anything he could himself supply.

Nonetheless I took Suleiman's explanation with a grain of salt. I had noticed that Barzani's army was chronically short of funds. It relied largely on collections made by the Kurdish Democratic Party from Kurds in the Arab-populated areas to the south. Landlords and other persons of means wherever they lived were expected to contribute. And from time to time the Barzani forces had the good fortune to seize an Iraqi army payroll, funds held by a police post, or the like.

The guerrilla fighters themselves received no pay. And indeed most of the time there would be little on which they could spend their money. When opportunities to spend did arise, in a small town for instance, the men were arbitrarily given some money.

In some places army dependents are taken care of by the Kurdish Democratic Party. Thus, a man from Kirkuk or Baghdad fighting in the mountains might expect the party to provide his family with enough money to keep them alive, but little more.

The women and children in the villages suffered less from the absence of the man of the family than one might suspect. After all, even in times of peace the women did much of the farm work.

One way or another, the fighting man eats well—a matter of special importance in a situation where there is so little entertainment to maintain morale. Barzani strongly endorses Napoleon's famous dictum that "An army marches on its stomach." While snacks, sandwiches and other abbreviated forms of nourishment—other than fruit gleaned along the way—are unknown, every meal takes hours. It may include many steaming bowls of boiled rice, grown in irrigated valleys of Kurdistan, and some kind of meat—mutton, goat's meat or chicken. With this there is likely to be salty and rather strong cheese, and yoghurt known as *mast*. An essential part of every meal is the flat, unleavened bread known as *nan* which the Kurds often use in place of spoons to scoop up their rice and *mast*. To drink there will be cold spring water, the colder the better, and very often *doh*, which is yoghurt from which the butterfat has been removed by the Kurds' system of churning —shaking it back and forth inside a goatskin. The *doh* can be boiled down into hard cakes which are kept for the winter. Then they can be dissolved in water like a milk powder or warmed in the oven and eaten like hard cookies.

Whenever possible the meal also includes fruit—grapes, or figs, or melons, all available in abundance throughout the Kurdish territory according to season and altitude. Sometimes there are plums, sometimes pears, sometimes peaches, sometimes apples.

And then, of course, there is tea served from a samovar before and after the meal. Coffee, it should be noted, is rare except on special occasions. These are tea-drinking people.

Kurdish guerrilla tactics stress speed, endurance, deception, movement by night, and dispersion. Compensating for their lack of heavy equipment, they can move faster than any regulars over difficult ground, indeed over sheer mountainsides that the Iraqi army wouldn't dream of trying to negotiate. They will try any kind of rock climbs to get a shot at the enemy—or, to get their pictures taken.

The Kurdish guerrilla's endurance is sometimes startling. Eight- to ten- to twelve-hour marches are routine. And that means strictly on foot. Kurdish cavalry belongs to the romantic past. Horses are too vulnerable to modern weapons.

Mules are used mainly for baggage, not for human transport except in the case of such privileged visitors as Apo and myself. General Barzani, although he has an exceptionally fine mule and sometimes rides a horse, makes a point of walking almost as much as his men. I remember one fellow, who delighted in the fact that his name was "Kassem," marching for ten hours in blistering heat one day in old shoes whose ragged condition caught my eye. At the end of it he was still singing boisterously and ready to leap like a circus performer onto the back of a pack mule.

Marksmanship is the boast of nearly every Kurd. This ability, and the relative absence of baggage, puts every Kurd in the front line. My friends were forever setting up cartridges or pieces of paper as targets. And one day we made a feast of a fish shot by one of our men who sat for half an hour in a tree by the Greater Zab river to get his chance.

As for the tactics of deception, there are no rules. Opportunities are as good as the imagination. One guerrilla officer described to me a rebel trick which he said always worked:

"We surround the enemy and worry him with sniping. But we leave one avenue of escape as though we had overlooked it. Sooner or later he finds it. And sooner or later he tries it. We let him go. Then when he is on the move we close in from the rear, as close as possible. If we get in close his heavier weapons are of little use." The guerrillas love to tell stories about how they outsmarted the Iraqi police or army. Typical was the case of the army post at Rayat on the road between Rewanduz and Khaneh. The guerilla command captured a building adjoining the Iraqi army barracks and tunneled from there under the barracks. After a few days the regulars got the message that the tunnel was ready and that their barracks would be blown up. They surrendered.

A former policeman who said that until a few weeks previously he had kept up a regular flow of arms and ammunition from his police post to the rebels told how he and his friends had taken over the police post at Taktak. When the Iraqi officers, determined to halt the flow of arms to the mountains, decided to lock up all weapons, the Kurds in the post decided the time had come for drastic action. They obtained pistols from associates in the town of Taktak. At night they overpowered the sentinels, broke down the door to the arms depot, loaded the entire stock of rifles, semiautomatics and automatics onto a truck and, with forty-two men, disappeared into the mountains.

The Kurds are not above harassing isolated police or army garrisons, which are usually brilliantly lighted at night. A few random rifle shots toward the lights usually unleashes a fireworks display of answering shots from machine guns and even artillery vainly blasting the surrounding darkness. The practice has the advantages of keeping the enemy on edge and sleepless, and of wasting his ammunition. Most of the time the guerrillas move and fight at night, partly to avoid the heat and partly to avoid the danger of aerial attack. Perhaps because they know the Kurds will be on the move, the Iraqi army or police rarely venture forth at night.

Dispersion is in the very nature of guerrilla movements, for the guerrillas necessarily operate in small numbers and in remote places. Apart from that, however, Barzani's men make a point of always keeping well spaced out so as to make a less attractive target for possible Iraqi air attack and so as to draw less attention generally. They also avoid camping in any center of population, such as a village. In consequence, although there are exceptions, the guerrillas suffer hardly at all from Iraqi aerial attack. It is the villagers who suffer.

Another characteristic which the guerrillas have elevated to the level of a tactic is secrecy. In contrast to Iraqi regulars, who disclose their every move in advance by sending messages about them in an easily broken code, the Kurdish guerrillas, before undertaking any major move, first freeze the movement of the villagers in the area affected. They know that even the friendly villagers might let something slip without intending to. In addition, they make a policy of putting about false reports as to what they are going to do next.

Hand-to-hand combat does not occur frequently. For that reason not all Kurdish guerrillas nowadays carry the traditional *hanjar*, the dagger wrapped in the cummerbund around their waist. In the northwestern region around the Turkish border I hardly ever saw a *hanjar*. They were common only in the eastern and southern sectors. Indeed I recall only one story of men fighting with *hanjars*. That concerned a fort at Shivakal in the eastern frontier area which the Kurds took by swarming up chutes normally used in winter for evacuating snow, and knifing the Iraqis inside.

To understand the Kurdish guerrillas' tactics, one must know not only what they do but what they don't do. They don't try to take territory as such and they don't try to take towns. Territory is meaningless to them and towns are a burden. The towns must be fed and they must be defended, both costly operations. Much better to leave the army and police and civil administration, cowed by raids and kidnappings, and prestige-bound to supply the populace.

The Kurds usually let supplies go through. At times, however, they are so bold as to require the government's civil and military authorities to obtain permits from the rebel authorities before they pass. Then the Kurds come into the towns and buy what they need, or, if it suits them, they may stage a raid and take what they need without paying. In some places where army or police garrisons are entirely cut off, the Iraqi army sends in supplies by parachute, much to the delight of the guerrillas, who know that many a delivery will fall wide of its target.

Barzani's forces do nothing to preclude the eventual reintegration of the Kurds into an Iraqi state. They avoid overtly flouting the Iraqi government's sovereignty. Some party leaders have experimented with uniforms but none has been adopted. The army has not attempted to set up border controls or to assert their independence on the frontiers of neighboring countries. Nor have they attempted to contact foreign governments. But General Barzani has tried unsuccessfully to approach the United Nations and international humanitarian organizations, such as the International Red Cross, in hopes that they might make efforts to prevent the bombing of defenseless Kurdish villages.

Opposed to the Kurds was the Iraqi army with its *josh*

auxiliaries, the Iraqi police, and the Iraqi air force. The Iraqi army consists of five divisions with 50,000 or 60,000 men. As it fought the Kurds up to the ceasefire of February 1963, 30,000 to 40,000 were in the north. During the second phase of the war, beginning on June 10, 1963, as much as four-fifths of the entire army has been concentrated in the north. Of the five divisions only three are complete. The fourth, an armored division, is divided, one-half at its base at Habbaniya, the other half scattered in support of other units. The fifth is largely on paper. Of its two brigades one is usually stationed in Baghdad, the other in Kurdistan. The second division has long been regularly centered in Kurdistan with headquarters at Kirkuk, while others have been divided between service in the mountains and at more comfortable garrisons to the south.

The Kurdish area is divided by the Iraqi army into two sectors, the northern sector extending from the Syrian border to Amadiya and Akra and the eastern sector extending generally from Rewanduz to Suleimaniya.

Supplementing the army there were until early summer, 1962, about 10,000 police and about 7000 Kurdish mercenaries. As explained in greater detail toward the end of the next chapter ("The War for Autonomy"), these numbers have been heavily reduced by casualties and desertions. The desertions continued during the rest of 1962 and during 1963, and in growing numbers, for between one-quarter and one-third of the Iraqi army and police force has been Kurdish. During the second phase of the war the army transferred many of the Kurds to the south and at the same time organized a new Kurdish mercenary force called "The Saladin Cavalry."

The Iraqi army is fairly well equipped. Soviet arms include guns up to five inches in caliber, armored cars and tanks. This in addition to the old army equipment consisting of British light weapons, Bren and Sten guns and 25-pounders. Some Iraqi officers have complained, however, that they have never had time to become fully skilled in the use of their

Russian weapons and that they were better off with their old British equipment.

The air force had about 40 MIG-15's and 17's, but some of these were destroyed or damaged in the coups of February 8 and November 18, 1963. It has 12 Ilyushin bombers, and late in the fall of 1962 acquired ten TU-16 jet bombers. These were added to the older British-made Fury fighter-bombers to make up a total air force of about 100 planes. The bombers operate out of Baghdad, the MIG's out of Kirkuk and Mosul, the Furies out of Mosul. Some Hawker Hunter jets are expected to be delivered from Britain in 1964.

As for the MIG's, it has been observed that they fly too high and too fast to be very useful in the close support work in the attacks upon villages in high mountain valleys, for which they are needed. The Ilyushins, operating at great altitude, seem to be extraordinarily inaccurate. All types have suffered from shortages of ammunition since the Soviet Union greatly reduced deliveries following the Ba'athist coup of February 8, 1963.

Since the Iraqi government dissolved the Assyrian levies, who were as good at fighting in the mountains as the Kurds, the Assyrians have identified themselves with the Kurdish population, so that in one unit of 200 Kurds there were, as I recall, about 30 Christians. As a result the Iraqi army has no effective mountain troops except for the dwindling *josh*. It is obliged, therefore, to stick very much to the valleys, the roads and the towns. It rarely attempts to penetrate the mountains. All in all Barzani figures the Iraqi losses, compared to his own, at forty to one.

6

The War for Autonomy

With the remarkable little army described in Chapter 5, the Kurds of Iraq between September 10, 1961, and February 8, 1963, waged a war for autonomy. What were the strategy and operations of this war, and what did it accomplish in military terms?

Politically the point of departure must be Article III of the provisional constitution of the republic headed by Abdul Karim Kassem which emerged from the revolution of July 14, 1958. Article III asserts that: "Iraqi society is founded on total cooperation among all citizens, on respect for their rights and their freedoms. The Arabs and the Kurds are associated in this nation. The constitution guarantees their national rights within the Iraqi entity."

The successive governments of Nuri Said under the monarchy had made some concessions in the realm of cultural expression to the Kurds. A few Kurds had achieved prominence in Iraqi public affairs. But the monarchy was far from having solved the problem of the Kurds. The revolutionary republican regime undertook to do so by making them brothers and equal partners.

However, in the spring and early summer of 1961 a series of delegations representing both the tribes and the Kurdish Democratic Party appeared in Baghdad to protest that the regime, far from having carried out its promises, was oppressing the Kurds in many ways.

Mustafa Barzani was in Baghdad at the beginning of this period, but did not participate in these delegations. He declined to do so because his relations with Premier Kassem were at that time growing tense, and he felt that his sponsorship would diminish the whole movement's chances of success. Barzani did, however, sign a notable petition which declared that if the Iraqi government did not settle the Kurdish question the Kurds would be obliged to follow the example of the Algerian people. Copies of the petition were circulated all over Baghdad.

In a series of long memoranda the Kurds charged that they were suffering cultural, economic, political and military oppression.

On the cultural side, the problem of language, for the Kurds perhaps the most sensitive of all problems, stood out. The Kurdish leaders complained that the government promise to recognize Kurdish as an official language in government offices in Kurdish districts had never been fully put into effect. Although the constitution assured them of their right to use their own language, not all Kurdish primary-school children and only a few in secondary schools could get education in the Kurdish language. In the regions of Suleimaniya and Kirkuk, where Kurdish schooling was strongest, the regime seemed bent on restricting it. In the region of Mosul, teaching was in Arabic at all stages. Furthermore, the Kurds complained, there were pathetically few schools of any kind in the Kurdish mountains.

Premier Kassem was reported to have asked for suspension of the appropriations for the Directorate General of Kurdish Studies and transformation of the directorate into a mere office of liaison between the Ministry of Education and the Directorate of Education at Suleimaniya and Arbil. Premier Kassem had furthermore canceled the 1961 annual meeting of Kurdish teachers at Shaqlawa near Arbil. The 1960 resolution for development of Kurdish culture voted by the annual Kurdish teachers conference at Shaqlawa had been ignored.

A related complaint was that Kurdish newspapers and

magazines had been suppressed. These included publications named *Khabat*—the organ of the Kurdish Democratic Party, *Kurdistan, Roja Nu, Zheen, Ronahi, Azadi, Sawt al-Akrad, Rasti,* and *Hatav.* Special Kurdish-language broadcasts on Baghdad radio had been cut down.

And there were smaller things that rankled. In Kurdish areas signposts designating names of streets had been put up in the Arabic language in place of older signposts in Kurdish. The campaign against the Kurdish language had gone to such farfetched lengths as an order of the Ministry of Agriculture changing the name of so-called Kurdish wheat to "northern" wheat.

Another category of complaints concerned official appointments. Not only had the government refrained from appointing Kurdish officials in the Kurdish regions, or promoting those already in office to higher posts, particularly key posts, but hundreds of Kurdish officials had been dismissed or transferred to the south of Iraq.

In another attempt to disperse the Kurds, the complaints went on, the training center for Kurds called to military service had been moved to the southern part of the country.

There was discrimination also on an economic level, the petitions charged. The Kurdish districts had not received their fair share of government revenues. Industrial and agricultural investments had been diverted from the Kurdish areas. Even certain projects contained in the economic plans of the previous regime, such as a sugar factory planned for Suleimaniya and a hosiery and underwear factory intended for Arbil, had been moved to new locations in the south of Iraq. The Iraqi-Soviet technical assistance treaty included building radio and television stations all over Iraq, but very few in Kurdistan.

The Kurdish Democratic Party had been persecuted, it was charged. Many members of the party, as well as other Kurds, particularly teachers, had been arrested or deported from the Kurdish area.

Finally—Premier Kassem refused to receive the Kurdish delegations and ordered the staff of the Ministry of Defense not to receive petitions from the Kurds. Even post-office personnel were ordered not to accept letters addressed to the government.

In the rebuffs suffered by the Kurdish delegations to Baghdad the political origins of the Kurdish war for autonomy came to a head.

Tipped off by Kurdish employees in the prime minister's office that Premier Kassem had ordered their arrest, some Kurdish leaders escaped from Baghdad. Orders to confiscate the property of Kurdish leaders and attempts to arrest them in the districts of Kirkuk and Suleimaniya followed.

In March 1961 Mustafa Barzani realized that his stay in Baghdad was no longer advisable. To avoid arrest he left Baghdad and returned to his home near the village of Barzan in the Kurdish mountains.

Meanwhile Kassem turned to the age-old tactic of arming some Kurds against the others. He even tried to use one of the strongest tribes of Arab Bedouin, the Shammar. But these, while happy to receive weapons from the government, had little interest in fighting the Kurds.

Correctly discerning that Barzani would be the heart of their Kurdish opposition, the government stirred up three tribes in northwestern Iraq against him—the Rikanis, the Zibaris and the Barwaris. These tribal engagements preceded and overlapped the outbreak of hostilities with the Iraqi army. As long as he could, Barzani took the attitude that this was a tribal fight. He said that he did not want to fight the government and advised the government not to involve the regular army in a conflict that could be confined to the tribes.

In the summer of 1959 Barzani had, incidentally, got a hint of the war to come when Barzani tribesmen, acting on a tip from Baghdad, intercepted four trucks on their way to Mahmoud Agha, chief of the Zibaris. The trucks were loaded with rifles and automatic weapons and accompanied by a letter from General Abdi, the military governor-general. At the time Barzani had complained to Kassem, who denied all knowledge of the arms shipment.

The first clash between two tribes took place between Barzanis and Rikanis during the summer of 1961. Determined to prevent this from going further, Barzani raided the Rikani strongholds and destroyed them. He drove about 500 Rikanis across the border into Turkey.

Next came the Zibaris, who took up arms against Barzani even though their chief had given his daughter in marriage to Barzani. They raided a number of villages under Barzani's protection, including a number of Christian villages in Nahla. They looted the great Dominican convent at Mir Yacub. In October–November 1961 as a result of the Zibari raids, 5000 or 6000 Chaldaean and Nestorian Christians fled from the valleys of Sapna and Berwari near the Turkish border. Barzani's men retaliated by raiding the rival army's strongholds. The Zibaris fled to the protection of the Iraqi army at Mosul and Akra.

In the third tribal clash, which took place in midwinter of 1961 in the vicinity of Amadiya in the district of Mosul, Barzani's men defeated the Barwari tribe, whose leaders Tahseen Barwari and Mohsen Barwari were prominent Communists. Tahseen was one of the most fanatical members of the Communist Party in Iraq, and Mohsen had been a leader of the Peoples Resistance Organization in Iraq after the July 1958 revolution. In the ensuing fighting, according to the Barzanis, 98 Barwaris were killed and 200 surrendered. Some escaped to Turkey, while others under the leadership of Tawfiq Barwari joined the Barzanis, bringing with them a goodly supply of arms, including 200,000 rounds of ammunition.

According to Barzani's own account, he did not want to fight the government, at least not yet. Some of his associates say that while he realized that the time to fight was approaching he wished first to establish, somewhere in the Kurdish mountains, a radio transmitter that would be able to carry the voice of the Kurds to the world in spite of all obstacles raised by the Kurds' neighbors. The Kurdish Democratic Party and one of Barzani's brothers, Mohammed Sadik, are said to have attempted to obtain the necessary equipment, but in this they failed.*

* During the summer of 1963 the Kurdish forces acquired a radio transmitter which could be heard in parts of the Kurdish mountains.

Events forced Barzani to fight before he was ready.

He blamed "irresponsible young members of the Kurdish Democratic Party" for precipitating open conflict with the government, while the Kurdish Democratic Party blamed "irresponsible aghas"—the feudalistic tribal leaders—for setting off the fatal spark.

What really happened, as I have pieced the story together, was this:

Five months before the fighting between the Iraqi army and the Kurds broke out, and about a month after Mullah Mustafa had withdrawn to the mountains, on April 16, 1961, the central committee of the Kurdish Democratic Party met in Baghdad to discuss a vital question.

The government was sending reinforcements of army and police to Kurdistan. About this there was no doubt. Nor could the Kurds have any doubt that it was the government's intention sooner or later to impose its will upon the Kurds by force. The question was therefore whether the Kurds should take the initiative and choose the time and place for the start of fighting, or whether they should wait and let the government start.

The majority of the committee, including Ibrahim Ahmed, the secretary-general, felt that the Kurds should postpone the clash as long as possible; they should build up their strength and, if possible, acquire a radio station. But Jelal Talabani, an ardent young editor whose influence was strong in the Suleimaniya-Kirkuk area, the southern part of Kurdistan, argued to the contrary. He insisted the Kurds should take the initiative.

In July the politburo of the KDP agreed, with Talabani's persuasion, to send him to consult Barzani, to set forth his own and the committee majority's views.

Talabani met Barzani at Shirin, in the mountains above the village of Barzan, in mid-July. Barzani ruled for delay. "It is not time for revolution," he said. "We must acquire arms and organize."

But up to early 1964 it could not be picked up in neighboring countries.

Just before Talabani reached Barzani he had received another delegation, emissaries representing the tribal leaders who, in the name of both peasants and landlords, were ready to revolt against Kassem's decision on the one hand to raise taxes on cigarettes, beer, arrak and gasoline, and on the other to impose on the Kurdish mountain areas the same kind of land reform that had been decided for the Arab population in the plains. To them, too, Barzani had given the advice not to fight.

The tribal leaders had, however, gathered their forces threateningly at certain places—at Khalakhan, Surdach, Darbandikhan and Darbandibazian. Worried that they might take some precipitate and irreversible action, the politburo of the KDP sent Omar Mustafa, who was called "Kebaba," or "The Tank," to the north with this message: "These tribal groups must not fight."

Meanwhile the KDP continued the political struggle. It presented another memorandum to the government, outlining Kurdish demands, and on September 6 it staged in Kurdish towns such as Suleimaniya and in the Kurdish sections of Baghdad and other places a general strike meant to dramatize the Kurdish demands.

On September 9 an army brigade wanted to move through Darbandikhan to Suleimaniya. It seems probable that the army expected this to provoke conflict, and moved because it wanted to begin the war. On the outskirts of Darbandikhan the brigade did in fact meet opposition, the nature of which will probably always be a matter for argument. Some say that the tribal forces opposed the army and that local KDP men rallied to their support; some say it was the other way around, that young KDP members took to arms and that the tribal forces were drawn in later.

In any event, there was a fight. Aircraft bombed the Kurds and artillery bombarded them. Blaming the party people, one of Barzani's aides recalled the occasion in these terms: "These young people had never seen MIG's or bombers," he said. "They went out into the open highway with old rifles and tried to fight the aircraft. Of course they were machine-gunned and suffered losses, and had to take refuge in the mountains."

This was apparently the pretext the army wanted. On September 10, 11 and 12 the army attacked at many points—but for the time being not at Barzan, where Mullah Mustafa was living. On September 12 the army by means of a trick regained the crossroads at Jalola near Darbandikhan. Army officers made contact with the Kurds, who were probably a mixed tribal and party force, and declared that they were turning against Kassem. The officers said they would bring the Kurds arms and ammunition. And the inexperienced, naïve rebels allowed themselves to be tricked. The Iraqi officers came with their troops. Once in the crossroads, like soldiers within a Trojan horse, they turned upon and overpowered the Kurds and reasserted control of the crossroads for the government.

On September 18, the Iraqi air force bombed the village of Barzan; the neighboring Zibari tribes, acting on behalf of the government, at the same time attacked Barzani territory and burned some villages. Then Barzani decided to fight. He parted company with his older brother, Ahmed, the much-revered senior tribal leader of the Barzanis, who was determined to avoid fighting and who declared his neutrality.

Recalling this moment, General Barzani said to me in an interview: "I could not follow my brother's decision. Anyway the government would never have believed in my neutrality. So I said to the men of Barzan: 'Those who would follow me, come,' and seven or eight thousand men followed me."

Barzani explained that if efforts to obtain a radio transmitter had not failed he would have moved off to the higher mountains of the Rewanduz region, where the equipment could have been set up safely. But in the absence of this equipment he moved west into the Mosul region, which was richer and where he had the confidence of a great proportion of the people. This was an area he knew well.

The day after Barzan was bombed on September 19, the politburo of the KDP met and decided to fight. It ordered some KDP men north to form partisan units. Others would remain underground in government-controlled territory, their tasks to collect money and information and to establish and maintain the political contacts that might ensure a "reasonable" government in Baghdad once Kassem would have fallen.

These were the very things that Barzani lacked, which neither his tribal forces nor the party were ever able to produce in sufficient quantity. Barzani was never satisfied with the party's role, whether on the fighting front or on the political front. He alleged that for seven months after he moved into the Mosul area this was the only militarily really active part of Kurdistan. Not until April when he moved eastward and took active command in the east did the other area become active. "Hah, they are beginning to fight now that they can see our red Barzani turbans," he declared to a British newspaperman, David Adamson of the *London Daily Telegraph*, who interviewed him in December 1962.

To be fair to the KDP one must consider that when Barzani decided to fight he could draw upon a reservoir of experienced tribal fighters, many of them already armed, some with fighting experience dating back to the 1930's. By contrast the party had to start from scratch. Thus Jelal Talabani has described to me the situation he faced in September 1961 as a party leader in the region of Suleimaniya and Kirkuk where it was his task to form partisan units:

"We were about thirty men, and they all wanted to go home. I had eighteen with me at Chem y Rezan [a gorge which is still a major Kurdish base]. Twelve of these were without arms. I had a bird gun which Mullah Mustafa had brought me as a gift from his last trip to Moscow. Twelve other men were stationed near Mawet."

Out of hundreds of little operations and a few big ones between the summer of 1961 and February 1963 Barzani shaped a grand strategy. First he defeated the tribal enemies whom the government had set against him in the northwest, between Mosul and the Turkish frontier. Then in a long series of raids and ambushes, he earned the serious respect of the Iraqi army and shattered the morale of the isolated police posts and the *josh* whom the army used as a mountaineering auxiliary. He won a host of new recruits from friends and former foes among the Kurds and equipped them with arms he took from the forces of the Iraqi government.

Then, with most of the territory between Zakho and Arbil and the Syrian and Turkish borders under his control, Barzani turned eastward. In mid-April he moved with the hard core of his men via the Zibari, Surchi and Bradost territories toward the northeastern corner of Iraq between the Iranian and Turkish borders. Here again his first task was to destroy tribal opposition, a task completed in May, June and July. Cooperating now with party forces to the south, Barzani's men and an ever-increasing force of other tribal and party figures in a rush of operations in July and August moved in a great arc north of Rewanduz through the high mountains, then southward. They reduced army and police posts as they went, and cleared the *josh* from the mountaintops. Finally moving westward again at a point south of Shaqlawa, Barzani closed the circle on about 12,000 soldiers and police of the Iraqi forces. These positions Barzani maintained the rest of the summer of 1962 and through the winter, thereby immobilizing a considerable portion of the Iraqi army. During the late summer and winter, until the Iraqi coup d'etat of February 8, 1963, the General's tribal forces and Kurdish Democratic Party forces consolidated control of the areas around Khanequin, Suleimaniya, Kirkuk and Arbil.

Those are the big lines of operations in the "War for Autonomy."

Mustafa Barzani's military genius probably showed itself most brilliantly in the tactical details of the hundreds of small operations. These I will now set down as I heard about them from various leaders whom I met before, during, and after my travels in Kurdistan.

By late summer 1961 the operations against various tribes already described had put Barzani into a dominant position in northwestern Iraq. He controlled the routes leading to the Syrian and Turkish frontiers. The Iraqi forces operating mainly out of Suleimaniya moved up along the only routes open to them, toward the Iranian border via Arbil, Shaqlawa, Rewanduz, Khalifan, Balakian and Zewa.

These movements had already been completed when the first major clashes between Kurds and the Iraqi army took place near Darbandikhan on September 9, 10, 11 and 12.

The first big fight in the west was dubbed Operation Geli Zavete, and it lasted from November 4 to 11. Barzani's forces destroyed two Iraqi police battalions comprising about 1000 regulars and about 1500 *josh* mercenaries. Geli Zavete is a narrow pass near Zakho, which in the course of history has been the scene of many scores of ambushes. Having got wind of the Iraqi forces' plan for movement, the Kurds hid themselves among the rocks on the slopes of the pass during the night. When in the early morning the Iraqis' convoy was strung out in the pass, the Kurds swarmed down from their hiding places, blocked the narrow entrance and exit with boulders and fell upon the Iraqis at point-blank range.

During the winter activity diminished, but there were more than twenty clashes up to the end of January 1962. Although the Iraqi air force did not develop its full activity until the following summer, the Kurdish officers estimated up to January 1962 that about 500 places had been bombed and about 80,000 persons had been made homeless.

Tribal strife continued sporadically. The Zibaris raided and looted a number of Christian villages west of Dohuk. The new Chaldaean church of Amadiya was partly destroyed by bombs.

For the spring of 1962 the government planned a major offensive to destroy Barzani's positions in northwestern Iraq. A force of twenty army battalions and six police battalions was prepared. According to the Kurds' intelligence, fifteen of the army battalions and four of the police battalions were assigned to an offensive due to begin on May 15. But, by a brilliant ambush on April 1 in a place called Galliespi near Zakho, the government's plans were badly disorganized. The Kurds believe that as a result of it the government's spring offensive was launched prematurely, on April 29.

A 600-man battalion was moving back from Zakho

through the Galliespi pass, on its way to Mosul to prepare for the planned offensive, when the Kurds struck. This was the first really profitable Kurdish victory. The colonel commanding the battalion, many of his officers, and about 150 men were killed. Four officers and 173 soldiers were taken prisoner and a great quantity of equipment captured. The equipment included 36 armored cars, which were burned because the Kurds had neither drivers nor fuel to operate them, four 3-inch mortars with 270 mortar bombs, six 2-inch mortars, 11 Bren guns with ammunition, four wireless sets, 260 rifles and automatic weapons with 40 boxes of ammunition, six machine guns and a large quantity of sidearms.

In another important engagement between April 25 and May 1, the Kurds dislodged the Iraqi police from Fish Khabour, a village on the Tigris river near the Syrian border. The Iraqi police fled across the Tigris to Syria. Barzani's Kurds thereby gained free access to the Syrian border.

On May 12 a battalion column moving north from Dohuk was cut off by Kurdish guerrillas who flooded the valley behind the Iraqis. After nineteen days in ankle-deep water the battalion surrendered.

When I moved through northwestern Iraq in July I saw the results of another battle that went on sporadically for twenty-one days beginning on June 18 on the road to Batofa: blood-stained rocks, charred remains of Iraqi armored cars, a crisscross of trenches hastily dug, and piles of used shell casings. Hoping, apparently, to reach the Kurdish headquarters in the northwest and perhaps to reach the Turkish frontier, a powerful striking force had moved out of Zakho toward Batofa, a mountain village where the Kurds had occupied one of the more important police posts. At a place called Bersevi, about ten kilometers south of Batofa, the Kurds had intercepted an Iraqi force composed of 21 tanks, 12 armored cars, a company of artillery and 920 *josh*.

One of the officers in command of the Kurdish forces described the battle to me as follows: "At Bersevi our forces were very weak. On the second day our commander brought reinforcements from the Turkish border. He ordered us to dig trenches across the road. He stopped the Iraqis from going any farther. All day long there were three Iraqi planes strafing us and artillery firing, and armored cars and tanks ahead of the infantry, and *josh* coming up behind them. The fight went on for four days.

"There are only ten kilometers from Bersevi to Batofa, and each day they moved forward two and one-half kilometers. When at last they got there we cut the road behind them. They had to supply themselves by helicopter. It was not enough. So we held them for twenty-one days until they asked for reinforcements.

"At last our commander ordered us to leave the road open for them to go back—but not forward. They withdrew. We figured they lost two hundred and ninety. We suffered eight deaths and sixteen wounded."

In mid-April Barzani decided that his strength had reached a point that permitted him to extend operations to the eastern side of the Kurdish-populated area, near the Iranian border.

As in the west, here again his first concern was with a few Kurdish tribes still in the service of the government. Before he took on the army and the police forces on this side of the country, he had to eliminate the fighting strength of three tribes with about two thousand men who threatened his flanks and rear. These were the large Bradost tribe, the nomadic Harkis led by Sheikh Mehai Harki, who spend their summers in Iran, and the Lolans, really a group of families whose aged chief, Rashid Lolan, had with his sons succeeded in extending his influence to both the Bradosts and the Harki tribes. In late April and May Barzani struck first at the Bradost tribe, then at the Harkis. Three hundred of the Harkis fled across the border into Iran and about a hundred others across the border into Turkey. Among the latter was old Sheikh Rashid Lolan, aged ninety, who, it was said, had to be carried on a litter.

In an unusual show of vindictiveness Barzani went on to burn the villages and the crops of the tribes who supported Sheikh Lolan, a leader who, in cooperation with either the British or the Iraqi government, had opposed him ever since the 1940's. He wanted to be sure that the Harkis would not be tempted to return. Then, leaving behind enough men to prevent trouble in the Bradost and Harki territory, Barzani moved on to eliminate a series of small garrisons on the road between Rewanduz and the Iranian border at Kaneh.

In a quick succession of bloody battles Barzani's principal commanders drove the Iraqi army and its *josh* from a series of high mountain ridges north and east of Rewanduz. Mahmoud Kawani surrounded enemy forces on Mount Seri Bin Kehlan. Sheikh Hossein Boskeni attacked at Suleiman Nabi, the mountain resort Haji Omeran, and Mount Koshi Spi. Abbas Mamand Agha surrounded and destroyed an important government force attempting to relieve Haji Omeran. In a battle at Simwi Marwili a force of 80 men under his command surprised a force of 200 police, two battalions of troops totaling nearly 1000 men and 300 *josh* auxiliaries. When 104 of the Iraqi forces were dead, the rest withdrew to the garrison at Zewa. The bodies of the dead lay scattered at the sides of the gorge where they had been caught and shot down. The stench was so overpowering we traveled several miles to avoid both sight and smell. According to my escorts no one could be found in the whole region willing to bury the Iraqi soldiers at any price.

Most important was the siege and capture of Rayat, already mentioned as a classic example of military deception. Here, after a siege of thirty-six days, the Kurds brought about the surrender of an Iraqi garrison by digging a tunnel under their barracks. Informed that they were about to be blown up, the Iraqis ran up the white flag. The Iraqi army attempted to supply the Rayat garrison by parachuting in supplies, but most fell into the hands of General Barzani's men, who made good use not only of the supplies but of the parachutes. Village women sewed the silk into shirts, tobacco pouches, sacks for carrying sugar, and coverings for binoculars.

At Rayat the Kurds took 120 prisoners, whom they released on the Iranian border. The Iranian authorities returned them to Iraq at Khanequin, a hundred miles to the south, because Khanequin was the nearest point at which they had contact with the Iraqi government. En route the Iraqi prisoners passed through a dozen Kurdish-populated towns, including Mehabad. Although the Iranian authorities undoubtedly did not intend it as such, this extraordinary tour was for the Kurds of Iran dramatic evidence of the successes being scored by their brethren on the Iraqi side of the border.

Moving in a great arc around Rewanduz and Shaqlawa in August, Barzani took Hiran village in the Khushnaou valley and occupied the Selaheddin range and Safin mountains to complete the envelopment of an estimated 12,000 Iraqi troops in the areas of Rewanduz and Shaqlawa. In addition to the purely tribal elements, Barzani had on hand for these latter operations some units composed of urban volunteers of the Kurdish Democratic Party.

These movements climaxed the year's operations, and I had the good fortune to be on hand to witness some of them. After that, during the rest of the summer, fall and winter, there were no more major movements.

Day after day we heard the reverberations of bombs and mortars, mostly in the vicinity of Shaqlawa. Night after night we looked down upon the Iraqi army encampment in the valley with barracks and tents and vehicles all set in a sea of what the Iraqis hoped was protective light.

By day we spent much of our time under cover while the Iraqi air force MIG's, Fury fighter-bombers, and Ilyushin bombers came over again and again, no doubt seeking Barzani's army but in fact bombing the Kurdish villages. As a rule, but not always, Barzani's men had the good sense to keep away from villages during the daytime.

While I was visiting Barzani's headquarters we got word that the Iraqi air force had begun to bomb Barzan, the tribal area of the Barzanis which up to that point had been maintained by the neutrality of Sheikh Ahmed as a kind of privileged sanctuary. "What about the neutrality of your brother Ahmed," I asked, "especially now that Kassem has bombed Barzani territory?" He replied as follows: "Last year I, too, was neutral. I was in Barzan. Then my brother went to Baghdad.

And I went to fight. Now he has been hit again. We will see what he does."

What Sheikh Ahmed did was to send a long telegram to Kassem pledging his loyalty and neutrality anew. Ahmed Tofiq got me the following account of this telegram: "I was and I am loyal to the Baghdad government. I promised to take no part in this revolt. I kept my word, and you promised to leave my region intact. I promised my people that if they stayed quiet the government would do them no harm. Unfortunately, you acted contrary to your promise. You have done them so much harm that the people of Barzan no longer believe me. I am no longer responsible for the acts of the Barzanis whose villages you have destroyed."

The neutrality of the Barzani territory is an important strategic element in the conflict between Kurds and Iraqis. General Barzani tolerates his brother's neutrality partly for sentimental reasons. But for both the Kurds and the Iraqis this neutral area is of value. Through this territory they can always communicate with one another. For the Barzanis it is a "privileged sanctuary" in which their families can live in peace while the men are fighting. It is also undoubtedly a source of supply. For the Iraqi government, on the other hand, the neutral territory offers a means of maintaining a semblance of governmental authority in the heart of the Kurdish area. If the government must refrain from using this territory for military operations it can also rest assured that its garrisons and police posts will not be attacked.

The men around Barzani at his headquarters felt that Sheikh Ahmed's neutrality must now be finished. But they were wrong. The police and army posts in Barzani territory still remained inviolate, and after a few weeks of bombing, Kassem's air force returned to its previous practice of respecting the inviolability of this area.

I was told that friends in Baghdad had sent Ahmed a warning that the bombings were going to take place. At a great meeting with village leaders from throughout his tribal area, which took place annually, Ahmed was able to warn that bombings should be expected and that all villages should be evacuated from dawn until dusk. Thanks to this warning the casualties from the attacks that followed were low.*

By comparison with Barzani's predominantly tribal force the achievements of the purely party forces in the southern areas of Suleimaniya and Kirkuk were slender.

The first notable party-sponsored operation mentioned by Jelal Talabani took place in December 1961. This is Talabani's account: "We heard the government was bringing money from Arbil to Kirkuk. We intercepted the transport, which consisted of two armored cars containing thirty thousand dinars. I sent ten thousand to Barzani, ten thousand to the party, and kept ten thousand for our operations around Arbil and Suleimaniya. This was on December twenty-fifth.

"Soon after this my group grew from thirty to seventy men. We decided in cooperation with Kurds in the army and police to occupy Suleimaniya, and devoted two months to preparations. In the meantime we did nothing else, so that the government got the impression that our activities in that area were all over.

"In early March I went to Suleimaniya with my men. But the police did not carry out their part of the plan, and we failed."

The degree of the partisans' inexperience is indicated by this abortive attempt to take Suleimaniya—a move which, even if it had succeeded, would have been contrary to Barzani's policy of avoiding the capture of large localities.

During the next few months—until Barzani appeared on the scene—the partisans concentrated on taking police posts. On March 19 a force of 870 partisans attacked six police posts. These were Choarta, Mokaba, Gapillon, Girgasha, Basna and a post at the Regaran bridge near Kelachualan. Some were captured quickly, others changed hands several times. Within a month seventeen police forts had

---

* During the Ba'athist offensive beginning June 10, 1963, the Iraqi army and air force again assaulted Barzani territory. A task force in helicopters even landed at the village of Barzan and burned it. After that Sheikh Ahmed for a while joined his brother in the fight. But after the November 18 coup he reverted to neutrality again.

been emptied and six hundred police—all of them Kurds—had joined the partisans.

In May the partisans, with the help of a tribal commander, Hamid Kawani, took the town of Penjwin, on the Iranian border. According to Talabani, 176 armed police surrendered here after they had been harassed and kept bottled up by seventeen partisans for eleven days. In this operation the Kurds gained twelve thousand dinars from the police garrison's strongbox, but lost the life of their commander. The Iraqi army detached an entire brigade of troops from Suleimaniya to reoccupy Penjwin a few days later.

Other partisan operations included the occupation of Mawet, where fifty-two policemen and 180,000 dinars' worth of tobacco were captured. To the west of Suleimaniya the partisans also harassed government forces at Surdagh, Dukhan and Gashkali. Also the police post at Shwan, near Kirkuk. By the time Barzani had shifted his operations from east to west and was operating in the northeastern part of the country the partisans were attacking in a number of places to the south: at Karadagh, Turweila, Biara and Argeler. Near Kaladiza the partisans liberated Merga Sangasar.

By the end of the summer of 1962 Mustafa Barzani had reached the height of his military success. He was in a commanding position. Although he hesitated to do so for reasons I have explained in the chapter about the Kurdish army, he probably could have taken one or more of the Kurdish towns—Suleimaniya and Kirkuk and Arbil and perhaps even Mosul. Omar Mustafa, the General's aide, said that the Kurdish forces had from time to time cut subsidiary pipelines of the Iraq Petroleum Company. "This indicates that we could cut the big ones," he said. These carry Iraqi oil from Kirkuk and Mosul to Syria and the Mediterranean. The Kurds also demonstrated their ability to impose their will in the oil fields by kidnapping two British technicians. Derek Dankworth was taken in August 1962 from the oil fields at Ain Zalah, near Mosul. Frank Gosling, a geologist, was taken near Kirkuk in November. Both were released six or eight weeks later with gifts and apologies from General Barzani himself.

General Barzani claimed that his forces had since the previous September killed about 4000 and of course injured a considerably larger number of the enemy. The Kurds estimated that by the end of the summer of 1962 only 3000 *josh* were left. The rest were either casualties or had quietly disappeared to their villages. In addition, the Kurds calculated, about 1000 soldiers and 2000 police had deserted and joined Barzani's forces, and they continue to come in increasing numbers.

Until a short time before the February 1963 ceasefire the Kurds' practice was to let all prisoners except officers go. This encouraged surrenders and relieved the Kurds of the necessity of caring for large numbers of captives. Barzani claimed in February that his forces had taken altogether 10,000 prisoners but had released all except 500.

If one adds to these figures Barzani's claim that his forces had cut off and surrounded 10,000 to 12,000 Iraqi troops one may get some concept of the impact of the Kurdish rebellion on the armed forces of the Iraqi republic.

The extent of the Iraqi army's demoralization was indicated by some of the messages intercepted by Kurdish monitors while fighting was at its height during the summer of 1962. Here is one sent by Colonel Hadi from a position on the road between Bazian and Agheler (between Kiruk and Suleimaniya) to the commander of the twentieth brigade on August 17, 1962:

"Our position is very bad. The soldiers do not obey us. The radio operators say the signals are weak. They cannot take the messages. The tank drivers do not follow orders because they say the heat is too great. The armored-car drivers say the vehicles are old, so how can they operate. The soldiers' morale is destroyed. All this is because they have seen terrible things. They weep. The road is torn up. There are two hundred revolutionaries in the path. For the reasons given we cannot attack."

Another message from the same officer indicated some of the terrible things the soldiers had seen. He said a tank had blown up on the road to Agheler and the body of the colonel in the tank had been left dismembered on the road, a leg detached from the body.

Another telegram sent by the army commander at the town of Amadiya to second division headquarters at Mosul on July 22 reflected a similarly desperate state of mind outlined as follows: "Since yesterday neither soldiers nor civilians have had water. There is a fountain at the base of the wall of the city. To get to it it is necessary to bring us several aircraft to drive the enemy away. Yet this water is not enough to quench our thirst.

"We are in a serious situation. Our greatest effort night and day is to get a few drops of water to drink. For ten days we have been in this condition and we have found no way out. Our forces have lost all hope. Our soldiers have no more strength.

"Above all, it is a matter of thirst. Tell us what you are going to do for us, we beg you. We will show you their emplacements so you can bomb them. Above all, bomb the front trenches. There is another trench across the middle of the road. That one, too. Make haste."

In another telegram the same commander at Amadiya said: "It is impossible to explain our situation. For five days we have called for help. You have not come. Since you have not come we have remained isolated. Tell us the truth. We beg you not to hide the truth. Our men hear that our future will be like that of Brivka, Rayat, and the others. For the sake of God and our children, help us."

So we have opposing one another in Iraq two very different forces: on one side an irregular force of guerrillas whose numbers are growing, whose organization is being steadily refined and whose morale could hardly be higher. They are riding a wave of optimism sustained by an unbroken series of military successes, by the knowledge that their losses are light and their enemy's heavy, by their sense that they have the confidence of most of the Kurdish people, and by their own great faith in their leader, Mustafa Barzani.

Air attack has inflicted severe losses on Kurdish civilians.

But its effect has been not to diminish the Kurds' will to fight, but to stoke the fires of their anger, to wipe out tribal differences in the sense of common disaster, and to bring new recruits to Barzani's forces from villages that might otherwise have remained indifferent.

On the other side we have a regular army and police force demoralized by a multitude of small, and some not so small, reverses; by distaste for their assignment; by internal political dissensions. These forces cling unhappily to outposts which they cannot abandon for reasons of prestige or which the Kurdish guerrillas are not yet ready to take.

Toward the end of the Kassem era the Kurds were attacking. The Iraqis seemed to have lost the will and ability to attack. General Barzani observed: "When an army loses the ability to attack it is finished."

This is undoubtedly true and in a sense Barzani's army had won. But it was also true that Barzani's force composed basically of mountain guerrilla fighters did not have—and probably never will have—the military capacity to defeat the main body of the Iraqi army stationed in the plains south of the Kurdish mountains. On the other hand, the Iraqi army could not then—and probably never will—defeat Barzani in the mountains. In its attempt to do so it has suffered severe defeats that shook the republic to its foundations. These clashes were among the factors that led to Premier Kassem's fall.

In June 1963 the Iraqi army, under Ba'athist inspiration, tried again, and failed again. Its failure was one of the most important causes of the army coup of November 18, 1963. Thereafter the military situation in northern Iraq developed into an armed truce.

7

The Barzani Story

On a chill misty morning in February 1963, in an open field outside the town of Kala Diza in Iraqi Kurdistan, Mullah Mustafa Barzani, general commanding the Kurdish revolutionary forces, stands alone and allows himself to be "shot" at all angles, by a visiting photographer. Here is a man of exceptionally powerful build, but lean, of grave demeanor and penetrating eye, yet for the moment smiling with a slightly quizzical, humorous look.

Respectfully at a distance of about a hundred feet stands a group of perhaps a hundred officers of the Barzani forces and local notables. The General walks slowly toward them. He moves deliberately with a kind of stiff-legged swagger. He smiles. The ranks of the men part before him as though in awe. They have to be told to come closer and to stand next to the great man so that he may be photographed in their midst.

Barzani is dressed like any one of them, in gray and white tribal dress, a double cartridge belt around his waist and the red and white turban of his tribe on his head. He is of medium height. But he towers above his men like a giant in their midst. Barzani, the symbol of the Kurdish national cause; Barzani, the operating head of the Iraqi Kurdish revolution, the military leader and the political leader, the heart and the brain, the man most loved and the man most feared in Kurdistan.

This day Barzani is victorious. He is awaiting the return from Baghdad of his emissary. His emissary has gone not as a petitioner but to outline the Kurdish demands, the Kurdish conditions for their autonomy within the Iraqi state.

At this moment Barzani feels and looks supremely confident. What do we know about this man?

Barzani is an aristocrat. Although his account has not been confirmed to me from any other source, he told me that the Barzanis had been the leading family in their territory for twelve hundred years. Their ancestors had been the princes of Amadiya, but there came a time when an eldest son did not choose to reign. He stepped aside in favor of a younger brother. Later, however, finding his successor's rule severe and unjust, he regretted his decision. He withdrew from Amadiya to the region of Barzan, and there, although neither he nor his successors exercised authority as rulers, the family retained moral authority. The princes of Amadiya disappeared as the centuries passed, but the Barzani family, proprietors of considerable mountain farmland, continued their leading role, some as military leaders, some as religious leaders. But always the Barzanis were fighters. They lived up to the old Kurdish saying that "The male is born to be slaughtered." They fought the Turks, they fought the Iranians, they fought the Arabs, and they fought their Kurdish neighbors.

Early in the nineteenth century the Barzani family became the leaders in their region of the Sufis, or mystics, of the Nakshbandi sect, an emotional variation of Islam which originated in Turkestan in the fourteenth century. Mawlana Khaled introduced the sect to Kurdistan early in the nineteenth century by converting Sheikh Taha of Shem Dinan, who passed leadership of the group on to Sheikh Taj ad-Din of Barzan village. Barzan village had been established about this time by the Barzanis, who moved from the other side of the Zab river and drove out the earlier Christian and Jewish residents.

Sheikh Taj ad-Din's son and successor was Abdel Salam I, who was hung by the Turks at Mosul. He had led a revolt and had gone to Mosul in an attempt to negotiate a settlement.

Abdel Salam I was succeeded as head of the Nakshbandis by his son Mohammed, who was distinguished for his mystical religious leadership, for his sons, who included the remarkable Mullah Mustafa, and for the extraordinary circumstances of his death.

The story is that Sheikh Mohammed built up a group of fanatically devoted followers. To these he spoke at length about the Mahdi—"the Islamic Messiah" and the Dajal— "the anti-Christ" or in this case "the anti-Mahdi." One day he told his followers that the Dajal would have a horse that could travel in one day the distance of one year's travel on ordinary horseback. "How then can the Mahdi escape?" asked his followers. "Of course," replied Sheikh Mohammed, "he will fly."

Now his followers had long been wondering whether Sheikh Mohammed was not in fact the Mahdi himself. Had not the Sheikh said that the Mahdi would be a learned man? Had he not said that he would be wise? And had he not said that his name would be Mohammed?

"If he is the Mahdi," one of them observed, "then he must be able to fly." And so the followers decided to put the matter to the test. Over the old man's protests they picked him up and flung him from an upper window of his house in order to see whether he could fly.

It is hard for me to believe that these followers were not ill-intentioned. However, that is the story.

The eldest of Mohammed's eight sons, Abdel Salam II, succeeded to the religious leadership but was hung by the Turks at Mosul in 1914. Mustafa Barzani told me that his brother had joined with some other Kurdish notables to resist new laws imposed by the Young Turk regime in Constantinople. But when the Turks sent their forces into the mountains to enforce these new laws only Abdel Salam resisted. And he paid the supreme penalty.

Next in line for the religious leadership was Mohammed's second oldest son, Ahmed, who embarked on a career of Nakshbandi mysticism rivaling that of his father. His youngest brother, Mullah Mustafa, twenty years his junior, became the military leader of the Barzani tribe. He was named "Mullah," it should be noted, not for any religious reason but after a maternal uncle.

The Barzani tribe itself consisted in 1906—when Mullah Mustafa was an infant—of only 750* families, but was expanded soon thereafter from various additional tribes who looked to the Sheikh of Barzan as their religious guide and master. These were the Shirwani, who in 1906 comprised 1800 families, the Mizuri, with 120 families, and two small tribes called the Barushis and the Dola Mari.

Young Mullah Mustafa's childhood was marked by violent events.

When one and a half years old he was imprisoned with his mother in an Ottoman jail for nine months. That would be about 1905. Then as he grew up he heard about the hanging of his grandfather by the Turks; the violent death of his father at the hands of religious fanatics in 1908; the hanging of his eldest brother Abdel Salam by the Turks in 1914.

Mullah Mustafa got his first six years of primary education from private tutors in the village of Barzan; thereafter he studied theology at Barzan for four years. Later, during a period of exile from Barzan, he continued his theological studies at Suleimaniya to the point known in Islamic theology as *tefsir* and *hedis*. (*Tefsir* is the ability to recite and explain all the Koranic verses. *Hedis* is the ability to recite the verses of the Prophet.)

But perhaps he learned more of the simple, hard virtues of his tribe, more of what he needed to know later as a revolutionary leader while roaming as a boy in the mountains around Barzan.

To get about this rugged mountain terrain one must travel by horse, by mule or on foot. Here are open mountainsides for grazing flocks, sheltered orchards and vineyards, and a little irrigated agriculture at the bottom of the valleys. Because the roads are so bad and markets so inaccessible the people of Barzan have remained self-sufficient in many ways. Sheep and goats can provide both food and clothing. Little

* William Eagleton, Jr., *The Kurdish Republic of 1946.*

remains that must be brought from the distant towns except for tea and sugar, rifles and ammunition.

For many inhabitants of this region life is just above the subsistence level. Life is possible at all only because the inhabitants, like the Scottish highlanders, are frugal, hard working, and imbued with high standards of personal conduct. The authority of a sheikh is absolute, whether on questions of religion or of war. And war there was, almost continuously, against Turks, against Arabs, and against Iranians, and against neighbors—the Zibaris, the Bradost, and the nomadic Harkis, the Rikanis, and the Barwaris.

Like every Kurdish boy, Mullah Mustafa learned to hunt. He shot the partridge that run so quickly among the scattered oak trees of the Kurdish mountains. He also shot wild boar, wolves and bear.

Mullah Mustafa worked on his father's farm. He learned to plow. He followed the goats and sheep through the hills like any shepherd boy. He even learned to gather the gallnuts of the wild oak tree that are collected and sold by the peasants of the high mountains for use in tanneries farther south.

In the late 'twenties Mullah Mustafa married a cousin, as is the custom among the Barzanis. She bore him three sons and a daughter. The sons are Obeidullah, born about 1927, Lochman and Idriss. Much later he married a second wife, daughter of Mahmoud Agha, chief of the Zibaris. Although this marriage was presumably arranged for political purposes it did not result in diminution of hostilities between the Barzani and Zibari tribes. She bore Mullah Mustafa another four sons: Mesoud, born about 1945; Sabir, a year younger; Nahad, born in the late 1950's; and since 1960 there has been another baby boy. (The Kurds are characteristically vague about their ages.)

Mullah Mustafa appeared in the role of fighting leader for the first time in 1931, at the age of twenty-seven, when he and his tribesmen defeated the forces of Sheikh Rashid of the Bradost who had declared a "holy war" against Sheikh Ahmed, Mullah Mustafa's brother, twenty years his elder and the senior tribal leader. Sheikh Rashid accused Sheikh Ahmed of propagating a heresy.

There were some who regarded Sheikh Ahmed as a holy man, but there were others—particularly the adherents of the rival Qadri sect—who maintained that the prayers and chantings by which the leader of the Nakshbandi sect at Barzan presumed to link his powers with those of religious forebears were intended to show that he was himself the "Mahdi" or, indeed, that he was himself God. It may be also that the government in Baghdad encouraged such allegations because it regarded Barzan as a dangerous center of tribal strength.

In any event, the government ignored Sheikh Ahmed's complaints about the raids of Sheikh Rashid of the Bradost. It took a much more serious view of the reprisals taken by young Mullah Mustafa. Nor was it to be appeased by Sheikh Ahmed's offer to release the prisoners taken and to return captured arms and cattle. It seemed as though the government did not want peace with the Barzanis but sought an occasion to bring them to heel.

Assisted by tribes hostile to the Barzanis and by the R.A.F., the government mounted punitive thrusts into Barzani territory in 1932 and 1933. Although the planes used in those days were slower and the bombs smaller than those available today, they were quite sufficient to destroy Kurdish mountain villages. In some instances the damage is said to have been as high as eighty per cent of all living quarters.

The Barzanis struck back hard, but by the spring of 1934 they were exhausted. Sheikh Ahmed and some of his men took refuge in Turkey, where some of them were hanged. Sheikh Ahmed himself was turned over to the Iraqi government. As a result of talks carried out in the meantime with a British officer whom the Kurds knew as "Captain Violet," the Iraqi government agreed to take no further action against the Barzanis on condition that Sheikh Ahmed, his brother Mullah Mustafa, and the entire family leave Barzan territory and submit to "restricted residence." This meant that they were confined first to southern Iraq, later to the town of Suleimaniya.

Thus the Barzani family was exiled for a decade, most of the time to Suleimaniya, a penalty which proved more bearable than the Iraqi authorities may have realized because Suleimaniya was the spiritual capital of Kurdish nationalism in Iraq. From the late-eighteenth century until 1848, Suleimaniya had been a center of sturdy Kurdish autonomy. During this period of rule by the Baban family, visitors to Suleimaniya heard recitals of Kurdish poetry, admired the ruler's Kurdish guard, and enjoyed hearty displays of swordsmanship, horse racing and wrestling. Of these days Sheikh Reza Talabani dreamed when he wrote: "I remember Suleimaniya when it was the capital of the Babans. It was neither subject to the Persians nor slave-driven by the House of Usman [the Turks]."

Here also the British recognized Sheikh Mahmoud as an autonomous Kurdish ruler in 1918. They turned against him soon thereafter, partly because his ambitions became excessive, partly because British policy, which had toyed with the idea of an autonomous or independent Kurdistan, shifted to a policy favoring Arab hegemony.

In November 1943, Mullah Mustafa decided to break out of his forced residence in Suleimaniya. With the help of Kurdish villagers he escaped, returned to the mountainous region of Barzan and raised his followers.

He and his tribesmen routed both the Iraqi police and the army regulars who were sent north to bring him to order.

On the advice of the British, who were still at war and anxious to eliminate troublespots in the Middle East, the government in Baghdad decided at this point to give up attempts to subdue Barzani and instead to try to negotiate a settlement with this troublesome Kurdish leader. The government sent to Barzani a minister of state named Majid Mustafa, a man of Kurdish origin. Majid Mustafa conceded the main Kurdish demands. Kurdish would be taught in the schools. Kurdish would be recognized as an official language. Kurds would be appointed to public offices. The Kurdish region would be developed and endowed with schools and hospitals. Premier

Nuri Said endorsed the agreement. Barzani himself appeared in Baghdad and was well received. He was allowed to return to Barzan with all of his exiled family. Premier Nuri Said in a speech at the officers club of the second division at Kirkuk declared that he believed the Kurds were entitled to their rights.

Soon thereafter in a shift of Iraqi domestic politics Nuri Said had to resign—at least temporarily. He was succeeded by a nationalistic government, fearful of Mullah Mustafa's growing influence and not disposed to make concessions to the Kurds.

It was now late 1944. The British, seeing the end of the war approaching, had apparently lost interest in pressing the Iraqis to come to terms with the Kurds. The new government, having rejected Majid Mustafa's agreements, began tightening police controls and reinforcing garrisons in the Kurdish north.

Tension rose. While Mullah Mustafa was touring the Dohuk region in an effort to settle old tribal conflicts an incident occurred at Mergasor. A Kurdish tribal leader named Ulu Beg had gone to a police post near Mergasor to obtain tea and wheat. A disagreement led to fighting in which Ulu Beg was killed. Tribal reprisals against the police post, and army reprisals against the Barzanis ensued. In spite of Barzani's urgent pleas that all differences could be settled amicably, the government seized the occasion to resume large-scale operations against the Barzanis.

Mullah Mustafa now turned all his energies to the defense of Barzan territory. Apart from the immediate region around the village of Barzan, he drew his forces from surrounding tribes including Mizuris, Sherwanis, Barushis and Dola Maris. In addition he was supported by the tribes of Rejukeran and Goran in the region of Akra, and by the tribes of Silevani in the Zakho region and Bradost in the Rewanduz region. Altogether he had 4000 or 5000 men.

Against him the Iraqis concentrated a force of 30,000, about half of the whole Iraqi army, plus 12,000 gendarmes and a considerable air force backed by the R.A.F., all under the command of Major General G. M. L. Renton, a one-armed

British officer, who had previously commanded a British army in North Africa. With him was Mustafa Omeri, minister of the interior, whose special task was to buy off some of the tribes. The Regent Abdul Illah also appeared at headquarters near Akra. By July 15, 1945, these forces had moved up into the mountains. On August 7 they attacked. They suffered heavy losses.

The Kurds seized the military posts and barracks at Bire Kepra, at Mergasor and Billeh. They occupied the surroundings of the town of Akra, Amadiya and Rewanduz. On one occasion a Kurdish force even advanced to within twenty kilometers of Arbil but was turned back there by a concentrated attack from the Royal Air Force.

At Nahlla the Kurds ambushed four battalions. Eight thousand troops were trapped by a force led by Mullah Mustafa. At this point the fortunes of war turned against the Barzanis. The encircled troops escaped as a result of betrayal by Mahmoud Aga of the powerful Zibari tribe, who till then had been allied with Mullah Mustafa. It is said that Mahmoud's brother Ahmed was bribed by the government. About this time Mahmoud Beg, Khalifa Samad of the Bradost tribe, also was bought off by the government.

In the course of these operations Barzani claimed to have captured 2000 rifles with 100,000 cartridges and eight larger guns, not to mention eight radio transmitters. He claimed also to have shot down nine aircraft. But in the end, the defection of powerful tribal allies and the intervention of the Royal Air Force were too much. Barzani recalled, in talking to me, that the British planes used to come "thirty-six at a time" to obliterate Barzani villages. He expressed the opinion that their pilots had been better trained than those of the present Iraqi air force because they came lower. Certainly they were more numerous.

Mustafa Barzani and his elder brother Sheikh Ahmed were now under great pressure from the British-backed Iraqi army. Mullah Mustafa believed the British were determined to crush his forces in order to prevent them from uniting with a developing area of Kurdish autonomy in Iran. In consequence

Mullah Mustafa was all the more drawn by glowing reports about the area of "autonomy by default" which had developed since 1941 around the town of Mehabad in Iran in the neutral zone between Soviet troops in the north and Iranian and British troops in the south. At Mehabad, which had been a center of Kurdish autonomy, like Suleimaniya in the eighteenth and nineteenth centuries, the Kurds in the 1940's made their most successful assertion of nationhood to date.

On September 16, 1942 a group of fifteen Kurds decided to form a committee for which the Kurdish word is "Komala." The Komala became the counterpart in Iran of the Hiwa society in Iraq and of the Hoyboun society which rallied Kurdish nationalists in Beirut, Damascus and other places outside Kurdistan.

In August 1944, after an exchange of Kurdish emissaries between Iraq and Iran, a historic affirmation of Kurdish aspirations to a greater unity took place at Mount Dalanpar, where the frontiers of Iraq, Iran and Turkey meet. Kurds from Iraq, Iran and Turkey signed the "Peman i Se Senur," the "pact of the three borders," providing for mutual support and sharing of material and human resources.[*]

Mullah Mustafa and Sheikh Ahmed decided to move, with their women and children and their flocks, out of Iraq to this region of relative freedom and safety which, in January 1946, was to become the Kurdish republic of Mehabad.

Although Eagleton in his book has set their number at only 10,000 including 3000 who could bear arms, Barzani himself has said that 35,000 men, women and children of the Barzani tribe and various associated tribes moved eastward in the late summer and fall of 1945. They left their villages empty. But in the mountains of Iran they did not find that they were immediately welcomed. Although the figure seems high, Barzani has estimated that 4500 of his people died of sickness, cold and hunger in the three months of winter from 1945 to 1946.

The reluctance with which Barzani's people were at first received was caused not by rivalries among the Kurds but by the pressure of Soviet agents on the Kurds of Iran to keep the

---

* William Eagleton, Jr., *op. cit.*

Barzanis out. The Soviets called Barzani "a British agent" (an epithet which they used as persistently at this time as certain American publications have more recently used the epithet, "the Red Mullah").

In the spring of 1946, however, the Kurds succeeded in overcoming Soviet objections, the Barzanis moved into more favorable locations in the valleys and Mullah Mustafa became one of the Mehabad republic's four generals. Soviet support for and pressure on the Mehabad republic were of a curiously equivocal nature. The Russians unquestionably did toy with the idea of supporting and using the Kurds. In October 1945, before the Mehabad republic was proclaimed on January 22, 1946, Kurdish leaders from Iran, including Qazi Mohammed, the future president of the Kurdish republic, were brought to Baku for a conference. The Russians approved the Kurds' plan for a republic, but reluctantly. After the republic was formed the Russians supplied some arms, a printing press and a little additional material support, including material for the uniforms in which the officers and leading officials of the Mehabad republic were clothed. But promised tanks, artillery and financial support were not delivered.

The Russians were really more interested in the neighboring Iranian Azerbaijani republic, which they would have liked to extend to include the Kurdish areas. And in the end, lured by the prospect of oil concessions in northern Iran, and under international pressures demanding their military withdrawal, they abandoned both the Azerbaijanis and the Kurds.

The Kurds' difficulty in dealing with both East and West was that they desperately needed help but wanted to maintain their independence. From the West they got neither help nor interest. Although there were a few American visitors to the republic, and Archibald Roosevelt wrote a fair and thorough report on it in the *Middle East Journal,* the official United States attitude was one of indifference touched with suspicion that the republic was controlled by the Soviet Union.

The Russians meanwhile, in return for their limited assistance, tried to exert much more influence than the Kurds wanted them to have. The Russians were not happy about the course the Mehabad republic was taking. In contrast to Tabriz, capital of the Azerbai jani republic, Mehabad experienced no "revolution," no terror, no Communism.

During my interviws with Barzani I asked him about the origins of the Mehabad republic and why it did not succeed. "You must surely know," he replied, "that when a people is oppressed it seeks opportunities to redress the wrongs that it suffers. When the Russians and the West occupied Iran we thought this was an opportunity to express the rights of the Kurds, for they left an area between their armies in which we could freely operate. If we did not succeed, you should seek the reasons from those two governments, the United States and Russia. When we asked the Americans to help us, they said, 'You are Communists.' When we asked the Russians, they said: 'You are Colonialists—Imperialists. You are with the United States.'"

Barzani recalled that toward the end of the life of the Mehabad republic, during a truce in the fighting between Kurds and Iranians, he spent forty-six days in Teheran. He said he went to see the American ambassador (it was Ambassador George V. Allen, although he did not remember the name) and asked whether the United States would be willing to permit him and his men to take refuge in the United States. But the Americans, he said, were suspicious. They would not hear of it. As Barzani interpreted the Ambassador's answer, he regarded the Kurds as instruments of the Soviet Union.

"In the situation of the world as it was then," he said, "I thought this was tantamount to telling me to go to Russia."

Ambassador Allen, who is now retired, has given me his personal recollection of the meeting with Barzani. In a letter from Washington dated May 10, 1963, he said that he agreed to see Barzani at the request of General Razmara, who thought that the American ambassador might convince the Kurdish leader that he could expect fair treatment from the Iranian government. Ambassador Allen wrote:

> I agreed to see him on condition that Razmara understood that I could give Barzani no guarantees on behalf of the Iranian government.

A rendezvous was arranged on this basis, at the residence of Colonel Sexton [the American military attaché] in Shimran, 7 miles out of Tehran. It was agreed that the meeting would be kept entirely secret. I tell you about it now because you have heard about it from Barzani and because the facts should be kept straight.

When I arrived at Sexton's house, Barzani and an Iranian who served as translator, were already there. I have forgotten precise details, having given little thought to the incident for 17 years, but I recall that Barzani was dressed in a typical Kurdish chieftain's costume, which as you know is quite dashing, and I think he must have had an ornamental dagger in a silk scarf bound around his waist, but he was a rather somber-looking figure, probably in his late 30's, huskily built, with a bull neck that went square into his shoulders. His complexion was swarthy and his black hair was cropped short. By far his most conspicuous features were deep brown eyes, which flashed from side to side as if on the constant alert. He was perched on the edge of a chair, and reminded me of a caged lion or hawk, watching for prey or to be preyed on.

After a few amenities, during which I inquired, with some purpose, whether he planned to remain long in Tehran, he launched into an impassioned plea for the Kurds to be allowed to live their own lives. (I had heard the same plea a dozen times from Qashqai and other tribal chieftains and knew the theme well.) He maintained that the Kurds were peaceful, quiet shepherds who had no designs on anyone else's land or property and simply wanted to be left alone.

I expressed pleasure at hearing his views but said I was doubtful that the United States, a country 4,000 miles from Iran, could be of much assistance. We could hardly undertake responsibility for Iranian internal affairs. He said he did not trust Iranian promises and declared that the U.S. could exert great influence over the Iranian government, by granting or withholding aid and through other means, if we wanted to.

I told him that his inference was natural and admitted that we might exert considerable pressure on the Tehran authorities if we went all out to do so, but I reminded him that just as the Kurds prized their independence, the Iranians did also and would bitterly resent our trying to tell them how they must conduct their internal affairs.

Mullah Mustafa expressed conviction that it would never be possible for the Kurds and Iranians to live together amicably and that the best solution would be for the Kurds to leave Iran. When I asked where he thought of going, he said, "We'd like to go to the United States."

I asked, "Do you mean all the Kurds? That means many hundred thousand." He nodded affirmatively.

I remarked, pleasantly, that the thought was very flattering to the United States but that it was difficult to see how it could be carried out. Transportation problems alone would be well-nigh insurmountable, even if the Kurds could manage to get to a seaport with their wives, children, and possessions. Suitable places to settle in the U.S. similar to those to which the Kurds were accustomed would be hard to find, not to mention the large sums of money involved, the problems of getting a special immigration act through Congress, acquiring adequate land in the United States, etc.

It is quite probable that Mullah Mustafa, a nomadic chieftain accustomed to moving his tribe with household equipment and animals from one place to another, did not consider the difficulties as great as I did, but he did not argue the point and let the matter drop. I got the impression that he had not advanced the idea with great expectation that it could be realized. He certainly did not press the point, and the conversation on this subject lasted only a few minutes.

In response to your specific question, I did regard Mullah Mustafa's inquiry as serious, and I gave him a serious and reasoned reply. I was aware that he could hardly appreciate the difficulties involved, for him and for us, in carrying out his suggestion, and I did not want to encourage false hopes, but I gave no indication of treating his inquiry lightly. . . .

We might have been willing to take a few dozen Kurdish leaders —those whose continued presence in Kurdistan might involve dangers either to themselves or the friendly governments—but neither Barzani nor any of the chieftains would settle in America and leave their tribes behind, and we would not have suggested it. He said nothing about a visit, for himself or anyone else.

There was no discussion of the U.S.S.R., as far as I recall, in my talk with Barzani, and if he had brought up the subject of going to Russia, I would probably have suggested that he try the Russians out and see if they would take him and his tribe. Any threat on his part to look to Russia for support if we turned him down would not have impressed me. A few months later, when he did go over the border, I am frank to say that I was not unduly alarmed. I was not unhappy to let the Russians wrestle with the problem for a while.

Ambassador Allen went on to express the opinion that the most important thing that Barzani could do for his Kurds at this stage of their development would be "to emulate Sequoia and educate his tribe. Otherwise, the Kurds will always be oppressed by someone."

Regarding the Soviets Allen added:

> Their support of Kurdistan is entirely opportunistic. They will pull the rug from under the Kurds in the future, as in the past, whenever better picking seems to lie in a different direction. We Americans must keep trying to maintain a reasonable degree of friendship with all groups and avoid setting one off against the other. This is not an easy policy and, as in the Arab-Israeli dispute, is likely to please no one, but it is a policy to which the honest and just can repair, which is as much as we can ask.

In his letter Ambassador Allen also told about his efforts to save the lives of Qazi Mohammed, the president of the Kurdish republic, and his brother. He said that Archibald B. Roosevelt, then a secretary of embassy, had visited Mehabad, where he found Qazi Mohammed and many other Kurds working "hand-in-glove" with the Soviets. They had received from the Soviets a small radio station and help in publishing a small newspaper in Kurdish. But, Ambassador Allen continued, Archie Roosevelt was confident that they had done these things solely because they thought Russian help was necessary to enable them to achieve Kurdish autonomy. The Ambassador wrote that Roosevelt urged him to "go to the Shah immediately and urge him to go easy on the Kurdish leaders." He continued as follows:

There were only a very few educated Kurds with knowledge of the outside world, and it would be tragic, Archie felt, for the handful of intelligent leaders to be done away with. . . . Archie could understand why honest and even anti-Communist Kurds would nevertheless be grateful to Russia. If the Iranians would offer the Kurds similar encouragement to maintain their own language and culture Archie believed the Iranians could go far towards solving the Kurdish problem.

I asked the Palace for an appointment with the Shah as soon as possible. It was arranged for that evening. I told the Shah I was concerned about Kurdistan. He professed surprise and asked why. I said his sending Razmara there seemed to indicate strong measures were to be taken. He asked why I was so concerned about a group of tribesmen who had been hand-in-glove with the Soviets. I said they felt they had no other alternative. I referred particularly to Qazi Mohammed as an educated Kurd with whom he could try to work. The Shah made a wry face and said he had put matters in Razmara's hands. I said that was what disturbed me most.

The Shah then asked me, straightforward, "Are you afraid I'm going to have Qazi Mohammed shot?" I said yes, I was. He smiled and replied reassuringly, "Don't worry. I'm not going to." I expressed pleasure and went home.

Two or three days later I read in a Tehran newspaper that Razmara had ordered both Qazi Mohammed and his brother executed, and they had been put before a firing squad that morning.

The Shah never mentioned the subject to me again, and I did not broach it to him. I was angry, but the men were dead and no one could bring them back. I presumed that Razmara, who was difficult to deal with, had taken matters into his own hands. (Two years later he was assassinated while serving as Prime Minister.)

Barzani maintained that he did not have any particular predilection for going to Russia. He said he tried "many other countries." He recalled that the Iranian government at this time offered to settle the Barzanis, once disarmed, in the southeast corner of the Kurdish area of Iran, in the Alvand mountain region, near Hamadan. But Barzani regarded this as a trick to put him and his force out of action. Also he approached the British for help in returning to Iraq. But the British were no more helpful than the Americans. The Iraqi government of that time was willing to permit the return of Sheikh Ahmed and his ordinary tribal followers. But the government made it clear that if Mullah Mustafa and his top officers fell into their hands they would be executed.

Barzani said that he did not seek these ways out until "I had been betrayed by my fellow Kurds." And, indeed, it does seem that disunion among the Kurds made it impossible for them to resist the Iranian government in its advance northward on the heels of the withdrawing Russian army at the beginning of 1947. Old tribal rivalries were accentuated by adversity.

At this time the president of the Mehabad republic, Qazi Mohammed, proposed to quit the battle and to surrender to the Iranians. He did, and he was hanged on March 31, 1947. Mullah Mustafa's brother Sheikh Ahmed, having obtained a written amnesty for himself and his people from the Iraqi government, decided to return home. While many ordinary Barzani tribesmen with their women and children were, in fact, allowed to return peacefully to their homes at the beginning of 1947 and in trickles for years thereafter, the promise given Ahmed was dishonored. He and many other leading Barzanis spent the next twelve years in prison. Four former officers of the Iraqi army who had fought in Barzani's forces were hanged on June 29, 1947.

Barzani selected five hundred "good fighters" and determined to march to the Soviet Union. But first he spent April and part of May waiting at Argosh on the border while the greater part of the rest of the Barzani tribe and affiliated tribes moved slowly across the border back into Iraq.

Then, Barzani and his men took off northwestward into the Iraqi mountains. The Iraqi army and air force were already out to intercept him, but he kept going. Recalling this episode with satisfaction, Barzani says: "We marched for fifty-two days. In the high mountain passes the late spring

snow was six to twelve feet deep. We fought nine encoun-
ters, lost four, and had seven wounded. The four were buried,
and the seven we took with us." He and his men moved from
Iran through Iraq into Turkey. Then, dodging the Turkish
army, they moved back into Iran, where the Iranian army had
already been alerted to cut them off. Between June 16 and
18, 1947, Barzani and his men crossed the Soviet border at
a point south of the Soviet frontier post at Sarachlu. In their
final dash from the mountains north of Barzan to the Soviet
border they had covered two hundred and twenty miles in
fourteen days.

"How did the Russians receive you?" I asked. "How can
I say how they received us?" he replied. "They did not receive
us. But at least they did not send us back to Iraq. Every government has its laws concerning frontiers and refugees. They
accepted us as refugees. They dispersed us in the country.

"At the beginning," he recalled, "we spent some months
at Baku. Later we went to Tashkent. At the beginning when
we needed anything we had to ask those responsible and one
or two persons would go with us to market or wherever else
we wanted to go. They would not let us just go here and there
as we pleased. But later we were more free.

"We were divided into groups. I went one place. Others
went other places. We asked for instruction and were given
teachers according to our abilities—whether as carpenters,
or mechanics, or in agriculture or some other subject. Some
studied geology, some science, some economics. I asked to
go to the Academy of Languages in Moscow and I was sent
to Moscow."

I asked whether he had studied at the Soviet Military
Academy as has frequently been reported, but he insisted that
the only school he went to was the Academy of Languages,
where he learned not only Russian but was able also to study
economics and geography and science.

Alluding to the story that he had been trained at the
Soviet Military Academy, Barzani recalled mischievously that
the Iranian General Razmara had excused his inability to
catch him by writing that General Barzani had been graduated

from London University and taught military science by Lord Montgomery himself. And, he continued, still grinning mischievously, the Iraqi government later complained that it was also unable to subdue Barzani, because he had learned his military science in Russia.

The truth, Barzani explained, was that he had got his military training by fighting. If he was called "General" it was a title that had been conferred upon him by the Mehabad republic. The Russian-looking general's uniform in which he had been photographed in those days was the uniform of the Mehabad republic—not of the Soviet Union. In his interview with Richard Anderegg, the Swiss Broadcasting Network correspondent, Barzani added, however, that after an initial period of nine months' internment most of Barzani's men were given, at their own request, a course of Soviet military training. They were put in a special unit for this purpose. Those who could qualify were given advanced training on the level of noncommissioned officers, or officers, but without rank or commission. Military training was suddenly halted after one year.

Barzani himself was permitted to travel a good deal. During the summers he visited his Kurds—scattered around the Soviet Union. Those who had finished their training worked in factories, a few went on to higher institutions. A few were used in farming or as *kolkhoz* guards. About eighty got married, mostly to Moslem Turkoman girls, a few to Christian Russians. Some of the latter adopted Islam.

The treatment accorded the Kurdish refugees improved markedly after Lavrenti P. Beria, Stalin's secret police chief, and Premier Bagarov of Azerbaijan were hanged in 1953. The Kurds believed that Beria had shaped his policy toward the Kurds on the basis of advice from Bagarov, whom the Russians regarded as an expert on the area and who was reputed to have harbored the traditional Turkoman hostility toward the Kurds.

Early in 1954 Barzani got permission to move to Moscow and attend the Academy of Languages. He and his two closest associates of this period, Assad Hoshewi and Mir Haj, were given apartments in Moscow. Other Kurds found themselves assigned to better jobs and living quarters.

I asked him whether the Russians had not tried to indoctrinate him and his men politically during their time in Russia and whether the fact that after more than eleven years in exile he was allowed to return to Iraq with his men was not evidence that the Soviet Union expected some advantage from his return. To these questions his replies were oblique, perhaps because he felt an implied slur upon his integrity. He said that the Soviets did not try to convert the Kurds to Communism, "because they already have their Communist Party in Iraq." He added that, "We are Moslems and good Moslems cannot be Communists." And he implied that if the Russians thought they would gain some advantage from sending the Kurds home again they were misled.

"I spent twelve years in Russia," the General observed. "And I did not become a Communist." He alleged that for this very reason the Communists had at one time plotted to kill him in Iraq following his return from Russia. From other sources I have learned that in fact only a few of the Barzanis were influenced by Communist indoctrination. These included Sheikh Suleiman, one of Barzani's nephews, with whom he has since then broken off all contact. Two or three others remained in the Soviet Union when Barzani returned to Iraq. In talking with many of these men during my travels I gathered that they were grateful to the Russians, who had given them not only a refuge but, in many cases, their first chance to learn a trade and their first formal education. Many of them lived in towns for the first time. But most seemed to have been immunized against political indoctrination by the combination of their religious feeling, national feeling and tribal pride. These qualities would perhaps not have been sufficient safeguards but for the fact that these were men who had been picked by Barzani not merely as fighters but for their personal loyalty to him. Although Barzani had to be careful in his public pronouncements his men could always sense their chief's reservations about Communism. He and most of them remained practicing Moslems living for the day when their chief would lead them home again.

Barzani was in Prague enjoying a holiday when Abdul Karim Kassem on July 14, 1958, took over in Baghdad. Although, as he confided to me, he was suspicious of Kassem from the start, he telegraphed immediately asking permission for him and his men to return, and permission was granted. A delegation representing the Kurdish Democratic Party flew to Prague in September to inform Barzani about the situation he would find in Iraq. It consisted of Ibrahim Ahmed, the secretary-general of the party; Major Nuri Ahmed Taha, a Kurdish officer in the Iraqi army; Barzani's son Obeidullah and his nephew Sheikh Sadiq.

Barzani, Assad Hoshewi and Mir Haj were sent back to Baghdad by air in September. The rest of the Kurds traveled aboard a Russian ship from Odessa to Basra early in 1959. About eight hundred persons returned, including nearly five hundred of Barzani's original group of fighters, most of the eighty wives whom they had married in the Soviet Union and their children, and a few of the Kurds from the Mehabad republic who had taken refuge in the Soviet Union.

Barzani's route home to Iraq led through Cairo. He traveled with Mir Haj and Assad Hoshewi. I asked him his impression of President Nasser. He said that although Nasser had received him he unfortunately had no real conversations, so he could not express an opinion. I sensed that he had in the back of his mind the possibility of an eventual entente with Nasser and was exercising the utmost care in what he said. Later when Nasser received Barzani's representatives, in the summer of 1963, he pointed to a chair in his study and said: "That is where Mullah Mustafa sat."

Barzani recalled that an aide of President Nasser came to his hotel to apologize that he did not know Barzani was coming. Otherwise he would have made him an official guest. The Egyptian government did, however, pay the Kurds' hotel bills. After a day at Port Said, Barzani flew on to Baghdad. He gave this account of his first meeting with Kassem:

"Kassem received me on the third day. I returned home

and my nephew asked me: 'What did you think of Kassem?' I said: 'He is worse than Nuri Said.' But I told no one else this at the time."

The thing that Barzani particularly disliked about Kassem was his practice of calling himself "Sole Leader." "Doesn't that mean that he could not be good for us?" Barzani asked me. A little later when there were disturbances in Kurdish territory Barzani was irked also because Baghdad authorities printed leaflets with Kassem's and his own picture side by side and distributed them in the Kurdish territories. "I protested against this," he said. "He calls himself the Zaim of the Iraqi people. I am not Zaim of the Kurdish people." The word "Zaim" means "leader" in Arabic with a connotation of greatness, uniqueness.

In Baghdad both Premier Kassem and the Communist Party laid claim to Barzani. Both wished to exploit the popularity which was reflected in the large and noisy reception he was given by the Kurdish community in Baghdad. Premier Kassem installed him in the villa that once belonged to Premier Nuri Said. The Communists talked as though the twelve years in Russia had made Barzani a Communist.

Barzani, who had no faith in Kassem and disliked the Communists, had to play a delicate political game. As long as Kassem showed any signs of carrying out the promises to treat the Kurds as partners, and as long as the Communists were tacit partners in Kassem's regime, he had to play along with both. Political statements he made during this period are full of praise for Kassem and gratitude to the Soviet Union for the hospitality it had showed his Kurds. In public he avoided ideological questions but in private he made no secret of his opposition to Communism.

Little by little in 1959 and 1960 Kassem turned against Barzani, whose following among the Kurds he began to fear. Barzani also began to complain more and more openly that Kassem's promises had not been fulfilled. The Communists meanwhile tried to infiltrate the Kurdish Democratic Party and found that the hard core of anti-Communism within the KDP was Barzani.

This was the time—from his return to Baghdad in September of 1958 until he took to the mountains of the Barzani territory in March 1961—when Barzani learned Iraqi politics from the inside. Ahead of him lay eighteen months of battle against Kassem's regime and beyond that more fighting, but also more difficult tasks. More difficult because more subtle. The future would call for political negotiation and maneuvering in the world of the Kurds, in the world of the Arabs, and in the world of the great powers. For this Barzani would need all the cunning and wisdom, the training and experience of his long fighting career as a Kurdish nationalist.

8

The Kurdish Democratic Party

In a garden belonging to a man named Haji Daud near the Chom i Sauj Bulaqeh river outside the town of Mehabad in Iranian Kurdistan fifteen men met on September 16, 1942, to form a Kurdish political party.

Although at first a secret organization called simply "Komala" meaning "committee," this organization was the predecessor of the Kurdish Democratic Party, or, as it was officially renamed at the party congress of 1956, the Democratic Party of Kurdistan. The men in Haji Daud's garden had for months been discussing the need for such an organization to help hasten the development of the Kurdish nation, to take advantage of the circumstances that had left Mehabad in a kind of political no-man's-land between the Russian army to the north of Iran and the forces of the Iranian government and the Western Allies farther to the south.

On hand for the occasion was a Kurdish captain of the Iraqi army named Mir Haj, who passed on his experience in forming a secret party in Iraq called "Hiwa." "Hiwa" is the Kurdish word for "hope." In line with his recommendation, the new party in Iran was formed of cells of five or six persons each. In consequence, although the Komala gathered about a hundred members in Mehabad during the next six months the names of the members were known only to a few. Members swore to the following: 1. Never to betray the Kurdish nation; 2. To work for Kurdish self-government;

3. To guard the secrets of the party whether oral or written; 4. To remain a member of the party for life; 5. To consider all Kurds as brothers and sisters; 6. Not to join any other party or group without permission of the Komala.

By April 1943 the Komala had spread through the neutral zone of northern Iran around Mehabad into the Soviet zone north of Miandoab, and as far as the Soviet frontier. To the south its influence extended as far as Saqqiz. It did not elect a president or chairman; its leading members in those early days were Rahman Zabihi, Muhammad Yahu and the poet Hazhar. In the next two years most of the Kurdish tribal chiefs and many others in the area joined the Komala. The new organization was strong enough to send representatives to Iraq to discuss possible joint activities with the Hiwa, and prominent Kurds from Iraq and from Turkey visited Mehabad. They marveled at what some have called "autonomy by default" in a place where the Iranian government was unable to exert its authority, and where the Russians refrained from doing so.

As mentioned earlier, in August 1944 representatives of the Kurds from the three countries, Iran, Iraq and Turkey, signed a pact, the "Peman i Se Senur," or the "pact of the three borders," providing mutual aid. The Iranian Kurds were represented by Qasim Qaderi of Mehabad; the Iraqi Kurds by Sheikh Ubeidullah of Zeno village near the Iranian border at Khaneh; the Turkish Kurds by Qazi Mulla Wahab. The Iranian and Iraqi Kurds in May 1944 adopted as their national flag a tricolor of three horizontal stripes, red, white and green—a simple reversal of the Iranian flag, which has green at the top. They adopted as their emblem a sun with jagged rays flanked by ears of wheat, with a mountain and a pen in the background.

The town of Mehabad awoke from centuries of indolent provincialism; became a crowded, lively, even excited national center. It became the scene even of an unprecedented performance of a patriotic opera called *Daik i Nishtiman* (motherland).

Up to this point the Komala had been a purely national

organization free from foreign influence. It had adopted a Communist Party style nomenclature—central committee, politburo, and so on—simply as a matter of convenience. It had no political significance, but the Soviet authorities, needless to say, had their eye on the Komala.

Active Soviet interest in the Kurds may be traced back to 1941, when the Red army was falling back on all fronts and Soviet authorities were eager to win Kurdish support against the Nazis then threatening the Caucasus. The Russians invited a group of Kurdish chiefs to Baku, where they met Jafar Baghirov, prime minister of the Azerbaijani Soviet Socialist republic. Although the Russians made no promises at that time, the tribal leaders got the idea that they could count on Soviet backing in their national aspirations. The basis for future Soviet policy towards the Kurds had been laid.

During a second visit of Kurdish tribal leaders to Baku in September 1945, Baghirov, after first attempting to persuade them to subordinate their ambitions to participation in the Azerbaijani republic, had to admit that the Kurdish leaders were determined to achieve their own separate autonomy. Making a virtue of necessity, he won the Kurds' emotional approval by banging his fist on the table and proclaiming that "as long as the Soviet Union exists the Kurds will have their independence." No one could be quite sure what that meant, but it served the general propagandistic purposes of the Soviet Union. More specifically, Baghirov observed that the Komala as then organized was ineffective; he recommended that the Kurdish movement should be transformed into a "Democratic Party of Kurdistan."

A few months later, in November 1945, the future president of the Mehabad republic, Qazi Mohammed, called together about sixty leaders of the Komala in the only public meeting place available in Mehabad, the Soviet Cultural Relations Center. In accordance with Baghirov's advice, they decided to abandon secrecy, come into the open as a democratic party, and change their name to Democratic Party of Kurdistan. Thus, the Russian hand appeared from the start in the affairs of the Democratic Party of Kurdistan, or, as it is more commonly known, the Kurdish Democratic Party. In those early days cooperation with the Soviet Union, whose armies were stationed only a few miles from the autonomous Kurdish territory, was a matter of necessity. It was also a great advantage in the limited extent to which the Russians provided material help, first to the party, later to the Mehabad republic.

The program of the KDP was as follows:

1. The Kurdish government of Iran shall have self-government in the administration of local affairs.

2. The Kurdish language shall be the official language and shall be used in education.

3. A provincial council in Kurdistan shall be elected immediately, according to Iranian constitutional law, and shall exercise its right of controlling and overseeing all public affairs.

4. All government officials shall be Kurds.

5. Revenues collected in Kurdistan shall be spent there.

6. The Democratic Party of Kurdistan shall make efforts to establish complete fraternity with the people of Azerbaijan and minority elements living there.

7. The party shall work for the improvement of the moral standards, the health and economic conditions of the Kurdish people by the development of education, public health, commerce and agriculture.

Very soon thereafter the Kurdish Democratic Party was also formed in Iraq by the merger of the Hiwa and the Jiani Kurd (Kurdish resurrection). At its first party congress, on August 16, 1946, the KDP of Iraq named Barzani its chairman, although he was at the time fighting in Iran. Despite the fact that Barzani was in subsequent years frequently to deprecate the value of the party and his ties with it, he willingly accepted the title of chairman in 1946 as a means of maintaining his links with the Kurds of Iraq. A group of left-wingers called Shoresh (revolution) held out and eventually joined the Communist Party. In Syria a KDP was also formed. Originally formed in Turkey, the Hoyboun (independence) had become the organization of Kurdish exiles in Syria, Lebanon and various European capitals. Hiwa replaced the Hoyboun in Iraq and KDP replaced Hiwa. Shoresh was a pro-Communist and pro-Soviet faction which split away from Hiwa. One party man explained it to me this way: "How could it be otherwise?" he asked. "The Communists were the only ones who paid any attention to us; no one else was interested in us. Only they recognized our claims to national rights. And if it is true that the Soviet Union let us down in Mehabad it is also true that the Soviet Union is the only country that did anything for us during that episode of independence."

From the beginning the Communists tried to exploit their advantage by penetrating or absorbing the KDP. But from the beginning also the KDP had its anti-Communists. Rooted in the Kurdish national movement, the party maintained its own distinct personality compounded of persons drawn from a broad spectrum of Kurdish life. It may convey something of this personality if I describe two men who played significant roles in the life of various parts of the party. One is from Diyarbekir in Turkey, the other from Mehabad in Iran. The first represents the old aristocratic element among Kurdish nationalists; the second, the new popular element.

Apo Jomart, the remarkable interpreter who accompanied me on my trip through Kurdistan, was born into a landowning family of Kurdish nationalists at Diyarbekir around the turn of the century. Families such as his have kept the flame of Kurdish national feeling alive through the centuries. He was educated with his numerous brothers and sisters at home, and in Kurdish. This family's lands were so vast that Apo's father spent weeks moving about on inspection. Within his domain were wide fields of wheat on the plains of Diyarbekir and flourishing orchards around the town, and even a plant where silk was made in the traditional manner, out of the silk spun by worms fed on mulberry leaves. Whatever was Kurdish this family cultivated avidly.

In 1908 when the Young Turks came to power Apo was in Istanbul, a student and eager member of the first Kurdish political clubs, and contributor to the first Kurdish periodicals.

He and his family organized a Kurdish political party at Diyar-bekir and other towns of eastern Turkey. They supported the great revolt of Sheikh Said of Piran in 1925. Apo also traveled from end to end of the Kurdish territories of Iraq and Turkey with British Major E. W. Noel on his assignment to inform himself concerning the extent and significance of the Kurdish national movement. Finally Apo was arrested and was lucky to escape with a prison sentence of a few years. After that he was too well known as a Kurdish leader, and could no longer live in Kemalist Turkey. In the late 'twenties he fled, and has spent the rest of his life as a refugee outside of Turkey, keeping in touch with the long and agonizing series of Kurdish revolts in Turkey, Iran and Iraq, waiting for and working for the day when Kurdish nationalism would achieve its ends. When I knew Apo he was seventy-two years old and still willing and able to fight for his cause.

Another member of the Kurdish Democratic Party was Ahmed Tofiq, who escorted me in Iraqi Kurdistan. Ahmed was a teenager in 1947 when he saw the bodies of Qazi Moham-med and his two brothers hanging in the city square, and the shock of that sight stayed with him for life. For Qazi Moham-med had been his hero. He had got a job running messages for the President and basked in the fact that twice he had earned commendations—once for refusing to admit to party headquarters a man lacking proper credentials, and again for helping to design the Kurdish national emblem.

For years after the executions young Ahmed ranged up and down the Kurdish territories of Iran organizing the Kurd-ish Democratic Party. At one time he held the title of secre-tary-general of the party in Iran. The Iranian police were after him, and he had many narrow escapes. Once, after he had been arrested, he found himself in the custody of a Kurd. He began to talk to the Kurd about his nation's struggle, about suffering and heroism, about the splendid future that awaited the Kurdish homeland—until at last the Kurdish policeman was in tears, and let Ahmed go.

In those days the Iranian authorities got the idea that

Ahmed was associated with the Communists. "But they were always wrong," he observed, adding with amusement, that the Communists at the same time imagined him an American agent.

In the early 1950's Ahmed managed to get himself sent to Prague on a mission for the Kurdish Democratic Party. He loved Prague and also Geneva, which he saw en route. These are the only cities outside Iraq that he has ever seen. He told me about the girls he met in Prague. "But really," he declared. "I have only one love. I am in love with my country."

In Prague, Communist Party officials tried to recruit Ahmed for the Communist Party. They forecast for him a brilliant future of leadership and prominence. But he turned them down. He told me that he was convinced that the Communist Party would always serve the interests of the Soviet Union and not of the Kurdish nation.

After his trip to Europe, Ahmed Tofiq did not return to Iran but settled down in Iraq, where he became a close observer of the evolution of the Kurdish Democratic Party of Iraq. He found that the party, two years after it had been formed in 1946, was split into two factions, one under Ibrahim Ahmed, the other under Hamza Abdullah. Ibrahim Ahmed's faction was called "Democratic Party of Kurdistan (Iraq)"; Hamza Abdullah's added the word "Progressive." Well-educated in Marxist dialectics, Ibrahim Ahmed conceded no points to the leftist intellectuals in his party. Although himself inclined to the left in his early days, as time went on he grew more nationalist. He tried to win the young people who were under the influence of the Communists to the cause of Kurdish nationalism.

Hamza Abdullah, on the other hand, persisted in his strong personal leanings to the left. He tried to win back the former Communists who had fallen under Ibrahim Ahmed's influence.

Although the two factions had attempted to unite under the title Union of the Kurdish Democratic Party and had even established a joint newspaper, Ahmed Tofiq found that they were working against each other. He branded Hamza

Abdullah an opportunist who played a pro-Communist line while exploiting his ties with the old tribal system. He accused Hamza Abdullah of misusing party money. And he advised the Iraqi party to expel him and his associates. This was in fact done but not until some years later. In the meantime Ibrahim Ahmed incurred Mustafa Barzani's displeasure and Hamza Abdullah enjoyed a brief period of favor.

This switch took place in 1958, when Ibrahim Ahmed flew to Prague with a KDP delegation to see Barzani. Barzani, the tribal leader, took an immediate dislike to Ibrahim Ahmed, the intellectual, a dislike which persists to this day and which plays an important role in the affairs of Kurdistan. To his aides Barzani spoke of Ibrahim Ahmed's "pride and vanity."

During the first half of 1959, while the Communists were enjoying a period of high favor in the Kassem regime, Barzani backed Hamza Abdullah, who evidently thought that the Communists were the real "wave of the future" and acted accordingly. In 1959 Abdullah even made the decision arbitrarily to unite various Kurdish organizations with the Communist Party; he proposed to transfer from the KDP to the Communist Party the organizations of Kurdish peasants, of Kurdish youth and of Kurdish women.

It was Ahmed Tofiq who alerted Barzani to these developments. Searching Barzani out at Shaqlawa he warned him that Hamza Abdullah was working with Kassem to destroy the Kurdish national movement.

Barzani called a conference of KDP representatives in Baghdad and this group decided to halt the activities of Hamza Abdullah until the annual national congress could decide on his case. The next day Barzani went to the central office of the KDP and placed it in the hands of a specially appointed party committee. This intra-party coup took place in the middle of 1959.

At the fourth party congress which followed on October 23, 1960, Hamza Abdullah and his closest associates were expelled from the party as traitors. At the fourth and fifth congresses Ibrahim Ahmed was re-elected secretary-general of the party. Mustafa Barzani did not oppose him, but did not support him either. This is the situation which continues to this day. Barzani voted for only four of the fifteen members of the central committee, indicating that he did not care for the rest of them.

Barzani's dislike notwithstanding, Ibrahim Ahmed has played a vital role in the evolution of the Kurdish Democratic Party and of the Kurdish national movement generally. He is a bookish man, a lawyer and editor of a magazine, "an intellectual." About fifty years old, he is small and frail with graying temples and a carefully clipped white mustache. Articulate, thoughtful, courteous, simple, he is very much the intellectual and the man of distinction.

A graduate of the Faculty of Law of Baghdad, he published his thesis on Arab-Kurdish relations in 1937 and was soon thereafter arrested as an anti-government agitator. In 1939 he started a periodical called *Galaweich,* which he published for a decade. At that time, although the Iraqi Communist Party criticized him as a man of the right, he was tried and sent to prison for "Communism." He was imprisoned for three years and subjected to "restricted residence" for three years thereafter.

When he got out of jail in 1952, Ibrahim Ahmed became secretary-general of the Kurdish Democratic Party for the first time. Now he became aware of the Communists not only as a political group who shared his interest in Marxism, but as competitors for the loyalty of young Kurds.*

Ibrahim Ahmed explained his attitude toward the Communist Party and toward Kassem in some detail in an interview with Eric Roulot of the Paris newspaper *Le Monde* in March 1963. Roulot made his way to the headquarters from which Ibrahim Ahmed was exercising general supervision over the KDP part in the struggle, located in a cave hidden between two high mountains not far from Suleimaniya. To get there he negotiated a series of well-defended

---

* The last few months of 1963 and the beginning of 1964 Ibrahim Ahmed spent in Europe. Like Jelal Talabani he succeeded in making his way by means that must remain secret.

obstacles—several streams and a well-observed winding path up a steep mountainside. No one would know that this path led to the headquarters of one of the principal Kurdish leaders. The entrance to the cave was so well camouflaged that it could be seen only from a few feet away. Inside, the cave opened up. Oil lamps revealed piles of boxes containing every kind of supplies—food, clothes, weapons and ammunition. And behind the boxes a flatbed printing press on which the party newspaper *Khabat* was still being printed regularly. In the back of the cave hung stalactites. Water dripped unceasingly. It was damp. Sounds echoed eerily. Ibrahim Ahmed sat in a well-lighted corner surrounded by books ranging from Dostoevski to Harrison Salisbury, from Shakespeare to Harold Laski and Marx and Lenin.

Ibrahim Ahmed complained that the Communist Party was skimming off many of the best young KDP members. According to an explanation he gave Eric Roulot, in order to resist this drain upon his membership he adopted a kind of tongue-in-cheek advocacy of Marx-Leninism. "I proclaimed that our party was inspired by Marx-Leninism. These words acted like an open sesame to the world of Kurdish youth who at that time were fascinated by Communism. The reactionaries treated us as agents of the Kremlin, but the Communists were not fooled. They denounced us as *agents provocateurs* and demanded that we cease all references to Marx-Leninism. Nonetheless since then we have lost no members to the Communist Party." He pointed out that the Communists consider the Kurdish Democratic Party representative of the Kurdish bourgeoisie and quite distinct from the proletariat led by the Communist Party.

Ibrahim Ahmed went on to explain his party's attitude toward Kassem. He pointed out that the important thing about Kassem for the Kurds was that his coming to power broke up the "holy anti-Kurdish alliance" which at that time united Baghdad with Teheran and Ankara in the Baghdad Pact. In return for the support of the Kurdish nationalists, he added, Premier Kassem recognized the claims of the Kurdish Democratic Party. He liberated hundreds of prisoners who had been imprisoned by Nuri Said and authorized the return of Mullah Mustafa and his companions from Russia. Above all, he agreed to include in the constitution an article recognizing the equality and the rights of the Kurdish and the Arab peoples.

"But," he noted, "the honeymoon of Kassem and the KDP was short. The former dictator recognized the Kurdish nation only with his lips." Ahmed observed that Kassem had used the Communists and the Kurds to put down the insurrection of Colonel Abdel Wahab Shawaf at Mosul in 1959, but, having used them to save himself, had then turned against the extreme left on the one hand and the Kurdish Democratic Party on the other. Leaders of the KDP have told me that they gave Kassem the first information that Shawaf was collecting arms in preparation for the rebellion. And it was the Kurds' swift intervention that enabled the government to put down the rebellion.

As Kassem's relations with the Kurds deteriorated, he prohibited all activity of the Kurdish Democratic Party and ordered the arrest of Ibrahim Ahmed for a murder which he had not committed. He put Mullah Mustafa under "restricted residence." Looking back over this period the KDP official observed: "Kassem was a fool to alienate us. We were his most faithful allies."

Kassem's insincerity, the opportunism of his professed support of Kurdish claims, became all too apparent by the beginning of 1961. At the same time the equal insincerity of Communist Party support—which was restrained by the Soviet Union's efforts to cultivate Kassem on a governmental level and to infiltrate Iraq by means of economic and military aid—also became apparent. As they fell out with Kassem the leaders of the KDP began to feel the disadvantages of their long association with the Communist Party. Quietly they began to try to mend their bridges with the other Arab parties, after September 1961 even attempting to form a national front of political parties against Kassem. But they discovered that they were not trusted. The Istiqlal, the National Democratic Party and others regarded the KDP with suspicion both because of their previous overt commitment to Kassem and their past close association with the Communists. The Ba'ath Party was particularly reserved in its attitude. As described in the chapter "The Great Double Cross," the gulf between the two parties was temporarily bridged during the period of active struggle against Kassem. But the bridge was not strong enough to last for long once the common enemy had been eliminated.

Kurdish national leaders could see that the government was steadily strengthening its position in the north and arming tribal enemies of the Barzanis in a manner that would make an eventual clash inevitable. For them the problem was whether they should take the initiative in launching a rebellion, or whether they should wait for Kassem to launch a repressive military campaign. But the Communists would not hear of armed action. In place of rebellion the Communists offered only words. They proposed "the formation of a vast peaceful gathering of the peoples founded on a common struggle of Arabs and Kurds."

The "war effort" of the Kurdish Democratic Party has been severely criticized not only by Barzani and his associates but by members of the party itself. The main points of criticism are the following:

1. Ibrahim Ahmed was slow in organizing a real KDP war effort. The party's efforts have at all times and in all respects been inadequate.

2. The party failed in the realm of foreign propaganda. The first successful effort to reach the foreign press was made by an emissary of General Barzani. The KDP could have made contact with foreign correspondents in Syria, in Iran or even in Baghdad if it had tried. It had access to the Kurdish intellectuals who, if their effort had been organized, might have raised their voices in a variety of publications around the world.

3. The party did not recruit medical personnel or acquire medical supplies urgently needed by the fighting men in the north. If the party recruited any doctors they were not sent to the tribal forces I visited in the summer of 1962. I met

my first Kurdish doctor at Talabani's headquarters at Chem y Razan in February 1963 and was given to understand that other doctors had in the meantime been sent to Barzani's men.

I remember the day the little party with whom I traveled through Kurdistan was bombed in the village of Bindar. When the planes were gone and the dead lay bleeding and the wounded screaming in the village I noted one man who seemed to be cursing. I asked my interpreter to translate. "He is saying, 'Where are our doctors?'" my interpreter translated.

4. While it continued to inveigh against "imperialism" and particularly against CENTO, the party's newspaper *Khabat* remained silent about the Soviet Union's deliveries of arms to Iraq. Such an organization as the Committee for the Defense of the Rights of the Kurdish People, in Lausanne, Switzerland, had sent telegrams of protest to Moscow, but the KDP had done nothing to protest the Soviet deliveries. Since every Kurd fighting in the mountains knew that bombs, and rockets and bullets being used against him were being supplied by the Soviet Union and deeply resented it, the KDP's attitude seemed out of line with the will of the Kurdish people.

5. The KDP's lack of military activity compared with that of the tribal forces was apparent to all.

Most of the KDP's inadequacies were probably related to its early association with the Communist Party. The Communists did not want to fight and the KDP wasn't quite sure. Ibrahim Ahmed has admitted that until December 1961— when Barzani had already been fighting for three months— he did not really believe in the possibility of armed resistance to the Iraqi army by partisans of the KDP. Until then his idea was that the main brunt of the fighting should be borne by tribal forces while the party devoted itself to gathering funds, supplies and information, to sending recruits to the mountains, and to engaging in political activity. Only after December did the party step up its own military effort. In defense of the KDP some of its officials have pointed out that many of its activities were of the kind that do not show, that it did gather funds, that it did deliver supplies, that it did obtain information, that it did send recruits to the mountains, and that it was Ibrahim Ahmed of the KDP who made the contacts with the Free Officers who finally overthrew Kassem. Among their activities they mentioned that in some urban areas the KDP has a system of supporting dependents of men fighting in the north. It pays their rent and 1.5 dinars per dependent per month. In rural areas the amount of support is one dinar per month.

As the struggle against Kassem went on, the political orientation of the KDP shifted to the right. The KDP partisans went on singing a song, the words of which are as follows: "The aghas and the sons of beys suck the blood of the workers. Side by side with all workers we fight against the common enemy, the exploiters." The party stood against monarchy and dictatorship, against the feudal lords and the landowners, as well as for Kurdish national rights. But the really important political development during the eighteen months of the first phase of the war was that the Kurdish Democratic Party succeeded in supplanting the Communist Party in all of Kurdistan except perhaps in some of the bigger towns, where the extreme left retained some followers among intellectuals and workers.

In the second phase of the war, against a Baghdad government controlled by the Ba'ath Party, and after the fall of the Ba'athist regime, the problem of relations between the KDP and the Communists seemed more delicate than ever. The Soviet Union and its propaganda organs, such as the Peyke-Iran* broadcasting station, embraced the Kurdish cause without reservation. And the Ba'ath Party waged its war not only against the Kurds, but also against the Communist Party of Iraq. As a result many Communists fled to the mountains of the north.

But in fact, now that the KDP is fully committed to its war against the Baghdad government it is also keeping the

* Peyke-Iran is a Soviet "clandestine" station broadcasting from East Berlin mainly to Iran, secondarily to the Kurds.

Communists at arm's length. More than that, in March 1963, Barzani's forces actually fought and broke up four pockets of Communists who had attempted to form armed groups in the northern area. At Kelkar Smak near Dukhan about 200 Communists were driven into a cave and captured. Near Shanderi, between Halabje and Suleimaniya, another 70 Communists were captured after a fight in which a number were killed. At Mount Bemo, between Darbandikhan and the Iranian border, a group of 120 Communists was broken up with many killed and injured. Finally, at Hornawazan near Kirkuk, the largest group, amounting to 500 men, were isolated in a valley. They surrendered to Barzani's men after suffering severe casualties.

These pockets of Communists and others were fugitives from the Ba'ath. Where they have been willing to submit to the authority of Barzani's forces they have been given places to camp and have been supplied with food, but they have not been given arms and have not been asked to participate in battle. During the second phase of the war the KDP has grown and adapted itself to the needs of the struggle. It is working with the tribal forces whose military commanders are the very aghas and beys mentioned in the party's songs. It has accommodated itself to new ideas, more nationalist, more right wing. In time there will have to be a new definition of the KDP's ideology.

9

The Spirit of a Nation

A nation's spirit lives in its songs—its poetry, its legends, its stories, and in its religion. That is why the Kurdish nationalists make so much of their folklore and literature. In these they find reflected their people, whose lives and loves, whose struggles and wisdom are bound up with the mountains among which they live, the animals, the trees, the rocks and the sparkling streams.

These things probably seem more real and more important to the Kurds than to Americans because the Kurd leads a simpler life. He has fewer sophisticated distractions. While the American child may learn his folktales from neatly bound and illustrated books or from television, and the tales may seem pretty unreal to him, the Kurdish child hears them told by members of his family, he lives and breathes the spirit of these tales.

Here are tales about hunting and brigandage, about Bunyanesque feats of strength and Robin Hood-like acts of generosity, about marksmanship and sangfroid, about chivalry, about honor and vengeance, the romance of battle, magnanimity and hospitality, feats of valor, the beauty, the courage and the wisdom of women.

Two tales about the origins of the Kurds establish the emphasis on the supernatural, the weird, the magical and the frightful that run through much of Kurdish folklore. They say that once upon a time, no one knows when, there lived an evil king named Zahak. From this man's shoulders there grew two monstrous snakes. Each snake had to be fed the brain of a young man or maiden each day. One of the king's ministers got the idea that he could save the lives of some of the victims by mixing a calf's brain with each human brain. Thus he was able to save the life of one youth or maiden each day. Those who survived fled to the mountains and there became the ancestors of the Kurds.

Another story traces the origin of the Kurds back to the days of King Solomon. It is said that there was once a time when King Solomon ruled the supernatural world of fairies and elves and all manner of wondrous creatures whom the Kurds called *jinni* or *div*.

King Solomon sent five hundred *div* to Europe to search out the most beautiful maidens and bring them back for his harem. Upon their return, however, they found that the monarch had died and so, of course, they kept the young ladies for themselves. Their offspring were the ancestors of the Kurds.

They tell a story about the younger brothers of the Emir Mohammed of Bohtan who, rather than violate the Emir's order not to shoot, wrestled a bear down and tied him up with belts and turbans. And about the shepherd who killed a lion by smiting him between the eyes with his staff, thereby earning a reward from his prince.

Marksmanship, sangfroid and the spirit of generosity are extolled in another tale. The princess of Bitlis had the habit of sitting at a window of her castle smoking a pipe that consisted of a long tube of jasmine wood. Opposite the palace was a building in which were installed the men of the Kurdish chief Hemedo. Whether these men suspected the princess was in love with their chief, or whether they just didn't like the way she stuck the tube of her pipe out of the window and watched the smoke curling upward, all the while paying no attention whatsoever to the men opposite her palace, I do not know. In any case, her manners did not please Hemedo's men. One of them, named Mijo, asked his chief for permission to fire his rifle and knock off the bowl of the princess's pipe. At last he consented and Mijo fired and knocked the bowl into the air. The princess got up, got another pipe and continued smoking. Three times the feat was repeated. And three times the princess returned to her place with another pipe. At last, however, she moved from the window and next day she asked her husband to organize a great feast in honor of the marksman who had performed so great a feat, and she gave him presents.

While the more favored among the Kurds might spend their excess energies in killing bears and lions and in exercises of marksmanship, less favored men have since time immemorial turned their energies toward brigandage. But usually not in any mean or vicious manner. The Kurdish brigand maintained certain forms of chivalry. He respected the ladies and returned to them particularly cherished objects. He might rob the rich but he helped the poor.

The Kurds' sense of honor is epitomized in some proverbs. They say "Life passes, honor remains." "Better to lose property than honor." "It is worse to suffer dishonor in this world than death." "A defenseless nanny goat has no rights when a horned billy goat is around."

They tell about the bandit Rezgin, whose men one day waylaid a rich young traveler who carried a fine Martine rifle, "shoes of Diyarbekir leather," "a broad belt from Gire Mousse," and "a fine cloth from Mosul" upon his head. The young man did not resist, gave up all his possessions and was allowed to proceed unharmed. Soon thereafter an old man driving a donkey came the same way. Rezgin sent his men to take the donkey. But this old man would stand for no nonsense. He raised his sword and rushed the bandit before he could fire. Charmed by this show of spirit, Rezgin invited the old man to come and sit with him. It took some persuading, but at last the old man came and accepted food, and while he ate Rezgin's men loaded his donkey with all the things they had taken away from the young man who had not defended himself.

Although the lives of the Kurds and their stories are full of examples of mercy and honorable forgiving, the Kurds like to assume a hardhearted pose. They say: "Do not hesitate to let vengeance fall upon the head of your enemy." "The enemy of the father cannot become the friend of the son." "Though the beard may grow a yard long never shall the sworn enemy become a friend."

But they also tell the story of Qedir Agha, whose youngest and most beloved son was killed by an assailant named Sayid Weqas. After four days of flight Sayid Weqas decided to seek Qedir Agha's pardon. Qedir Agha was still receiving the condolences of his friends when Sayid Weqas appeared. In consternation the servants alerted the father and an elder son. Filled with emotion the father declared: "My son must not injure or insult our guest!" For his part the son thought: "Because he is so filled with paternal love will not my father refuse to pardon the man who killed my brother? And will he not thus put an end forever to our family's reputation for generosity and hospitality?" Father and son met in the central hall of the house and they spoke the same words to one another: "Sayid Weqas is here and he asks forgiveness. We must give it to him."

The Kurds can also be tender. In one of their verses a girl declares: "I am slender. My body is fine like a swan. My movements are like those of the swans upon the rivers. My throat is white as the first jet of milk in the morning. My charms are like the apples of Malatia, like fire in the winter's night, bitter and sweet at once."

The Kurdish woman appears concerned with her charms, her house and her man, alert and gay in all family matters but capable also of dealing with larger things. Women have headed tribes and taken part in battles. And women are given credit for heroic deeds. They tell about twelve-year-old Perixan, whose father Musa Beg Kasani had in 1907 organized a secret-resistance committee. One day their village was surrounded and Perixan's father was taken away and shot. Perixan said that she would avenge her father and her people. Six years went by. The little girl had become a young lady. But she had only one love, which in no wise resembled the love that moved the hearts of her friends. Came a Turkish national holiday. The governor of the province was to review a great parade, and Perixan was chosen to present to him a bouquet. In the bouquet she hid a bomb. The smiling girl entered the governor's tent. When he reached out to take the flowers Perixan hurled them to the ground with all her strength and perished along with the governor.

The story of Perixan, based on fact, is the stuff of which legends are made. More recent, real-life heroines among Kurdish women may make the legends of the future. One is Fatima Khan, who following the death of her husband ran a group of eight villages near Rewanduz for many years. I found a picture of her on the walls of an inn near Ranieh when I was going to visit Barzani in February 1963. Another is "Lady Adila" of Halabja, a small market town near the Persian border. She acquired her title from the British, who admired the authority with which she bossed the men of the Jaf tribe, including her easygoing husband Osman Pasha.

Recently we had the example of a Christian girl, Margaret George, who for several years led a unit in combat in the Akra region. Late in the summer of 1963 the Pej Merga decided she was too impetuous to lead troops, and she was withdrawn and is now at home in a village near Akra, taking care of her father. But thousands of Kurdish guerrilla fighters still carry her picture in their wallets along with that of Barzani.

There were also at least six women who took part in the great national Kurdish conference at Koisinjak in the latter part of March 1963.

When Kurdish families sit around of an evening, when they have put away their transistor radios, someone may start to tell a story. The stories ramble on while the audience gazes dreamily into the dim oil lamp, and may be prolonged to last half a night or three nights. The stories are full of non sequiturs, unaccountable magic and sudden death. They show a people's imagination at work. Here is one told by Jamil:

Two centuries ago there lived in Kurdistan a rich man named Ahmed Bey Shelazi, but he had bad luck and lost everything. Because he was now so poor he had to go to the mountains and make a living gathering gall-nuts. One day he had gathered enough nuts to load a mule and started for the village to exchange them. His son of twelve years wanted to go along. The father did not want him to come as the season was cold and rainy. But the boy begged until the father consented.

On the way home the rains started. As they hurried along they came to a cave called al-Kuska. Ahmed Bey decided to spend the night there. Then he observed to his surprise that the cave was full of rich young travelers who were singing and joking around the fire. They would not let the old man and his son come in. They declared that he was dirty and might steal.

"At least," Ahmed Bey begged, "let my boy come in to sit by the fire." But they refused.

When the old man saw that they would not relent, he remembered his gun. He took position and called out, "Very well, we will fight." Then the men in the cave relented and let the old man and his son enter.

The travelers said to him: "You are old and alone except for your boy. We are younger and numerous. What could you have done to us?"

"Well," replied the old man, "I had to do it. I was obliged to."

The travelers did not understand his words, but they respected him. One of them suggested that the old man tell his past adventures and experiences. Ahmed Bey agreed on condition that each of the others, after first swearing not to lie, would also tell his adventures and experiences. "I will tell you my story when I have heard yours," he declared.

Every traveler told his tale: One said that he had loved a girl and had kidnapped her. Another said that he went hunting and was surrounded by bears and killed them all. Thus they boasted.

At last it was the old man's turn. And this is what he said: "When I was young I was rich. My only occupation was hunting. One day one of my neighbors wanted to come with me. I said, 'No, it is better that you stay at home. I do not have to

work but it is better that you should attend to your business.'
But the neighbor insisted and we departed for the mountains together. Toward evening we killed a wild goat, hauled
it into a cave, and roasted the meat. When we had eaten well
we lay down to sleep. I slept inside, my companion near the
entrance. Suddenly I heard a terrible yell from my friend. I
jumped up and saw a shadow, seemingly of a huge animal,
holding my friend's leg and pulling him out of the cave. I ran
after the shadow but it disappeared into the darkness, dragging my friend behind him. Then I heard the sound of a great
rock falling, and I knew that it had hit my friend.

"Next morning I found my friend dead. I could find
nothing else. I could not find out what had happened. I
returned to the village and told my story.

"Some of the villagers believed me, but others said,
'These are lies.'

"Now the dead man had a son named Tahir, aged eight
or nine. The villagers decided to leave the question of the
father's death until the boy was grown. Whether anything
need be done would depend on whether the boy decided to
avenge the death of his father.

"Meanwhile I returned to my hunting. When Tahir was
grown he wanted to be a hunter like me. He came to me, but
I refused. I told him how his father had lost his life. Hunting
is dangerous, I said. But the boy would not accept this advice,
and at last we became comrades. We often spent five or six
days together in the mountains. This went on for ten years.
In the autumn of the tenth year, at the season when the boy's
father had lost his life, we planned another trip. We took supplies for one week.

"Having killed four or five animals we decided to spend
the night in a cave. By chance the cave happened to be the
one in which my friend's father had been killed. But I could
not bring myself to tell him. We roasted the meat, ate it and
lay down to sleep.

"This time I lay down at the entrance to the cave, but
could not sleep. I remembered the night twenty years before
when this boy's father had lost his life. At midnight I dozed.

Suddenly I was awakened by a terrible cry. I saw a huge animal dragging my friend away. I rushed forward, but it was too late. The great beast disappeared into the darkness, and a moment later, once again, I heard the sound of a great stone falling. I knew that my friend was dead.

"How could I go back to the village now? The father had been killed, and now his son had died in the same way. I decided that I must catch the animal, and searched the neighborhood. Close to the cave I found a hole. With difficulty I squeezed in and found that it led into a large cavern. Cautiously I crept forward, rifle at the ready. Suddenly there loomed before me a terrible animal. I succeeded in firing my rifle and hit the animal, which fell down dead. But yet another animal attacked. With monstrous teeth it slashed at me. Now I fought with my knife. Slashing wildly I wounded the beast, and at last killed it. I was injured and exhausted.

"Now I looked about and saw two glowing eyes staring from the back of the cave. I approached. I heard a human cry. 'I am a human being. I beg you, do not kill me.'

"I drew nearer. 'Who are you?' I asked. 'I am a woman,' said the voice. Then in the dim light I perceived the creature, naked, her hair hanging down about her face.

"I left the cave and returned to my village. I told the story and invited the villagers to come and see. They brought clothing to clothe the naked woman. They found the dead animals and the naked woman.

"Back at the village the people asked the woman who she was. 'I am from Bikade,' she replied. 'When I was very small my mother died. My father took another wife who treated me badly. One day I went to my uncle and I came home a little late. My father's wife would not let me in. I was left outside. I wept and begged. But she would not open the door.

"'When it got dark I wandered away from the house. Suddenly a savage creature took me in its jaws and dragged me to this very cave. The creature was going to kill and eat me, but its companion protected me. This second animal was a female. It fed me on meat and would not let me out.'

Then Ahmed stood up in the cave and said to the rich

young travelers who would not let him into the cave: "And now you should know that this is the cave where these things happened. You should know that I married the woman I found in this cave and that the child with me is her son."

I heard another story one night in the village of Sheile Dze, told by the niece of our host Sadoula. It was called "Haspe Seling" or "The Horse with Three Legs":

Once upon a time there was a prince who had three sons. The prince fell ill. He called together his sons and gave them this advice: do not waste your time in tea-shops; do not drink liquor and do not gamble; above all, do not keep bad company. Then he died.

Soon after this, two of the prince's sons also died. Only Mirza Mohammed was left. Mirza Mohammed forgot his father's advice. He spent all his money foolishly. He spent his time in bad company, he drank liquor, and he gambled. When nothing was left he told his sister: "We will have to move." And so they went to live in a cave. Every day Mirza Mohammed went hunting. Whatever he brought from the hunt he gave to his sister to cook.

Some days went by, and while Mirza Mohammed was hunting his sister received a visit from an ogre who wished to marry her. And indeed the two did marry secretly, and after nine months she bore a son. Whenever Mirza went hunting the ogre came to his sister, and when Mirza returned the ogre hid in a hole below the cave with the child.

The girl told the ogre: "This is very difficult. My brother will find the child and ask where it came from." So the ogre took the child and left it where Mirza Mohammed would find it. Mirza did find the child and brought it home and asked his sister to care for it. She agreed, and she was very happy. She gave the child milk from her breast. Gradually the child grew. Then the sister and her husband hated Mirza Mohammed. "We must get rid of him," they said.

The ogre said to his wife: "I will change myself into a snake and hide over the entrance to the cave. When your brother comes back from hunting I will sting his head and he will die." Mirza returned home and the child ran out to him crying, "Oh, please, please carry me on your shoulders." Now the ogre did not want to sting his own son. So they failed in this plan.

Next day Mirza's sister said: "We will put a scorpion in his food and he will die." When Mirza returned from hunting that day he struck the floor with his hand so that the dust flew up, and while the dust hung in the air he turned his plate to the other side. Then he began to eat. When his sister began to eat her food she fell down and died.

Mirza cried out: "Oh, sister, what has happened to you?" Then the child told him the truth: "Your sister married secretly a long time ago. I am her son. If you don't believe me I will lead you to where my father is hidden."

Together they went to the ogre. Mirza drew his sword and slew the ogre. Then he told his nephew: "We will live as before. You will stay in the cave and cook. I will go hunting."

One day, a long time later, the fire in the cave went out. Mirza Mohammed sent his nephew out to get fire. Very far away he found a fire in a cave. He entered the cave and found in it an ogre.

"Please give me an ember from your fire," said the boy. But the ogre refused, and tried to kill the boy. But the boy was strong. He was himself the son of an ogre. He caught hold of the ogre, pulled the hair out of his beard and tied him up.

Then the ogre cried: "Please forgive me. Do not tie my hands. I hold in my hands a ball of string which I must unroll, and if I do not unroll it the dawn will not break."

But the boy would not listen.

A big pot was on the fire. The boy said: "For whom are you cooking this meat?"

"For my seven brothers," replied the ogre.

"Show them to me or I will kill you," replied the boy.

The ogre led the way to another cave where the ogre's seven brothers lay sleeping. The boy wakened the ogres and said: "Why are you living here and how long have you been here?" They explained to him as follows: "We came here because our brother wished to marry the ruler's daughter. The ruler refused to give his daughter and we were unable to enter the city in order to take her. Since then we have been camped here in the mountains."

The boy offered to help the ogres. "Get me a hitching post and I will climb over the wall into the city," he declared.

That night they came to the wall of the city. They put up the hitching post against the wall, and the boy said: "When I get over the wall I will throw back a piece of charcoal and then one of you will follow."

So the boy climbed over the wall and threw back a piece of charcoal. The first of the brothers climbed up, and over. As he came down on the other side the boy swung his sword and cut off the ogre's head. He cut off the ogre's ears and put them in his pocket. Then he threw another piece of charcoal, another ogre climbed the wall, and the boy cut off his head. He repeated this procedure until he had killed all seven of the brothers. Then he entered the ruler's city.

As the boy approached the palace he found a thief trying to steal the ruler's treasure. He took the thief and tied his hair to the top of a tree so that the thief was suspended in the air. Then he entered the palace and went to the ruler's chamber. There he found a snake preparing to sting the ruler. He killed the snake and cut it into pieces and put the pieces on a plate, and put the plate on the ruler's table.

Under the ruler's bed the boy found a scorpion. He killed the scorpion with his dagger and drove the dagger through the scorpion's back into the table. Then he cast a spell upon the dagger so that no one could draw it out except himself.

The boy entered another room of the castle where the ruler's daughter slept. He took off her blanket and bent over as though to kiss her breasts, but he did not touch them with his lips. When he bent over the girl a black spot appeared on her breast. "Oh," he exclaimed, "if I touched her what would happen to her then?"

Without harming the girl he went out of the city. He came to the old ogre with the ball of string whom he had tied up.

"What is this string of yours?" the boy asked. "If I unroll it," the ogre replied, "the darkness will go and light will come." "How long will it take you to unroll the string?" the boy asked. "Just half an hour," the ogre replied.

Then the boy released the old man so that he could unroll his string. He took an ember and returned to his cave and cooked for himself and his uncle.

When the ruler awoke he found the scorpion and the snake in his plate and a thief hanging in a tree and the dead ogres lying beneath the wall. He said to his servants, "Find out who has done these good things and I will give him my daughter."

Many people came and said that they had done it. The ruler said to them: "If you have done these things, take your dagger." But none of them could draw the dagger out of the table. "Have all the men in the city tried?" the ruler asked. "Are there no more men?"

"Yes," said his servants, "there are two men who live in a cave outside the walls of the city."

"Bring them here," said the ruler.

First came Mirza Mohammed but he, too, could not draw the dagger from the table.

"Where is the other one?" asked the ruler.

"He is my nephew," replied Mirza, "but he is only a boy and he cannot do it."

But the ruler insisted, and the boy was brought before him. "Have you done these good things?" the ruler asked.

"Yes, my lord," replied the boy. Then he easily picked up the dagger. He showed the ruler where the thief was hanging in the tree, grasped the tree and released the body. And he showed the ruler the ears of the ogres which he had in his pocket.

"Will you shake my hand and accept my daughter?" said the ruler.

"I will accept your daughter for my uncle," the boy replied. And so Mirza Mohammed married the ruler's daughter.

Mirza remained a long time with his father-in-law. One

day he went up on the roof and began to cry. The tears rolled down, and one of them fell on the ruler's hand.

"What is this?" cried the ruler. "My son, why do you weep?"

"I am homesick," said Mirza.

So the ruler gave him a sack of gold coins and sent him to his own country. But he advised him that on the way he would find a green field where there would be a horse with three legs.

"The horse will ask you to race," he warned. "Don't do it. If you do you will lose your wife."

That is just what happened. Mirza met the horse with three legs and the horse challenged him to a race. At first he refused but at last he agreed to a race around the green field.

Twice he raced around the field and the third time he saw a green flame in the field and the flame picked up his wife and carried her to heaven.

Now Mirza was filled with sorrow because he had not taken his father-in-law's advice. He was in despair. He mounted his horse and rode off until he came to a spring.

At the spring he met a woman who had come for water. She stood a little way off and gazed at him.

When the woman went back to her house her mistress asked: "Why were you so long?"

"I stood a long time looking because when I came to the spring there was a man who looked like you," the woman replied, "as like as two halves of an apple."

Then the mistress ordered her servant to call the stranger to her house. She called him and he agreed to come. At the house he discovered that the mistress was his sister. She embraced him and cried out: "How did you come here? Do you not know that my husband is a giant? When he comes back he will eat you."

To protect her brother she changed him into a needle which she stuck in her dress. But first he asked his sister, "Do you know about the horse with three legs?" She said, "No, but I will ask my husband." When her husband returned, he cried: "I smell the blood of a foreigner."

"Do you see anyone?" his wife asked. "No," roared the giant, "but I smell him."

"If you saw Mirza Mohammed what would you do?" his wife asked.

"Oh, I would be very happy," declared the giant.

Then the woman took the needle out of her dress and suddenly Mirza stood before them. The giant embraced him and welcomed him. Unfortunately he was so strong that when he hugged Mirza he broke three of his chest bones.

The giant's name was Black Ogre.

"How did you come here and for what?" he asked Mirza. Mirza told him and asked if he knew anything about the horse with three legs.

"No," the giant replied, "but I will call all the foxes and ask them, for they are very clever. All the foxes came, but not one knew about the horse with three legs.

Then the giant said, "I will send you to my brother." Mirza went to the giant's brother and on the way he came again to a spring. Again he found a woman preparing to draw water and the woman went back to her mistress. And the mistress sent for Mirza, and again Mirza found one of his sisters, and again the woman changed him into a needle which she stuck in her dress, and again the giant declared that he would be very happy to see Mirza. But this time the giant who embraced him broke four ribs. This was White Ogre.

Again Mirza explained he was looking for his wife who had been taken by the horse with three legs.

The giant said he would call together all the lions, for they were very powerful. But when the lions came none of them knew about the horse with three legs.

Then the White Ogre sent Mirza to his brother, Red Ogre, and the same things happened. The Red Ogre called together the birds to ask them if they knew anything about the horse with three legs, for the birds saw everything. But none knew.

They said, however, "There is one bird who is deaf and featherless and very old. Perhaps he knows." So they went and brought the old, deaf and featherless bird. He said, "Yes, when I was young I made my nest on the roof of the house in which lived the horse with three legs. I will show you where he is."

The horse with the three legs lived on an island in the midst of seven seas. The bird went away and Red Ogre took Mirza to the shore of the sea. By the sea was a herd of camels belonging to the horse with three legs.

Red Ogre took a camel and cut open its stomach and put Mirza inside. That afternoon when the horse with three legs came to take his herd of camels, he found one of them dead, and put it on his back. He put down the dead camel in front of his own door. His wife, who was really Mirza's wife, said: "When you go I will cook the camel." But she had already heard the voice of a man inside. When she opened the camel she found her husband. They embraced.

"What am I going to do with you?" she cried. "The horse with three legs will return and eat you." So she hid him in a cupboard. Then, when the horse with three legs went hunting they decided to escape.

They took a young horse and galloped away. But a dog warned his master, the horse with three legs, and the horse with three legs came running home. He asked his mare to give chase. But the mare said: "I cannot run as fast as the young horse. But if I neigh the young horse will return." The mare neighed once and the young horse slowed down. The mare neighed again and the young horse turned back. Then the horse with three legs caught Mirza and cut off his head. His wife begged the horse with three legs to send Mirza's body to the shore where someone might find it and bury it, and this he did.

When Mirza was dead Red Ogre's horse began to champ and kick. Mirza's sister, who was the wife of the Red Ogre, knew that this was a sign that her brother was dead. She asked her husband to bring back her brother's body. When the body was brought to the Red Ogre's house the Red Ogre's family found three mice quarreling. Two of the mice cut off the head of the third. But then the mice were sorry. They sought medicine to bring their friend back to life. They brought a special kind of grain, ground it up and made of it a paste. This they spread on the neck of the dead mouse. They replaced the head and soon thereafter the mouse came back to life. Mirza's sister asked her husband to take some of the special kind of grain, to grind it up, and put it on her brother's neck. Sure enough, when the head was replaced he recovered.

When Mirza had regained consciousness he asked: "What happened? Where am I?" Then his sister told him the story of the mice.

Mirza determined to try again to rescue his wife. His sister begged him not to, but he said that he must.

Again he came to the shore of the seven seas and again the Red Ogre put him inside the stomach of a camel. But this time when his wife had released him from the stomach of a camel he told her to ask the horse with three legs where his spirit was hidden.

"When the horse with three legs returned the woman said to him: "I would like to see your spirit so I will not be lonely when you are gone away."

So he told her: "My spirit is a worm covered with fur in a box, in the belly of a hare, in the stomach of a big bird, in the belly of a pig, on the top of a mountain. At the top of the mountain there is a spring and every afternoon the pig goes there to drink water."

The woman thanked the horse with three legs and the next day Mirza, who had been hidden in a cupboard, went to the top of the mountain with a bow and arrow. He shot the pig. He took out the bird which was in the belly of the pig. Then he took out the hare which was in the belly of the bird. Then he took out the box which was in the belly of the hare.

Just then, as Mirza took the box, the horse with three legs felt ill, and came home. There he found Mirza who held the box with the worm in his hand. He begged Mirza not to kill the worm, but Mirza cut it in two pieces, and the horse with three legs fell dead.

Then Mirza took his wife and returned to his father-in-law's city, where he lived happily ever after.

Our host's niece offered to tell us another story called Hamza's Battle. But it was too late. The children were asleep, and we were all groggy, especially Apo, who was giving me a running translation in French.

Proverbs and folktales are interwoven with religion—not only Islam but pre-Islamic religion. The great god of the pre-Islamic Kurds was Ahura Mazda, sometimes called Ormezd, the god of the good. He was opposed by Ahriman, the god of evil. In addition they worshipped Mithra, the sun god, and Anahita, goddess of water and fertility, and all the forces of nature, particularly fire. Certain trees and rocks were held sacred.

Presiding over the religious rites was the priesthood of the magi. Most of their ceremonies were held in the open, but they also built temples with square towers where they tended sacred fires and drank intoxicating *haoma*. They made bloody sacrifices.

The religion of the magi was reformed and developed by Zarathustra, who is believed to have lived between the years 660 and 583 B.C., or about a generation before Cyrus the Persian gathered the kingdoms of Gutium and Babylon under his rule. From his homeland in the Mukri region of what we know today as Kurdistan his teachings spread rapidly. Zerdest, as the Kurds called the new doctrines, or Zoroastrianism as it has come to be called in English, became the official religion of the Persian Empire under the Sassanians, who ruled from A.D. 226 to 636.

Zarathustra eliminated the bloody sacrifices practiced by the magi but retained the worship of fire as a symbol of justice and of the struggle of good against evil. The watchwords of his religion were "good thought, good words, good works."

While Zarathustra was reforming the religion of the magi an entirely new religion was penetrating the East—Christianity. There is a trace of it in the second chapter of The Acts of the Apostles in which there is mention of "Parthians and Medes and Elamites and residents of Mesopotamia" who had gathered in Jerusalem at the time of Pentecost and who came to hear Peter the Apostle.

The Apostle Thomas is said to have evangelized the Kurds. Mar Mari of Urfa preached in the region between the Tigris river and the Little Zab, and near Arbil converted the king Shahgert "who was worshipping trees and making sacrifices to a copper idol." In the time of Sassanian rule, during the third century A.D., organized Christian communities had been established with twenty episcopal sects in the empire of the Persians and the Medes.

Although during the reign of Sapor II in the fourth century the magi inspired savage repression of the Christian movement, by the year A.D. 486 the Christians had so far recovered that a synod was held at Beit-Adhre in Kurdistan. Christian convents, both Nestorian and Jacobite, scattered through the mountains of northern Iraq and eastern Iran, nurtured notable theologians, some of whom were former magi.

The troops of the Arab caliphs, who began to penetrate into Kurdistan and Persia around A.D. 636, converted the Zoroastrians by force, but the Christians, regarded as "people of the book," were for the most part left unmolested. Christianity continued to prosper within the empire until the dreadful invasions of the Mongols and Tatars between the years A.D. 1260 and 1405. The great Khan Mangu, his brother Hulaghu Khan, and Tamerlane devastated Persia and Kurdistan and destroyed the Christian convents. In Kurdish territory one may today find the ruins of about one hundred convents. The only ones that remain or have been built anew today are the convents of Rabban Hormez near Alcoche (Chaldaeans), and those of Mar Matta (Jacobites), of Mar Behnam (Syrian Catholic), and Mar Yakoub (Dominican), and a convent which has become the temple of Sheikh Adi, founder of the Yezidi sect. All but the last are still in Christian use.

The memory of conversion to Islam, forced upon them by the invading Arabs, is preserved in an ancient Kurdish text said to have been engraved upon an amulet, as follows:

The temples of Ormezd are destroyed.
The fires are extinguished.
The great men of the land are hidden.
The cruel Arabs have put the Kurds to flight.
The Kurds have withdrawn to the borders of Shahrizor.
The women and the girls have been taken prisoner.
The heroes have been slain in ambush.
The law of Zerdest is observed no more.
*No longer does the mercy of Ormezd live among men.**

Yet resistance to the Islamic invasions continued in the Kurdish mountains for some three centuries. Even today some Kurdish tribes have preserved traces of the ancient Zoroastrian faith in their veneration of certain trees and rocks. According to a Turkish proverb, "compared with the unbeliever, the Kurd is also a Moslem."

Technically the Kurds are Sunni Moslems of the Shafei rite. But they are not given to orthodoxy. Nor are they fanatics. They are tolerant of the Christians among them. Their Islam is heterodox. The average Kurd is not strict in the observance of daily prayer or the fast of Ramadan. Few Kurds make the pilgrimage to Mecca. It may be because the Moslem liturgy is in Arabic, which most Kurds do not understand, or it may be something about the mountains in which they live that makes the Kurds turn to the mystical dervish brotherhoods that seek emotional union with God.

Kurdish dervishism is organized on a tribal basis. The sheikh teaches and interprets it in his residence surrounded by his disciples, the best of whom carry his message to other tribes. Thus all of Kurdistan has been converted by a network of mystic cells. At first the sheikhs were only religious chiefs, but as their influence increased and gifts piled up, they became more and more also temporal leaders, until there were places where the sheikh exercised more authority than the hereditary chiefs.

Many Kurds have complained that the sheikhs abuse

* Mackenzie in the *Bulletin of the School of Oriental and African Studies,* Vol. XXVI, 1963, casts doubt upon the authenticity of this text.

their power. They say that some pretend to practice magic, that they keep the people in ignorance for their own advantage and exploit the credulity of women and girls. Yet among them have arisen some of the greatest Kurdish leaders—Sheikh Said of Piran who led the rebellion of 1925 in Turkey, Sheikh Talabani, Sheikh Mahmoud of Suleimaniya, and the sheikhs of Barzan, to mention but a few.

If tribal life sometimes makes it necessary to transgress the religious prohibitions against killing, stealing and lying, recourse to the sheikh is convenient. By him all is forgiven. Mothers go to the sheikh when their sons are sick or wounded. Girls who fear that love will pass them by turn to the sheikh. The sheikh has remedies for everything. His amulets and talismans are more effective than his advice.

The flavor of the activities of the sheikhs may be appreciated in the long national epic poem, *Mame Alam*. The hero of the story, Mam, falls ill because his fiancée, Zina Zedan, has disappeared. In vain his father calls together the sheikhs, the mullahs and the physicians. Each in his own fashion makes amulets and talismans. Some invoke the names of *jinni* and fairies. Others raise their hands to heaven in prayer. The sheikhs put up green flags in the windows. The roll of drums is heard. The clash of cymbals becomes deafening. The shouting of the disciples rises to the skies. But all this noise does not impress the young man. "Do not tire me with these things," he says. "I have never known rosewater to heal the wounds inflicted by lances. I am wounded in the heart and you bring me sheikhs and mullahs! I close my eyes to see the image of Zina Zedan. And you bring me this crowd of madmen?"

The dervish sheikhs favor sensuous allegorical poems such as the following by Sheikh Ehmede Nichani, who lived in the fifteenth century:

> *The sons of the magis, dispensers of wine, come in the dawn to dance.*
> *Draining cup upon cup they lie down beside the river.*
> *The young girls' tresses are the color of amber or brown.*
> *They are like jewels, like stars in the sky.*

The hair of some is blond and some is red.
Their eyes like pearls, their faces like fairies.

Farther on the poem continues:

She took me to dance. The dancing and the music would not stop.
She with the eyes like pearls said to me:
"We are yours and you are ours!
We are really one. But the problem is insoluble!"

And farther on:

All the letters have the same origin if you reduce them to their principles.
Every letter becomes a line; remove the line, the period remains.
Absolute unity, O Mela, is the light that irradiates our hearts:
The question is hard to understand, the mystics remain in doubt.

The first of the mystic orders was the Qadiriya founded by the Kurd Abdul Qadir el Gilani, who lived from A.D. 1078 to 1166.

The second of the brotherhoods was the Nakshbandi, founded by Beha-ud-Din of Bukhara, who lived from 1317 to 1389. It was popularized among the Kurds by Mawlana Khalid of the Jaff tribe, who was born in 1779. He began to preach at Suleimaniya about 1808. After initial opposition this order spread rapidly and is now more popular than the Qadiriya. Its uneducated members seem particularly given to eccentricity.

Given these characteristics it is perhaps not surprising that heretical sects, some of which seem to have strayed far from Islam, abound among the Kurds.

First and most important are the Yezidis, popularly known as "devil worshippers," who number about fifty thousand, mostly in Iraq, in the wooded valleys of Sheikh Adi and the mountains north of Mosul; also in a few dozen villages of northern Syria and in the region of Erivan and Tiflis, in what is today the Soviet Union. Although many critics have considered that the Yezidi faith was derived from ancient Babylonian religions and Zoroastrianism, its practitioners are in fact the followers of the Moslem Sheikh Adi to whose tomb they now go on pilgrimage. Partisans of Caliph Yezid I from whom they took their name, they drifted gradually into extremist forms of Moslem mysticism. They believe in transmigration of souls, and have developed a kind of cult of Satan involving the following beliefs: Satan, whom they call lblis and who is represented in their ceremonies by a bronze statue of a peacock, is an angel fallen from grace. Satan will some day be restored to grace and for this reason no word must ever be said against him, indeed one should not even pronounce his name.

The Yezidis have two sacred books, The Book of Revelation and The Black Book. Although their religion is secret, some of their prayers have become known. Here is one of them:

> O God, you are, I am not;
> You are the master of the law, I am a slave.
> You do not move and you are multiple,
> You are small and you are great,
> You have no voice and you are the word.
> You are suffering and you are balm.
> You are the judge of kings and of beggars.
> O God, you are the emperor who rules over thrones,
> You are the creator of oxen and fish.

The Kizilbash are another notable sect; they speak the Zaza dialect and are believed to number about one million persons. They live for the most part in Turkish Kurdistan in the provinces of Sivas, Diyarbekir and Kharpout. Their natural fortress is the Dersim mountain range, where lives their spiritual chief. They are extremist Shi'ites, that is, worshippers of Ali, whom they deify. They have no mosques and pray once a day only. They have no sacred book of their own but revere the Torah, the New Testament and the Koran.

A much smaller group are the Ahl-e-Haqq who, like the Yezidis, believe in transmigration of souls and have set forth other beliefs in poems in the Gorani dialect. They venerate Moses, Elijah, Jesus and above all, David. Most live in villages on the road between Khanequin in Iraq and Kermanshah in Iran.

All of the foregoing, the religion and tradition and legends of the Kurds, their poetry and stories, their proverbs and superstitions—all of this is the background against which the Kurds have produced a lively literature.

The first of Kurdish poets is usually said to be Eli Termuki, who sang of the things that have moved all subsequent Kurdish poets—love of the natural beauty of his country, the charm of its girls. In "Life Is a Dream" Termuki wrote:

> *Our religion teaches us to hope for a paradise*
> *Where the shadow beneath the trees is cool,*
> *Where the waters flow quietly and sweet as honey,*
> *Where beautiful girls preen themselves like angels.*
> *When I perceive the springs and the women of my country,*
> *I think that I have already entered into the promised land.*

Whether Termuki was really the first of Kurdish poets, whether, as some have said, he wrote in the tenth century, or whether, as more recent students have believed, he lived in the fifteenth or sixteenth, is not certain.

Authorities on Kurdish literature date its beginnings to the Mullah of Jezireh, who lived from 1407 to 1481 and wrote mystical religious poetry.

The giant of Kurdish literature, still the most universally loved and studied of Kurdish writers, was Ahmed Khane, 1650 to 1706, author of *Mem u Zin,* which is an Islamicized rendering of a pre-Islamic folktale concerning the love of Mem and Zin. The first written text of the tale may date back two or three centuries earlier. Khane made Mem's love symbolic of the Kurds' love of country, and his struggles the symbol of the struggles of the Kurdish people.

In the seventeenth and eighteenth centuries the princes of Ardelan in Iran, south of the area of Mehabad, encouraged the poets of their day. One of the most important of these, Mahzuni, who wrote in the years following 1783 at the court of Khusraw Khan, at the town of Senna, produced works of romantic poetry in a religious spirit and in the dialect of the Gorani.

In the nineteenth century there came a great outpouring of religious and mystic poetry. One poet of this period, Haji Qadir Koyi, 1815 to 1892, accused the sheikhs and mullahs of intellectual laziness. He said they had not kept up with the changing world and were not leading the Kurdish people toward the nationhood to which they aspired. His patriotic verses are still often quoted.

Another was Sheikh Reza Talabani, an agnostic and a skilled satirist. Always in verse, he stirred Kurdish national feelings and stung the enemies of the Kurds with sarcasm. A catalyst, an arouser, an inciter, an agitator, he wrote of himself: "There is a thorn with every rose—I am the thorn."

In all the years up to 1920 there was scarcely any prose literature in Kurdish, and no theater. Except when they wrote history, the Kurds wrote poetry. Greatest of the historians was Prince Sharafeddin of the Sharaf Khan dynasty of Bitlis, who wrote in the service of the shah of Iran at a time when the shah, at the end of the sixteenth century, hoped to arouse the Kurds' sense of kinship with the Persians. His *Sharafname* is fundamental history, but it was written in Persian and has never been fully translated into Kurdish. It has, however, been translated into French and into Arabic.

This was the period also when the heroic Kurdish epic of *Dim-Dim-Kala,* which has already been cited elsewhere, was first composed.

Since World War I Kurdish presses have been active at Suleimaniya, Arbil and Rewanduz. Suleimaniya has become the Kurdish literary center. Here many Kurdish periodicals have garnered works from all parts of Kurdistan. Among Iraqi Kurds one should note especially Bekes, 1905 to 1948, a fiercely patriotic poet whose tormented personal life is reflected in his poetic images of wine, women and struggle.

Another is Goran, a writer in free verse, he was acutely aware of social injustice. He defied the old stereotyped poetic forms just as he defied the old political and social systems.

In Syria, Kamuran Bedir-Khan produced some poems in the early twentieth century.

Jager Khwin was a notable agitator for nationalist objectives and social change. Son of a peasant, he was trained as a mullah and is accused by some of allowing Communist ideas to slip into his work.

In the Soviet Union (Armenia) two poets, Jasim Jalil and Mikhail Rashid, have written poetry about nature and love.

In recent times Kurdish writers have produced no novels, but a good many short stories. Among the short-story writers are Nureddin Zaza, the secretary-general of the Syrian Kurdish Democratic Party; Ahmed Bohti, who has written a number of fables; Kadri Jan, a teacher whose articles deal with social issues, morality and the problems of Islam; and Osman Sabri, in the opinion of some critics the most promising Kurdish writer.

Among recent Kurdish historians one should note Hussein Husni Mukriani, of Rewanduz, who died in 1947. A great collector of original documents, he printed his collections himself. Although disorganized, his work is a great storehouse of source materials for other writers.

Mohammed Amin Zaki has written a history of Suleimaniya, a book of celebrities of Kurdistan, a history of the Kurdish emirs in the period of Islam, and a general history of Kurds and Kurdistan.

Another historian of more limited scope is Rafiq Hilmi, who died in 1961. His memoirs of the revolution of Sheikh Mahmoud is a source book of vast detail.

Most notable of Kurdish literary critics is Sejadet, who has written a history of Kurdish literature.

The first example of modem Kurdish journalism appears to have been a periodical called *Kurdistan* published by members of the princely family of Bedir-Khan in the dialect of Bohtan. Other Kurdish periodicals followed in Constantinople after the Young Turk Revolution of 1908.

Among Kurdish periodicals in recent times the following are notable: Celadet and Kamuran Bedir-Khan, grandsons of the famous revolutionary leader, published the magazines

Hawar and *Ronahi* in Damascus before and during the Second World War. They published *Roja Nu* in Beirut. Under the protection of the French mandate Kurdish cultural life flourished, but after the final departure of the French, Arab nationalism asserted itself in such a way that periodical publication was no longer possible.

In Iran no truly Kurdish periodical is published, but the government produces a weekly newspaper called *Kurdistan* in the Kurdish language which is distributed abroad for propagandistic purposes. Except in the Soviet Union this is the only Kurdish periodical published regularly since September 1961. In the Kurdish mountains the Kurdish Democratic Party puts out *Khabat* from time to time. In Istanbul the Turkish government's suppression of Kurdish cultural life was so far relaxed as to permit publication of a Kurdish biweekly in 1962 and part of 1963. But it was suppressed after disturbances in Ankara in May 1963.

In the Soviet Union a periodical called *Rea Taza,* or "The New Road," is published twice weekly at Erivan. Another publication in Kurdish is the *Caucasus Review,* published in Tiflis.

At Erivan a Kurdish theater has also been active, while Erivan radio and Tiflis radio frequently produce Kurdish programs. This relatively active Kurdish literary and cultural life in the Soviet Union, encouraged by the authorities, naturally leads Kurds to make comparisons with the difficulties they find in expressing themselves culturally in other lands.

Although Kurmanj, the language of northern Kurdistan, may in the long run prove the purer and stronger dialect, the Sorani dialect spoken at Suleimaniya has become the standard vehicle of literary expression in Iraq. The patronage given by Baban princes to literature in the early part of the nineteenth century had something to do with this predominance of the Suleimani language. C. J. Edmonds points out that the Turks founded a military school at Suleimaniya so that more Kurds reached a high level of education from this area than from others. Under British protection in 1918 Suleimaniya became also the first place where Kurdish was recognized as an official language of administration.

Edmonds divides Kurdistan linguistically into northern and southern areas by "a line running from the southern shore of Lake Urmiya to the bend of the Great Zab where it changes direction from southeast to southwest, and thence down the course of that river to the Tigris confluence." In the north, in addition to northern Kurmanj, there are linguistic islands where a dialect known as Zaza is spoken; in the south, southern Kurmanj is subdivided into the MukriSoran and the Suleimani-Ardelan dialects. A markedly different dialect called Gorani is spoken in scattered areas of north and south.

A Latin alphabet devised by the Bedir-Khan brothers has been widely used by Kurds in Turkey, Syria and Lebanon, but in Iraq and Iran Kurdish is still usually written in Arabic characters. A Kurdish alphabet in Latin characters has also been published in the Soviet Union.

10

Kak Farzo's Progress

On July 21, our ninth day in Kurdistan, we arrived at Assad Hoshewi's headquarters. He commanded the western sector from a point near Zakho.

After the long and dusty trail it was a great relief to experience the simple open-air hospitality of this sensitive, thoughtful man. Here we rested in an atmosphere of rushing waters, cool breezes, croaking frogs and good news.

Assad Hoshewi welcomed us with a little speech saying that America was renowned for its democracy and that was surely its strength. He spoke of America's glorious past and of its powerful arms. He also spoke of the "evil man" who would destroy the Kurdish people.

He told me he belonged to the Mizuri-Bala, a subtribe of the Barzani, and it was evident that he was one of its leaders, a man who enjoyed immense respect. But beyond this I was not able to find out very much about him. He declined to be drawn out about his family.

From other sources I learned that he accompanied Barzani to the Soviet Union in 1947 and was one of Barzani's close associates throughout the twelve years of exile. While there are no formal military rankings in the Kurdish forces he was widely regarded in his present post as number two after Barzani himself.

In 1932 Assad Hoshewi's older brother, Khalil, was fighting with Barzani in the Kurdish mountains. When Barzani left the field of battle Khalil continued. He stayed in the mountains with his partisans for five years, until 1937. Some people say he was a bandit. Others call him a hero of the Kurdish national movement.

In the winter of 1937 there was very heavy snow. Khalil and the small band of his followers could find no more food. From the cave in which they were camped they went out to a village to try to exchange some guns for food. But the villagers denounced Khalil to the Rikani tribe, which was working with the government. The Rikanis surrounded Khalil. He ordered his men to disperse and was himself killed.

The small boy who played around us there at Assad Hoshewi's headquarters was also named Khalil, the grandson of the Khalil who held out so long in the mountains. Another brother of Assad Hoshewi was killed while fighting under Barzani's command in 1945.

Hoshewi's front was now fairly quiet. Major operations had shifted eastward. He was concerned mainly with the siege of Amadiya. He said that his forces had cut off the town's water supply and had brought up heavy machine guns to fight off the helicopters supplying the garrison. Although the town had suffered much, he added, there were still five thousand inhabitants in it.

The entire area of Dohuk and Akra was occupied by the Kurds, he said. Only the towns themselves remained in the hands of the government. Akra itself was so near to the mountains that his men could "almost fire a pistol into the town."

Hoshewi maintained that he could take these towns or even so large a town as Suleimaniya. But for the time being his orders were to stick to the mountains insofar as possible. Occupying a town would tie up too many fighting men in defensive positions, create too large a supply problem and expose the Kurdish inhabitants to merciless bombings.

I asked Hoshewi how after a battle the soldiers divided the booty. "We just carry it together," he explained, "and distribute it according to need. In each district there are hundreds of armed men, a kind of reserve for the army. When we get more arms, we hand them out to the men who lack them."

It was as simple as that. All without files, correspondence, or paperwork of any kind.

It was Assad Hoshewi who first told me about Margaret George, a Chaldaean Catholic girl who commanded a small unit of troops in the area of Akra. A former hospital attendant, she had taken up military service after the *josh* had attacked her village. She was reputed to have killed one of the top *josh* officers, named Ma'aviya. In addition I heard about a Moslem girl who was doing military service but was never able to get her name or other information about her.

From Hoshewi's aide, Mullah Hamdi, I learned about the Kurds' amazing ability to break the Iraqi government's codes. A man of exceptional intelligence, Hamdi knew the military codes so well that he could read them off, almost as though they were "in clear." Hamdi was an unusual young Kurd. In his case, "Mullah" was a real religious title. He had given up religious studies in favor of fighting. Fair-skinned with a wide, expressive mouth, he wore a costume of light tan, nearly white, and toyed constantly with a small string of Oriental beads. At Hoshewi's request he accompanied us nearly a full day's journey beyond the headquarters and we found him a most agreeable companion.

Before we left, Assad Hoshewi presented us with gifts. To Ahmed Tofiq he gave a coveted Brno rifle; to Apo Jomart and me, walking sticks of fragrant cherrywood. And to me he gave in addition a complete Kurdish national costume. Of course I had to put it on instantly and be photographed with everyone. I had to declare that I liked it, although actually it was extraordinarily hot and scratchy. Furthermore, the jacket was too short and so were the pants. It was a brown costume which I found rather less attractive than the gray style. The outfit included a proud red-and-white-checked cloth for a Barzani turban. Ahmed Tofiq showed me how to wind the latter around my head and how to arrange the long sash around my waist, but it took me weeks to learn how to do it properly.

Ahmed found this a suitable occasion to suggest that it was time for me also to take a Kurdish name. Henceforth, he declared I would be known as "Kak Farzo," which was short for "Kak Farzanda," meaning, I must confess, "The Intelligent One." I accepted this embarrassing title with good grace and from then on I was in fact called Kak Farzo.

As Kak Farzo mounted his mule he made the mistake of flourishing Hoshewi's cherry stick in front of the mule's nose. The startled animal zoomed away leaving The Intelligent One briefly suspended in midair. Ahmed rushed up to bathe my scratched right hand and arm with the only disinfectant readily at hand—our supply of White Label whiskey.

For several days our route led through a Shangri-La of lush valleys that brought to my mind the words of the old hymn "where every prospect pleases and only man is vile." We were reminded from time to time in these idyllic surroundings of the vileness of man by the distant boom of guns or bombs around Amadiya. But there was no evil surely in these valleys where generations of devoted labor had devised an intricate system of irrigation channels to water bright green fields of tobacco and rice and groves of graceful poplar trees.

As we moved through the little villages during the next few days I could not help but admire the Kurdish women, their proud, erect carriage and their manner of dress, so graceful, so fanciful, so colorful. Most wore extremely full sleeves which, so far as I could observe, were tied together across the back so as not to interfere with their work. As the women moved about, the tied sleeves slid gracefully back and forth across their backs. And so they went about their duties, flashes of color—blue and yellow and red and green and purple—all somehow blended harmoniously, a little grace in the midst of all the harshness of their world. How much more admirable were these proud village women with their colors and their open faces than the poor cowering creatures of the town with their black veils. These village women are in every way freer than those of the towns, even Kurdish towns. When they get the chance many of the Kurds send their girls as well as their boys to school. But most of the old people are illiterate.

Everywhere it seemed to me the children's voices were similar, soft and respectful. The Kurds love their children fiercely. But their discipline is rough and sure. The child's place is so much more humble and self-effacing than in our society that the problems of behavior to which we are accustomed simply do not arise.

In a village called Soriya I found a mullah who taught ten or twelve children the Koran. "They learn to read the Koran," one of the village elders explained to me, "but they understand nothing. It is purely an exercise in memory." As others had done throughout Kurdistan, he deplored the lack of teachers.

The women, incidentally, are not the only ones who love color in Kurdistan. Children and the lower social orders among the men, muleteers and the like, often affected costumes contrived of a marvelous collection of colored and flowered patches. I admired my muleteer's crazy quilt clothes. His brown jacket was patched with red and blue. The seat of his pants and other key points were covered with a pattern of little red and yellow suns. Another of my muleteers had also the virtue of song. Once I encouraged him and after that he could not be stopped. He made the mountains echo with something that sounded like a cross between a Swiss yodel and the Gregorian chant. The name "Barzani" kept recurring in his song.

One morning we moved through a heavily wooded valley, crammed with walnut trees. The air was full of butterflies. The villages were few and far between, surrounded by vineyards and orchards of apple trees, peach trees and walnut trees. Around noontime these Elysian surroundings were invaded by a great Ilyushin bomber soaring overhead, and Ahmed Tofiq hustled me into the shelter of two great rocks. He insisted I stay there until the plane had departed. In the cool shade of the rocks I listened to the bombs come down—one, two, three, four—each with a low deep boom about half a mile down the valley.

That evening we climbed into the most unusual geographical location we had yet encountered. This was Reshawa, a village that seemed to hang on the side of a mountain overlooking a valley inhabited by the not so friendly Zibari tribe.

Here I met Mohammed Tahir, the first fat Kurd I had seen. Tahir had an eight-months-old baby suffering, Apo said, from either dysentery or malaria or both. At their request I gave the father some sulfaguanadine pills. Except for some aspirin carried by Ahmed, that was the only medication we had with us, except for the White Label, of course.

This village of forty houses had given twenty men to the revolution, I was told. It had been attacked by air four or five times. Three houses had been destroyed and a fifty-five-year-old woman injured. Our host said that in the last few days sixteen villages around Amadiya had been attacked and many wheat fields burned. The village of Kane lost all its wheat. At Bawark village one Christian and two Moslems were killed. The villages of Bartche, Sagal, Segere, and Mere Sere were all bombed and strafed. Two men were said to have been killed while they were threshing wheat.

In the crotch of a tree at the front of a terrace on which we sat were lodged three or four sacks stuffed with provender and household belongings. They were things which had been evacuated from houses which were likely to be destroyed by air attack. They were lodged in a tree to keep them out of sight on the one hand, and away from wild animals such as foxes on the other.

In Reshawa we spent the night on a cool roof free of flies and mosquitoes. A welcome change. Up before dawn to avoid the possibility of air attack on the village, we moved swiftly down the steep hill to breakfast in our host's tomato patch. From time to time as we waited for our tea we could hear the dull boom of mortars or aerial bombs being fired at Amadiya on the other side of the mountain. Four more men from the village came down to bid farewell to our host, who appeared to be the leading personality in the village. They treated him like a master, kissing his hand obsequiously. I noticed that Ahmed Tofiq did not like it. I would have questioned him about the practice but it is always difficult to find a private moment for any purpose whatsoever on such a trip and in such company.

To give a practical example, I might say very quietly to

Ahmed, "Where is the toilet paper?" And he would repeat the question loudly for the entire group to hear: "Where is the toilet paper?" A general discussion would then ensue as to where the toilet paper might be, in which pack the toilet paper might be located, somewhat to my embarrassment as I was the only person in the group who used such luxuries. The others might use leaves or sand or water from some rushing brook.

In the village of Terwanish two young men came to talk to me in English. They were Anwar Moiza, aged twenty-three, and his brother Hossein, aged thirty-two. Anwar had started a school in the village. For nine months, he said, he had been teaching thirty young people to read and write. He said he had thus anticipated an army order to all villages to start reading and writing classes. He said he had got his idea from mobile schools which the Kurdish Democratic Party had tried to organize a year earlier. He said the KDP held a meeting in the village once a week. Party officials would tell about the progress of the national struggle and give the villagers advice on all subjects.

Anwar had learned his English working as an accountant for an American contracting firm building the Darbandikhan Dam and later in a similar job for the Iraq Petroleum Company at Mosul. His brother Hossein had served in the British army until 1955.

Anwar said his village was more progressive than most. Proudly he pointed out that most of the houses were built of mortared stone rather than mud. Nearby he said there was also a Jewish "ghost" village. He said as a boy he had known some of its Jews, before they all migrated to Israel in 1948–1949.

I asked Anwar what had been the economic effect of the war on his village. He pointed out that sugar which formerly had cost sixty fils per kilo now cost one hundred and fifty fils. But he maintained that the villages managed very well with the food that could be raised in the region. The main hardship was the danger of air attack and the necessity of going out of the village every day to take refuge in the hills. "Some of the young women say they don't want to go to the hills. They say, 'Never mind, we don't care if we get killed. The children catch cold in the caves. We would rather stay in our village.' But we make them go."

Anwar told me about a miraculous spring near the village called "Merkugi," or "Hopeless Spring." It was said that if a "good man" knocked on the rock above the spring it would flow. But if he was not a good man, it would not flow. I said that I wanted to see this wonder.

Next morning we set off for Hopeless Spring. On the way we photographed the wreckage of an Iraqi air force bomber that the Kurds said they had shot down, but which I suspected had crashed after it had been damaged by Turkish anti-aircraft fire on the other side of the border. We were only two miles from the Turkish frontier here and the Iraqi air force had on a number of occasions bombed villages on the Turkish side whose appearance is, of course, exactly like those on the Iraqi side. Anwar and others from the village assured me, incidentally, that for the past year the villagers had had no contact with the Kurds living on the Turkish side of the border, because the Turks kept their side effectively closed.

Late that morning we arrived breathlessly at the spring called Hopeless. We all tried our luck knocking on the rock above it, but it would not start for us. Perhaps none of us was "good." Someone remembered the story about a Kurdish prince named Sevin who was said to have camped beside this spring for twelve days waiting for it to flow. On the twelfth day he gave up and moved on. As he was leaving, the spring began to flow, but the prince refused to turn back.

Apo was disgusted. "I like history and I like science," said he, "but I have no time for these tales. The secret of Hopeless Spring is a matter of siphons." He explained that the spring filled up a natural bowl of water in the rock. If a good man knocked on the rock at the right time it would spill and start a prolonged flow of water. But if the water had not reached the top of the bowl it would not flow no matter how virtuous the knocker.

This did not prevent Anwar from telling about a cave

nearby said to be inhabited by an ogress named Ken Pirhave
who lived on human flesh. But that is all that I could find out
about her.

As we trudged on up the mountain we saw two small
boys coming down toward us. One of them carried a dishpan
which, when he reached us, we discovered was filled with cold
water. His mother in a shepherd's tent on the mountain far
above us had observed our quest for water at Hopeless Spring
and, knowing very well that we would get no water, had sent
her boys to us with this welcome refreshment.

We struggled up a very steep draw into an immense bowl
in the center of which stood the black tents of our benefac-
tress. Eight women and a swarm of children were living in
those tents surrounded by hundreds of goats. Four of the
women said their husbands were away fighting with Barzani.
The other four were in Iraqi jails. These were wonderful people, an independent breed of women, not in the least bashful.
Delighted that we should pass their way, they scurried about
with rugs and pillows to make us comfortable and produced
goat's milk in various forms, cheese and bread. One of the
children had a baby partridge with which he played. I tried
to make him understand that if he squeezed it too much it
would not last. But it was a lost cause.

We rested through the heat of the day and I watched
the women kill and cook one of the goats for us and milk the
rest. They drove them down into an enclosure from which
there was just one narrow exit. Two of the women squatted
at this exit and grabbed the goats as they crowded forward in
an effort to get out. The big milk pails of goat's milk looked
delicious as the milk, warm and foamy, squirted in from the
goats' udders. Unfortunately, dung and earth and dirty hands
were mixed in, too, while clouds of flies swarmed around man
and beast. The germ count in all the food produced there
must have been something frightful. No wonder my intestines
were rebelling.

One morning we watched the people of Bedoh village
leaving their homes. A young mother walked slowly up the
trail herding half a dozen children and four or five goats,

carrying a great pack piled high with kitchen utensils, driving a mule loaded with other household gear ahead of her, and knitting as she went. She was heading for the cave where she would spend the day and return at nightfall to the village in time to light the fire and to bake piles of *nan*. At dawn on the morrow she would be up to make yoghurt and then butter by shaking the yoghurt in a goatskin, back and forth in a rhythmic pounding movement. And then she would be off to the hills again in flight from those awful airplanes.

These poor souls have to hide in caves all day. Their fear is great, but on the other hand, so is their fortitude. The heroes of it all are, of course, the women, who put up with it and make it bearable for all. Over and above their natural fortitude I believe that the national ideal must have got through to these Kurdish women.

In one way these mountain people have an advantage: the time of their greatness lies ahead of them. Not like the Arabs and Turks and Persians who have so much behind them and must seek always to evoke past greatness. Because they have been consistently suppressed for centuries the Kurds have had no great flowering and no decadence, a great unspent human potential in the Middle East.

With their dauntless womenfolk behind them, literally and figuratively, keeping the home fires burning, the Kurds of Iraq were in this year of rebellion an astonishingly single-minded people. The men among whom I journeyed seemed to live for nothing else, no other interests, no amusements, no pleasures. Hardly ever even sweets with their food. Just the rebellion. Among them were men who had been fighting off and on for thirty years. To them, indeed, fighting seemed to be the normal state of man.

One of those who had fought all his life was Jamil, who acted as chief of our guard except when someone of obviously higher rank was around. He had joined Barzani in the 1930's, followed him to Iran in the '40's and to Russia in the '50's. Jamil, the old fighter, had lost a lot of his teeth and was getting old and stiff. Several times he fell off his mule and once injured his back. But he would not put aside the heavy cartridge belt which for him was a kind of badge of military honor and masculinity.

Jamil functioned as a kind of governess for us all, supervising the loading and unloading and the cooking, and seeing to it that we got up in the morning and stopped talking and went to sleep at night. He gossiped and argued incessantly except when he was taking notes in a notebook the use of which I could never discover. I suspected that this was a little trick of his to maintain his authority because the others imagined that he was going to make reports to some mysterious higher authority. Along with all these other duties Jamil carried my wallet and passport, neither of which I needed during this trip. I could find no place to carry them in my Kurdish costume, which contained no pockets, but Jamil wrapped my valuables in a cloth and somehow carried them safely in the folds of his costume.

Jamil had a wife, he said, at Sarsang, the resort town near Amadiya—a pretty Turkoman girl he had brought back with him from Russia. In some other village, among the Barwaris I believe, he had a second wife and his companions alleged that he had a third in Iran. Later I heard that after my departure he got leave and returned to the Zakho area to marry a fourth time. This was unusual; most of the Kurds I knew were monogamous.

He treated me like a favored guest, picking out for me the best pieces of meat or the best fruit. For me especially he barbecued chicken and to me he told endless and rather rambling tales.

One concerned a castle whose ruins we passed high upon the mountains above the village of Terwanish. "There was once a prince of the Kurds," he related, "who lived in this castle. For seven years he fought the Turks. The Turks could not destroy this man. His rule extended as far as Van, in what is now Turkey. Then the Turks gathered a great force to break down the gates to the castle and kill the Kurdish prince. A loyal watchman warned the prince and just before his enemies broke through the gate he escaped through a secret passageway and made his way to Amadiya. Thereafter he ruled from Amadiya for many years and was known as the 'Kind Prince.'"

His story may have lacked written corroboration; it served to illustrate the point that tales such as these live among the Kurdish people, nourishing their sense of past distinction and continuing struggle.

Soon after we left Assad Hoshewi's headquarters we got word that the Iraqi army had sent a force of a thousand men with tanks and armored cars to relieve Amadiya. All the villages were mobilizing men to reinforce the Kurdish siege and oppose the Iraqi relieving forces. Our guard had therefore been reduced to ten men. Partly for this reason and partly because we were now moving through or around areas not entirely friendly to Barzani, Ahmed Tofiq tried to put an end to the triumphant receptions I had been accorded as we approached various villages and command posts. Our movements became occasionally furtive. Apo Jomart and I, who habitually yelled at each other in French as we rode along, were instructed to keep quiet as we moved through villages, or around them—an order rather hard on Apo, who found it difficult to stop talking.

In the evening as we approached new villages, men would sometimes come out to meet us with flashlights and loud talk. Ahmed would be annoyed and order them back. He did not want our presence to cause so much attention. I realized that he was worried about the problem of crossing the neutral territory of Barzan. He was worried also about our dear Apo, who was having great difficulty making his way over rough terrain in bad light. One night after Apo had fallen from his mule and then fallen again as he tried to make his way down a steep gully in the dark, Ahmed raised the question as to whether we ought to leave Apo behind, or rather, send him back. He explained that we would have to cross Barzani territory by night, three nights in a row.

It seemed that there were three ways to get through this territory: by going around it over extremely difficult territory, by going through it by day but without arms, or by going through it by night so that the arms could not be seen.

Barzani territory, as I have explained elsewhere, was neutral, and Sheikh Ahmed, the tribal chief, insisted that his neutrality be respected in these ways. Hence the restriction.

I argued for Apo. I insisted that the success of my mission depended in no small measure on my having a really competent and intelligent interpreter like Apo. For me he was not just a translator, but guide and philosopher, a man who could provide me with the background of every facet of Kurdish life we encountered. Furthermore, it was thanks mostly to the unquenchable spirits of Apo that ours was on the whole a gay party, in spite of a slipped disk, various forms of dysentery, the Iraqi air force, heat, flies, obstinate mules and extreme fatigue. I conversed interminably with our seventy-two-year-old "Kind Uncle" as we rode along. Apo never stopped pouring out anecdotes and reminiscences of a lifetime of happy struggle, about his own experience of the birth of modern Kurdish nationalism and beyond that about the origins and history of the Kurds and their pre-Islamic Zoroastrian religion. He was an optimist who could turn all vicissitudes to joy, goodwill, good fellowship and laughter, a wonderful man to have along. My French surely improved and perhaps I even picked up a little of Apo's unmistakable Istanbul accent. For that is where he learned his French as a student back in the early 1900's.

Finally, it was decided that Apo would cross Barzani territory separately. While the rest of us went through by night with our armed guard, Apo would go by day, without arms, accompanied by only one other person and pretending that he was a merchant dealing in sugar.

The borders of neutral Barzan territory are formed by the Big Zab and Little Zab rivers. We made our way into a deep ravine above the roaring torrent of the Big Zab. Across the torrent there was a steep cliff-face honeycombed with deep caves. On our side the peasants had built passable steps and passageways above the rapids.

As our mules squeezed along the narrow trail hewn out of a rocky mountainside, the last of the White Label was crushed in the saddlebag. Apo said, "Never mind," he would make me some *smak*. This turned out to be like a very acid lemonade made from small yellow and reddish berries of a plant found alongside the rivers in Kurdistan. When liberally mixed with sugar it was delightful—and anti-laxative. We were following part of a route thousands of years old on the caravan trail from Basra into Kurdistan and on to Diyarbekir in Turkey and finally to Europe. Another route went farther east via Lake Urmiya in Persia.

We followed the course of the Big Zab up to a point where it is spanned by an old, broken Turkish bridge. Some later engineers had repaired a fallen arch by laying railway tracks across the gap. We crossed the bridge and wound slowly up the other side of the valley listening still to the thud of mortar bombs and possibly aerial bombs in the battle of Amadiya away on the other side of the mountain. Toward noon smoke began to drift around the mountain from the scene of battle. We skirted the territory of the Zibaris and stopped that night, at last, just inside Barzani territory, at the village of Sheile Dze.

11

In a Kurdish Village

I will never forget the village of Sheile Dze, for there we spent thirteen desperately worried days. We were worried because we seemed to be hopelessly stuck, and in some danger. In my case, I was also worried about the family I had left behind in Beirut.

We were delayed at Sheile Dze because Ahmed, who had gone ahead to reconnoiter the route across Barzani territory, did not return. Ahmed had said that he would be back in three or fours days' time at the most. Two days after he left we received a note from him by courier explaining that all was well but that he had found it necessary to go farther than he expected. After that we heard nothing. As far as I could see there were two kinds of problems: the military problem of getting through an area beyond Barzani territory where the fighting had become intense; the political problem of crossing neutral Barzani territory.

The courier who brought Ahmed's letter dramatized the military dangers with stories about the feats of the Barzanis. He said Barzani had absolutely defeated the Lolans and several other tribes who supported the government and had scattered a group of five hundred *josh* who were now fleeing to the protection of the army garrison at Mergasor.

Barzani was said to be moving up with his main force to try to cut off a large part of the Iraqi army in northeastern Iraq. He was supported by names famous among the Kurds such as Abbas Mamand Agha, one of the great chiefs of eastern Kurdistan, and Mahmoud Kawani, another tribal leader. And the Iraqi air force was out in full strength bombing and strafing everything in sight. One story had it that a group of *josh* had raided Barzani's personal headquarters and that he had joined in the fighting. The courier said that Barzani fired his automatic rifle so furiously that it soon became too hot to handle; an aide kept handing him fresh weapons. (While most of the courier's tales were based on fact the one about Barzani was apocryphal. Indeed, the Kurds often invented tales about the greatness of their leader.)

Apo tried to persuade me that the delay was caused purely by my friends' concern for my safety now that the war seemed to be swirling all around us. But I had the feeling that something had gone wrong which I did not know about. I got a hint of it from Apo's admission that part of Ahmed's task was to get permission from higher authority for us to cross Barzani territory. But it was not clear what authority was involved, although I suspected that the trouble was with Sheikh Ahmed who, to all intents and purposes, ruled this territory. Very likely he believed that my traveling through his territory could be interpreted as a violation of his neutrality— particularly because I had an armed guard. I proposed that the guard shed their arms for this part of the trip, but Barzani's men were horrified at the idea. To them leaving their weapons behind would be a kind of dishonor. I suggested that we go to see Sheikh Ahmed, who was spending the summer on a plateau high in the mountains near Barzan village. But Apo and Jamil felt this would just make matters worse, since he would then not be able to pretend ignorance.

The only good thing about the long delay was that it gave me an opportunity to get to know a Kurdish village.

We could settle down in Sheile Dze with our armed guard because it was in a kind of twilight zone, neither clearly inside nor outside of Barzani territory. Benefiting from the indistinctness of frontiers, it partook of both the neutral and the fighting worlds.

Most of the men of Sheile Dze were away with the fighting

forces. The twenty houses that were their homes might have been the original for the story about the crooked man who lived in a crooked house, et cetera. In these poor houses nothing was ever straight. Apo explained that they lacked tools for making boards smooth and straight. Thus the poles that support the roof were all knotted and twisted. The boards of a door were of different lengths, uneven and bent. The ladder they made for climbing up to the roof was lopsided and lacking several rungs. The windows were not quite square. The houses were built of uneven stones loosely fitted together, roofed over with crooked beams, branches and earth. Two or four houses were usually backed up against one another and the roofs joined so as to make a single surface.

The effect was picturesque, but the drafts in wintertime must be formidable.

All the houses bore painted dates with the letters DDT indicating the times when they were sprayed by Iraqi government DDT teams. The most recent date seemed to be in the summer of 1960. Now the flies and mosquitoes—but mostly the flies—were obviously avenging their former suppression.

We were well enough protected at night, for the villagers supplied us with good mosquito nets suspended on poles (crooked ones, of course) attached to the four corners of two iron bedsteads. The bedsteads were the only ones in the village. By day the flies were ever-present, buzzing around our ears and nipping at our ankles. Now I understood why the Kurds like those thick woolen stockings: they protect ankles and legs not only from thorns and briars but from biting flies.

Our host here was Mohammed Sadoula, who was given this land by the Iraqi authorities when he came as a refugee from Turkey thirty years ago. Sadoula devoted nearly full time to looking after us. I suspect that it was for him a welcome excuse for avoiding work. He provided the beds and bedding and we were fed from his kitchen.

Sadoula's village was very poor and we tried to minimize the burden of our presence on him and the other villagers by ordering meat, sugar and other staples from neighboring villages. We also had a few luxuries of our own which Ahmed obtained for us just before his departure. We sent his order in to Hoshewi's headquarters, from where a courier went south into Iraqi government territory—to Arbil in this case, I believe—and there delivered the things to us as surely as any American department store. These luxuries included the Nescafé, several cans of an extremely sweet and sticky Australian jam, some boxes of English biscuits, some canned New Zealand cheese, some toilet paper, and most remarkable of all a set of gleaming white bedsheets for me. I don't suppose that anyone in Sheile Dze has slept between sheets before or since.

Also on our shopping list were several dozen films, but unfortunately my camera had been damaged when I fell from the mule at Assad Hoshewi's headquarters and it would no longer work at all. And we were at our wit's end to know where to obtain another. In these poor villages nothing like that was to be found. (Later on in Barzani's home village one of his teen-aged sons offered me a fine-looking Russian-made miniature camera, but we had no film for it. I did not find a camera that could take my 120 film for another week. Then a soldier at Sheikh Boskeni's headquarters offered me a German-made box camera with a maximum shutter speed of one-fiftieth of a second. That was too slow for the Tri-X film. Finally at Barzani's headquarters I obtained an adequate replacement for my Rolleiflex.)

One day Sadoula sent off a party of hunters to the mountains, but they came back a day later empty-handed. They had hoped for wild boar or even a bear. Another party climbed for seven hours over the top of the mountain nearest us to a bowl where the snow lasts the whole summer through. They came back with packs loaded with snow. Usually this was done only when someone from the village was sick. But in this case it was done for me. I was not half so appreciative, however, as the village children who ate up most of the snow within a few hours.

Sheile Dze had been raided three times by the Zibaris, a neighboring tribe whose chief was allied with the government. This was the excuse, according to Apo, for the dilapidated condition of the village. Because the Zibaris during their last raid drove off all the animals except for some of the cows, Sadoula did not do his spring plowing this year. That was one reason why he was short of food.

Arguing that this village was indeed poor, Jamil proposed that we move to another one where we would be able to get better food. But I objected strongly, on the grounds that we should stay in the place where Ahmed had put us. Sadoula backed me up by arguing that the people of the next village could not be trusted, and proclaiming that we should have everything we needed in his village. He was outraged at the very thought of our moving. "For thirty years I have fought for the Kurdish nation," he declared. "To me it is precious to have you here. Do you think I am as other men?"

So we remained at Sheile Dze hoping that every day would be our last and yet appreciating the eager attentions of our host. Every morning at sunrise we hastened to be away from our place on the rooftop, to escape from the heat of the sun, from possible attack by aircraft and, most important, to avoid being observed by strangers who might report our presence to the Iraqi authorities. Under the arrangements for the neutrality of the Barzani tribal territory their police posts and some of their army posts were still intact. They still maintained radio communications with Baghdad and they could, at least theoretically, send out a patrol to try to arrest the American journalist.

Every day Sadoula led the way to a different camping place, usually on the banks of the river Zab. But even there he thought we might be observed by hostile Zibaris across the river. Our favorite place was a fine shady spot where a little creek flowed into the river. Apo and I were given the choice location in the densest shade while the others settled down a few yards away. In the morning when it was still chilly we immediately built a fire to make tea and—for me and Apo—Nescafé. Apart from Apo and me, our party now consisted of Jamil; and Mustafa, who was remarkably clever at such things as arranging baggage and saddling mules; Lasker, who fancied himself a great rifle shot and spent long hours sitting in a tree waiting for a chance to shoot fish; and

Anwar, the schoolteacher, who became a regular member of our party.

Anwar, as a village intellectual, did not fit in very well; he quarreled constantly with Jamil, to whom he was distantly related. Jamil made fun of the young man's pretensions to education and declared him to be totally useless at every practical task, including fighting. Whatever Anwar said Jamil would say the opposite, and vice versa. The truth is that Anwar was not very useful, since I could get a better interpreting job done by speaking French through Apo. I tried to maintain his standing and morale by asking him to translate some historical notes in Arabic that had been given to me by another schoolteacher near the beginning of my journey. The notes were supposed to concern the fighting in the Zakho area, but were in such high-flown and vague terminology that I found them useless. At least they had the merit of keeping Anwar busy for a few days. Most of the rest of the time he spent curled up in a kind of treehouse, a platform among the branches which he devised at the water's edge. He also spent much time reading a summarized edition of Dickens's *Tale of Two Cities* and in asking me questions about correct usage in English. He said that his great ambition was to become an aviator in the first Kurdish air force. But I'm afraid he may be overage when the day comes.

There were always two or three or more men from the village with us. They lay around gossiping or sleeping, washing themselves or their clothes, and occasionally swimming in the river. The boys from the village darted around us, shed their clothes in an instant, scampered over the rocks like little brown animals and plunged into the water. Some of them used gourds strapped to their buttocks, like misplaced water wings. Sometimes when they came out they found a sandy place on shore and covered themselves up with the hot sand. I typed with my typewriter on the ground, or balanced precariously on my knees, or on a rock, until Sadoula triumphantly produced a small rickety table and a chair with a canvas bottom. Although uncomfortable they were a great improvement.

Toward the end of the afternoon the sun streamed in

beneath the branches of the trees and the heat became particularly uncomfortable. Then Mustafa took out a curved knife and ruthlessly chopped down branches which he propped up in such a way as to keep the visiting journalist in the shade. Apo set off for the village ahead of the rest of us on the grounds that it was easier for him, with his bad eyes, to walk in the sunlight. Then the rest of us followed by the rays of the setting sun. At this time of day the flies clustered thickly on whichever side of our costumes was exposed to the sun. As we approached our crooked village we saw a crowd of little children rolling around on a rooftop, and I wondered why they did not roll off. But somehow they never did. One of the very little ones did a crazy dance for our benefit as we went by, until reprimanded by an older sister.

Back up on our rooftop as the sun was disappearing we had tea in the usual little hourglass-shaped glasses, and then one of Sadoula's boys brought trays of food, one for Apo and me, another bigger one for the rest. I was still watching my diet carefully, insisting that everything be either boiled or broiled. For the benefit of my health Sadoula got me a special kind of *doh*. It was very hard, dry and salty, really a kind of cheese made of concentrated skimmed milk, probably extremely rich in protein and minerals. Just before they brought it to me they heated it over the fire; only then could it be chewed.

Meanwhile the women baked bread, and black smoke rose from their oven and drifted over us. The oven was a hole dug into the earth. When the flames heated its bricked sides sufficiently the dough was slapped on the sides of the oven in light, thin, round pancakes, each about one foot in diameter.

During the evenings we sometimes walked down to the spring, half a mile from the village, from which the village transports its water in goatskins slung across the back of a limping donkey. Other evenings we walked nearly to the top of a hill outside the village, and, looking down at the village, jokingly discussed where we would build our houses and raise Kurdish families if we were forced to spend the rest of our days in this place.

Along the way we passed the village's big, brown, woolly sheepdogs, their ears cropped close to their heads. Usually they did not stir and I was tempted to pat them. But I had been warned they are not used to being touched at all and would be likely to bite anyone who tried to do so. Sometimes the dogs would rush out barking ferociously at us. Then our Kurds would hurl stones at them; when hit they would run away squealing like puppies.

Sometimes we would see Sadoula's smaller boys driving calves into a pen consisting of intertwined stakes and branches. They directed the beasts by throwing rocks at them with such violence that I expected their bones to be broken. An old bull, tethered beside the house, broke loose and blundered into a stable which was part of the house. This bull was suffering from severe diarrhea. Apo, as usual, had a prescription: Keep the bull out of the sun. Keep him quiet and cool. Give him lots of salt. And let him drink *smak,* the same drink that he had been preparing for me.

Toward the end of the day the wind often blew smoke from the region of Amadiya across the setting sun as though to remind us that our peaceful camping place was surrounded by war.

After dark we tried to make Sadoula's ancient battery radio work. Usually it was tuned quickly to a Kurdish music broadcast from one of the Iranian stations or from Baghdad. Only once I managed to get some news in English. It was about the death of Marilyn Monroe, and I hastened to announce it to my friends. "And who is she?" they asked. Their attitude brought home to me the utterness of my isolation. Not only was there almost no possibility of communicating with the outside world, no telephone or telegraph, no bus or train, but these people lived mentally in a totally different world.

To pass the time during the evening I asked Sadoula to tell some of the stories of his people. His niece obliged two nights in a row. Family and relatives and visitors crowded around in the light of an oil lamp. The flickering light, the Kurdish costumes, the farm animals and the crooked house created a setting to intrigue any artist. The woman's movements were reflected in vast shadows as she gesticulated to the audience squatted on the ground around her. Her story, "The Horse with Three Legs" (see page 139), rambled on without any reason for ending except the exhaustion of all concerned.

I also spent time trying to learn a little Kurdish, including such useful phrases as the following:

Kurdish	English
wera	come here
ravestan	stop
an haren male	let's go home
hedi here	go slow
hush here	go faster
zu here	go fast

Soon I became intrigued by the similarities between words in Kurdish and in European languages. Here is a list I worked out with Apo and Anwar:

Kurdish	English	French
av	(water)	eau
kiya lura?	(who's there?)	qui est la?
pantol	pants	pantalon
dran	(tooth)	dent
courte	(short)	court(e)
egnou	knee	genou
neh	nine	neuf
deu or dou	two	deux
niu	new	nouveau
non or nan	no	non
dlop	drop	
hek	egg	
leilac	lilac	lilas
mer	man	
brew	brow	
liv	lips	lèvres
ster	stars	astres
ribar	river	rivière
gully	valley, gully	
munk	month	mois
ling or lag	leg	

I found it much easier to learn Kurdish than Arabic because Kurdish, an Indo-European language, has more familiar sounds. I was intrigued by a Kurdish greeting that was meant to suggest complete submission. It is *"Lesser chawum, lesser serrim,"* meaning "On my head, on my eyes."

As the days passed without word from Ahmed I worried not only about our situation but the indefinite prolongation of my absence from home. I had sent off one letter and a telegram to Tania from Assad Hoshewi's headquarters, from which they had been carried out to be sent through the Iraqi postal system. The telegram, written in Arabic and addressed to a Lebanese friend, arrived. So did the letter which I addressed in Arabic to a neighbor. Presumably they passed unnoticed through the censorship. I had sent another letter from Sheile Dze just after our arrival. This one too got through, although I, of course, had no way of knowing it. For there was no way to send a reply. My last arrived in an envelope typed in Arabic with a post office box in Basra as return address, and postmarked Basra, at Iraq's southern end, more than three hundred miles from the place where I wrote it. But it did more harm than good, for it aroused false hopes of my early return. This is what I wrote:

> Darling Tania, another chance to write to you although I cannot at the moment tell you much except that I'm well enough and that I think I'll be with you again in about ten days [that would have been about August 6]. In spite of all my preoccupations here I have you and dear Shnoops [son Dana, aged eight] in my mind all the time.
>
> It is for you two that Daddy does these things. This time I'll really bring back something worth having, and I don't mean just a present. All my love my dearest darlings,
>
> Daddy

But now I began to wonder whether this trip could after all be so fruitful. I became quite desperate. Whatever the dangers, I insisted, we must move on. If necessary I would go myself to the tribal leaders of Barzan. I proposed to try to explain to them that by the standards of World War II it was

quite proper for a neutral territory to permit a war correspondent of either side to pass through its territory.

Then, on the twelfth day, a letter arrived from Sheikh
Ahmed's son, Osman. Osman apologized for the long delay
and invited us to move our camp to a place close to his home,
where he would be able to make us more comfortable and
help to put us on our way.

On the thirteenth day, before we could do anything
about Osman's offer, another courier arrived to announce
triumphantly that our own Kak Ahmed had returned and was
sleeping a few miles away after having marched almost continuously for three days.

When the word came at last that Ahmed had returned,
the despair that had settled so heavily over our little party in
the village of Sheile Dze was quickly dispelled. We all began
to vibrate energy.

There was a great flurry. We were all going together. The
scheme for sending Apo through Barzani territory separately
had been forgotten. We would risk it together. Even Apo, who
had begun to grow a vast facial adornment, thankfully shaved.
So did Jamil and so did I.

We were off at 4:15 in the afternoon, with our village
host Sadoula accompanying us with three or four of his men.
This is the usual form. First the honored guest is met some
miles from the host's home; then when he leaves he is accompanied as far as his next stopping place, if that is physically
possible.

We had become quite attached to this village, and were
sorry to leave them all. They gave us a warm farewell, the
women and children waving until we were out of sight.

We moved up the Behinda valley and crossed the Shin
(Blue) river. As usual my Kurdish friends made a great joke
of crossing through the deep water, some, stripped naked,
leading the mules, others, with pants rolled up, on the pack
animals. To be sure they were not lost, they carried the bigger
loads over by hand. I worried that my precious papers might
get wet. Apo and I were put on the two largest mules with our
pants rolled up to our knees, and the animals were led across

midst shouts of glee whenever a mule stumbled and it looked
as though we might get a bath.

As we were crossing, a thundershower bore down upon
us. Unusual at this season, even in these high mountains. We
took refuge in caves with a family who were camping beside
the river. To our amazement and delight Ahmed was waiting
for us here. We were so glad to see him that we hardly knew
where to begin. He told us that it had taken him six days to
reach Barzani. He had been delayed by a lame companion.
He had returned in three days. That meant he had spent four
days with Barzani. He looked completely exhausted. He had
had to go all the way to the great leader himself, for two reasons, as I understood it: to get Barzani to send a message that
would persuade his brother Ahmed to permit us to proceed;
and to organize a stronger guard for our journey through
areas where fighting was going on.

We gave Ahmed a letter we had received from Assad
Hoshewi's headquarters about the fighting at Amadiya. The
letter said that a unit of sixteen hundred Iraqi soldiers and
seven hundred *josh* and three big guns had tried to lift the
siege of Amadiya after a battle in which seven *josh*, seven Iraqi
officers and forty soldiers had been killed. After several days
of fighting the Kurds had let them go through, and then had
resumed the siege. This then was the not-so-brilliant denoue-
ment of the struggle for Amadiya we had been observing at a
distance for the previous few weeks.

When it stopped raining we set out immediately for what
was to be a fifteen-hour march with three rests.

I was learning more and more about the ways of mules.
Apo and I were not the only ones who fell off these beasts.
The others slid off and on, voluntarily or involuntarily, and
made very little of it. But Ahmed, who insisted on riding
the most nervous of the animals, hurt himself more than he
would admit in at least two falls. Jamil, who already had a back
injury, hurt himself again. Since at this time I was allowed
only a poor little creature deemed safe enough even for me,
my progress was often slow. I got tired beating him with all
manner of sticks. Apo, or whoever happened to be following

me, beat him from behind. Sometimes a muleteer pulled him from the front, except when we went through villages. Then I proudly steered him myself so that the villagers would not be stirred up unnecessarily by the presence of a stranger (anyone who could not manage his own mule obviously would have to be a stranger). I called this underpowered ass "Little Turtle," for which the Kurdish is *kucuk kuchi.*

We moved gradually up to a very high plateau where, according to Ahmed, there had once been many villages. But they had been abandoned some fifty years before and the inhabitants had migrated to Arbil and other towns. Apparently life had been just too hard and unrewarding on that high plateau. We enjoyed water in the middle of the night from wells on this plateau—a curious network of holes, quite overgrown and dangerous in the dark.

Ahmed was in poor shape. He complained about his "rheumatism," and had developed an unexplainable sore over his right shinbone. During one of our rests he fell asleep for fifteen minutes. Then he slept for two hours on the ground next to a spring. It was beginning to get chilly as we plodded on through the night, nearly falling asleep in our saddles at times. But the terrain was so rough, now up, now down, that no rest was possible.

We had to walk down one steep, long and nearly pitch-dark valley, too steep for the mules to carry us down. It was so dark that Apo and the rest of us were about even. Our better eyesight was no great help.

As the dawn crept into the eastern sky Ahmed told me to watch for a great oak tree with four huge branches, three of them dead, one flowering. And I did notice it and called to him. "You see," he explained, "the flowering branch is the Iraqi part of Kurdistan, flowering in revolt. The other three branches are still dead." He meant the Turkish, Iranian and Syrian parts of Kurdistan.

At eight o'clock in the morning we came to the village of Baban. I was struck immediately by the fair-haired children and blue-eyed men in the streets. These men seemed to be distinct Barzani types, slight and handsome. They must have been much inbred to produce such distinct types. This was suggested also by the presence of a village idiot. He shouted and threw rocks in a field in the early morning. Later, he came to stare at us.

The houses here were far superior to those of Sheile Dze. Adobe mud had been used skillfully and neatly to supplement the stone. Really exhausted, we crept into one of these neat, clean houses and slept gratefully until 2 P.M. I found that a pajama coat over my head served adequately as a mosquito net. They served us a good lunch, with boiled chicken and boiled eggplant and boiled rice and the inevitable yoghurt. I was feeling well again and ate heartily.

As we were leaving the village I noticed a particularly blond, broad-faced woman surrounded by a crowd of tow-headed children. I was told that she was a Christian woman, converted to Islam, who had married one of Barzani's men in Russia. I would have liked to talk to her but Ahmed did not think it was advisable. The villagers would not like to have their women interviewed, he said. The question kept going around in my head: "How was that Christian girl getting along in this utterly isolated, lost mountain village, so far from her own people?"

After lunch we were off again. Moving along the rim of a mountain and looking down on the village of Barzan, I could see nearby Iraqi police posts. We passed through the village of Hostan. Seventeen men from this village were with Barzani, the people said. Every village seemed to boast its quota. Obviously, no able-bodied young man could have resisted the social pressure upon him to serve Barzani. One of the men here had been married in Russia to a Turkoman girl.

I was amused by the different kinds of ways they cut the children's hair. At Sheile Dze the system was to leave a tuft like a mop at the top. At Hostan they kept parts of the neck and forehead strangely long, because they feared that if they cut it short while the child was growing the hair would creep down his neck and back and down his forehead toward his eyes.

Barzani had given Ahmed permission to let us visit his

sons in a village which I will not name. We met them in a
ravine outside the village.

The boys' names were Idriss, aged seventeen, who had
a mustache; Mesoud, aged sixteen; Sabir, aged fifteen; and
Nahad, aged three years. All fine-looking boys. Sabir was rather
fat. He struck up an immediate friendship with old Apo. He
wanted to be Apo's protector and struggled sweating over the
rocks, up banks and down gullies, to assist our old interpreter.

Idriss met us at the bottom of the ravine and explained
that it was not advisable that we enter the village, as there
were "malicious people" there and one could never tell who
might see us. The Iraqi authorities were, after all, quite near
in this area.

Excellent food—probably the most palatable of our
entire journey—was sent down to us from the Barzani house.
There were various kinds of chopped meat, meatballs mixed
with various herbs, honey, and some tasty kinds of cheese.

They all spoke a little English, but not much. They said
they were trying to keep up their schoolwork by studying at
home. They said their father wanted them to do a lot of reading, "especially Kurdish poetry."

Of course, a man like Barzani wants his sons to be
steeped in the tradition and lore and literature of the Kurdish people. But I hope that he will also see to it that some
of his sons get abroad and acquire a breadth of knowledge,
experience and perspective that is at present sadly lacking
among the Kurds.

The smallest of the sons was brought down to us as we
were leaving, wending our way through orchards and vineyards. He was a healthy-looking cherub who was delighted to
be placed on the back of a mule and waved gaily as we left.

Meanwhile we sent the three armed men now accompanying us ahead by another route, avoiding all villages. They
had to go a very difficult way through the hills to avoid being
recognized as "combatants." Obviously the neutrality of the
Barzani territory did have some substance. Although Barzani's
men could get through the territory it was made very incon-
venient for them to do so.

To maintain the privacy of our visit we waited until darkness before we left the old Barzani family property. We—that is, Apo, Ahmed, Anwar and I—rode slowly down an extremely long, gently sloping valley and crossed a river. On the morning of August 13 we reached the edge of Barzani territory and met the guard of fifteen men sent to us by General Barzani. They arrived as we, after a few hours' sleep on the hard-packed earth outside a shepherd's hut, were making our breakfast, including the precious Nescafé and Australian jam. The commander of our guard was a smiling fellow with an English type of military mustache who said he had been with Barzani in 1945 and 1946. Upon his return to Iraq, he said, he had been sentenced to death. But the sentence had been commuted to twenty years' imprisonment, and he had been given an amnesty after six years. As we sat eating, the shepherd, who looked a primitive fellow, surprised me with a picture album of Kurdish revolutionary leaders going back to the 1943 to 1946 campaigns. At the end were pictures of him in a group at an agricultural school in Russia.

We were now getting into an area of active military operations. Three scouts went ahead of us at all times. In the afternoon we got to a hilltop overlooking Mergasor. Our three scouts returned to us there with word that two hundred Iraqi soldiers had reinforced the garrison of Mergasor that morning. It was thought advisable for us to stay hidden until nighttime. That afternoon, in a well-camouflaged hiding place above Mergasor, we watched two Iraqi planes wheeling lazily in the sky as though they were looking for something. And we watched through field glasses while trucks came and went around the military camp of Mergasor.

While we waited, Ahmed told me this story. Last March, Mohammed Mirhan, the commander of the district of Sherwan, was seriously wounded in combat when he ran forward to pick up the body of an injured man. He was hit in the jaw and the chest. Mullah Mustafa, knowing that Mohammed Mirhan would die if he was not brought to a hospital, decided to try to send him to the government hospital at Mosul. So he sent the wounded man to Mosul with his son, aged twenty-four, and his sister.

The Republic hospital at Mosul accepted him, and within a few days his wounds seemed to be healing. He whispered that he thought that he would recover and fight again. But that evening someone put up ladders to Mirhan's window on the first floor. There was a sudden burst of automatic fire, and Mirhan was dead. His son and sister escaped. This was in section 2, private room number 1 of the private clinic of the Republic hospital.

That night, after our enforced daylong rest, was truly an aesthetic experience. We climbed first over curiously smooth and bare hills of gray earth, then up a long gradual slope studded with oak trees. The stars sparkled brilliantly. The moon was hidden behind the mountain. Our path led into a vast bowl where a woman's voice and a boy's laugh and a dog's bark carried from far away on the other side of the bowl, as though they were only a few feet away. But the sounds came not once, but twice and thrice, echoing around and around this bowl-shaped valley.

Then the moon rose over the top of the bowl and cast a ghostly light upon the scattered oak trees, upon the silhouettes of men marching by or riding. The echoes coming back again and again, of the woman's voice, the boy's laugh, the dog's bark; the sudden sound of a rushing stream superimposed on the night's noises, growing louder as we approached; the cacophony of louder barking, of a donkey braying; silhouettes of peasant huts, children sleeping like little corpses on the roof, all against the background of immense mountains; past a river reflecting the stars and the moon and the mountains, and then on up the mountainside again. Worried faces, because one of the men has disappeared. And the captain, cupping his hands, and calling with a long, eerie sound, "Ooo, Mel-laa!" The voice was soft, but somehow it filled the valley. And we looked down then, and before, and after, from the hilltops we crossed toward the Iraqi army posts with their lights blazing brightly, sometimes only five hundred yards away. After all, they did get reinforcements that day. Always there was that certain fear of possible ambush.

During the night we crossed the river Musaka, which separates Barzani territory from Bradost. We slept two hours on the other side, then went on at dawn to Halan village. Now we looked down on the lights in the distance, at the towns of Rewanduz and Diane, both heavily occupied by the Iraqi army. We could see the Iraqi army tents at the entrance to Gali Ali Beq pass.

In early dawn as we approached Halan village we could see three women in black running from the houses across a plowed field toward the path we would have to follow. They seemed in an extraordinary state of excitement, throwing up their arms and falling and uttering a strange sound between singing and moaning and weeping. They stood at the edge of an irrigation ditch that ran between them and our path, singing, moaning and weeping. The oldest woman kept bobbing her head up and down hysterically, weeping, shuddering, throwing up her arms.

Ahmed said they were a mother and two sisters. They had lost the two boys in the family and they were imploring Ahmed to help them, at least, to get back the bodies. They followed us to where we camped and the old woman seized Ahmed's hands, bobbing her head, crying aloud, shuddering and lamenting, and finally collapsing on the ground. It was a shocking experience.

As we prepared to leave this place at the edge of a village called Bebele later that day, Apo touched the hindquarters of his mule, which was suffering from sores from the ropes under its tail. It kicked him once in the shoulder, once in the arm and once in the leg. With an agonizing cry of alarm and pain he threw himself to the ground.

Ahmed was furious. He seized the mule and fought with it, beating it with a heavy stick. Then he held its left front foot doubled up while someone else held its ears and a saddle was put upon it. Only a short time thereafter as we were going down a steep hill, Apo's saddle slipped sideways and he fell again. He caught his foot in the stirrups as he fell and once more I heard his agonized cry. What an extraordinary old man. Despite all the knocks he suffered, he remained gay and vigorous.

My personal horsemanship had improved a little. One morning as I spurred my mule to something like a gallop in a race with Anwar, the chief of our guard raced after me: "Do be careful," he cried. "If you fall and hurt yourself Barzani will kill us all." And Jamil, our ever faithful Jamil, added: "You see, we want to carry you to Barzani like this"—and he extended his hands in front of him as though he were bearing a tray.

We were now entering Sorani-speaking territory. The dress differed a little, too. The pants were narrow at the bottom to fit easily into the socks. And the turbans had fringes like the bottom of an old-fashioned sofa.

Late at night we arrived at the headquarters of Sheikh Hossein Boskeni. Sheikh Hossein spoke the Sorani dialect, and sometimes I found we had to interpret in four stages—from his dialect into the dialect that Apo understood, into French and then, of course, I translated in my own mind into English.

All the leaders here seemed to be aghas. It was significant that here the entire Kurdish population seemed to have supported the Kurdish national movement, whereas farther west many had gone to support the *josh*. Sheikh Hossein told me a lot of stories about the fighting which I will not try to repeat. There was so much talk about the fighting, and so much evidence of it, that it became in my mind a nightmare of confusion. Parties moving off to join the battle. Wounded men coming back. Tense consultations. Detours to avoid places where the bodies lay stinking on the hillsides. Searching through field glasses from hilltops for Iraqi troops, for our own men. Watching for Iraqi aircraft. Taking cover when they swooped down to machine-gun something or drop their bombs.

Hossein said that during the past three months the Iraqi air force had used mostly incendiary bombs and rockets. He said they spent a lot of time setting fire to fields in Kurdistan.

To continue the first evening's conversation Sheikh

Hossein came to our lunch camping place. He apologized that we had been given only the regular "army fare." I asked him why he thought this rebellion would succeed. What was different from the many other Kurdish rebellions?

"In other times," he replied, "we served three nations. We served them sincerely but in vain. We awakened after many of us had been slaughtered and pillaged. Their oppression awoke us. The fact that we are awakened now has given us confidence in success."

And he added: "In other times the revolt was not so general. This time it is not just a few villages or even towns. It is all the Kurds of Iraq."

I asked one of Sheikh Hossein's men what kind of political organization was maintained among the Kurdish forces. Since this was a typical tribal force his reply was defensive. He said that the Kurds did not need any political organization, "as all the fighters have a clear idea of what they are fighting for. Our commander is Barzani, who voices all our political aims and has done so ever since 1932."

About Iraqi army tactics one of the men said: "They're always the same. First they bombard with artillery and aircraft, then they move forward. We do not answer until they advance. Then we move in behind them. They never learn and they do it over and over again." To this Sheikh Hossein himself added: "When their infantry moves forward our men sometimes cut the road behind them by rolling down big rocks. Thus they fall into a trap and often we are able to cut off armored cars."

On our last night before we reached Barzani's headquarters we visited Abbas Mamand Agha, chief of the Ako, greatest of the tribes in eastern Iraq. We reached his headquarters in the early evening and were escorted to a vast cave closed at the mouth by a wall of rock. A small stream flowed past the mouth of the cave. All around were camped his men and many refugees. I was reminded of the valley of the Guli which we had visited weeks earlier.

Abbas Mamand Agha is an extraordinary man in every respect. He stands about six feet five inches, the tallest Kurd I ever saw, and rules his tribe in a direct and autocratic manner such as one would hardly expect to encounter in these days. He is famous for having refused for years to permit members of his tribe to answer the Iraqi army's call for conscripts. "But during the last four years," he noted, "we sent them so they would get training in the use of modern arms." He is famous also for having declined an invitation to attend ceremonies marking King Faisal's coronation, for having declined an opportunity to have himself elected a deputy to the parliament in Baghdad, and for having declined to endorse the federation of Iraq and Jordan.

Abbas Mamand Agha had with him his son, a handsome lad of twelve or thirteen, who carried his own rifle.

Cross-legged as usual, I sat in the cave on Abbas Mamand Agha's right and tried to ply him with questions. His replies were dry, monosyllabic, and as soon as he had spoken he would turn and speak in Kurdish to someone on his left. His manner was almost insulting, although I am sure he did not intend it this way. More likely he was ill at ease under the questioning of a journalist.

I asked him the same question I had put to Sheikh Hossein: What was his concept of victory? He replied that it did not consist of destroying the Iraqi army, nor of occupying Baghdad, nor even of overthrowing Kassem. "It consists," he said, "of freeing the Kurdish territory." This, he added, had already been about half accomplished.

Abbas Mamand Agha told us that Barzani had inquired several times as to when we would be reaching him. He implied that Barzani was impatient to see me.

On our way the next afternoon we halted at a spring called Spindar, in the Bla valley, and there met a man named Kaukas, the distinguished-looking son of a remarkable father. As he was going our way, to Barzani's headquarters, he told us the story of his father, Sayed Taha. Sayed Taha had fought long and hard with a notable Kurdish leader named Simco. "Twice he was allied with the Russians, once with the Ottomans, once with the Assyrians, and once with the Iranians," said Kaukas, "but always in the service of the Kurdish cause."

In 1914, he said, his father and a friend named Abdel Raza Bey took refuge in Russia, attempting to win the Czarist regime for the Kurdish cause. When the Communists took over they returned to Kurdistan and tried to come to terms with the Turks. But the Turks were unfriendly. Abdel Raza Bey was poisoned and Sayed Taha, learning that he was to be assassinated, escaped first to the mountains, later to Rewanduz in Iraq. Under hospitable British authority just after World War II he became Qaimaqam, roughly equivalent to district commissioner, of Rewanduz. Several years later Reza Shah proposed that he come to Teheran and there he, too, was poisoned.

It seemed to me that whenever I dipped into a family history among these people I found violence, death, betrayal, struggle.

We lunched at Sara village, just over the top of an enormous ridge, in the shadow of the Karduchi mountains which Xenophon mentions passing. He wrote that the inhabitants of these mountains caused him more trouble than all the armies of Persia.

Trudging down and down endlessly from Sara we regaled ourselves with sweet blue grapes and the marvelous scenery. One or more of my guards would always be gleaning the best grapes, the choicest figs to right and left of our route, and bringing some to me. They were never at all apologetic about this, regarding it as the natural right of fighting men. As a matter of fact, I do not recall ever hearing a Kurdish peasant remonstrate with our men for helping themselves in the fields. On the contrary, very often they would help us to find the choicest fruit.

This business of gleaning is one of the lighter sides of war in the Kurdish mountains. The tastiest of all the fruit came not from farmers' orchards, however, but from the wild fig trees and vines. I will never forget the sweetness of the small black grapes that grow along "Hamilton's road," from Rewanduz to Kaneh, just across the border in Iran. A. M. Hamilton was the doughty British engineer who built this road in the 1930's and wrote a marvelously descriptive book about it called *The Road through Kurdistan.*

We made a detour to see this road and found that big chunks of it had been blasted or dug away, and boulders rolled down upon it, to prevent any possible movement by Kassem's vehicles—perhaps a little in the style of the people who gave Xenophon so much trouble about 2300 years ago.

That night we rode as long as the moon lasted, then slept and ate at the village of Gerawan Seri. Ahmed woke us with the happy news that a courier he had sent ahead had returned to say we were at last within a few hours of Barzani's headquarters, and that he was waiting for us.

12

Conversations with Barzani,
August 1962

For days we had been within one more day's journey of
General Barzani's headquarters. But he kept moving
as fast or faster than we did. This time the General would
stop and wait for us. On August 15 at 7:45 A.M., we arrived
at Barzani's headquarters. His son Obeidullah, about thirty-
five years old and a carbon copy of his father, and several
other officers met us about half an hour's march from the
headquarters.

Of course it was ridiculous, considering that Barzani
moved his headquarters every day and carried with him a
minimum of staff and baggage, but somehow I had expected
some kind of special show to indicate that this was a great
man. Yet the setting was almost the same as at many another
military command post. Rugs and mats were laid out on both
sides of a cement-lined irrigation channel beneath a canopy
of branches and leaves. On one side where the level of the
bank had been raised about twelve inches above the water a
place appeared to have been set aside for Barzani and for us.

Barzani, we were told, had been up until about three-
thirty in the morning, hearing and reading reports and giving directions, as was his custom. So he was sleeping, and we
must wait.

Twelve or fifteen men were gathered under the canopy, and beyond in a wider circle were scattered mules and

baggage and campfires and bedrolls and men in vast profusion. Among the men were three officers recently defected from the Iraqi army. They were Major Baqur Abdul Karim, Lieutenant Colonel Aziz Akawi and Lieutenant Aziz Atrusha. The Major, who had been with Barzani in Mehabad in the days of the ill-fated Kurdish republic, gave me a briefing on the composition of the Iraqi army. He said the army could be divided into four parts: "One part has joined us. One part has fled. One part is dead. And one part that is left has no morale."

Obeidullah and the General's senior aide, Omar, filled in the time with talk about our journey and with translations of radio-monitoring reports. These reports were always the "news," and most eagerly sought after among Barzani's officers. They were the best clue to the enemy's morale and intentions. On this occasion the telegrams dealt with the effects of Iraqi air force bombing. Omar said that a village called Gerawan had been bombed ten days earlier while Barzani was camped nearby. His men believed the bombers were directed by spies.

I felt a little as though I were in a theater waiting for the curtain to go up, only in this case I was on the stage with the actors. I noticed that somehow everyone in our party had found time the night before to shave.

Barzani appeared about nine o'clock in the morning, suddenly and unexpectedly, from behind the place where I was sitting, so that he was there and sitting down in the place selected for him even before I could scramble to my feet. He was unshaven and seemed to be preoccupied. He devoted the barest minimum of words to greeting us, a sharp and rather deflating change from the flowery greetings to which I had grown accustomed at every stage of my progress across the country.

I tried to establish some rapport with Barzani by recalling that I had interviewed him once before, in December of 1959, while he was still in Baghdad. He replied that he was sorry, he did not remember the occasion.

Feeling even more deflated, I launched diffidently into

a list of prepared questions. Nothing that I could think of seemed able to elicit from him more than general and pious comment. Thus, with regard to the area his forces had occupied, he said: "It was God who helped us." Concerning his plans for occupying the rest of Kurdish-inhabited Iraq, he declared: "My aim is to enable the Kurdish people to live in peace and security. May God help us." I had a clammy feeling that the interview for which I had come so far would be a bad one.

During one of the uncomfortable lulls in the conversation Ahmed prodded me to present to Barzani the pair of powerful binoculars I had brought along as a gift. Barzani accepted them with evident pleasure and spent the next few minutes trying them out. This helped to break the ice.

Little by little Barzani warmed up. In his own way he was perhaps seeking the psychological wavelength of his interlocutor. I felt about this man a sense of strain. A year and a half earlier in Baghdad he had been relaxed and affable and a good many pounds heavier. Now the lines in his face were deeply etched. He seemed to have an expression of gravity, as though the responsibility for the rebellion he led weighed heavily upon him. He wore the typical Barzani national costume in gray and white, neither better nor worse than that of his men. His only personal affectation was that he toyed alternately with a long wooden cigarette holder and with a small penknife. With the latter he shaved slivers of wood into what appeared to be oversized toothpicks.

After two hours of rather inconclusive talk I felt that I must be taking too much of the great man's time and suggested to my interpreter that we might withdraw. But I did not know my man. He was just getting started, just getting used to me, and he was far from finished.

We talked on until lunchtime and then, to my surprise, a tray was brought and placed between the two of us. It was rice and rather tough chicken. As I was to learn in the next few days food at General Barzani's headquarters is likely to be worse than in any village along the way. He does not pamper himself or those around him. Having eaten the

General rose, walked a few feet from the place where we were sitting, and waited for a soldier to bring him water and soap. He washed his hands just as he had before the meal, said he would see me later, and, without further formalities, departed.

Two hours later he returned. This time he was clean-shaven and seemed more relaxed. I saw him coming and rose, addressing him in French as *"Mon General."* He turned to Apo and declared, half humorously and half seriously, "I am not a general. I am just Mustafa. Tell your newspaper that I care nothing for titles. I am just one of the Kurdish people." But somehow I could not bring myself to call him Mustafa. His presence demanded some more respectful form of address. And I noticed that the Kurds around me also never addressed him in the ordinary way as "Kak," an expression that means something like "honorable brother" and takes the place of "mister" in ordinary conversation. They called him "Mamusta," which means something like "sir." So our conversation continued that day and the next and the next. I went off on a side trip to one of the Kurds' few permanent bases, at Betwata where there were prisoner of war camps, and a radio-monitoring station, repair shops, supply dumps and a small hospital.

I returned to Barzani in a new location, and followed him from there to a new camp in a deep cave and from there to another in the open air on the side of a lofty mountain where we sat and talked long under the stars. And again to a temporary headquarters set up in the middle of the night in the village of Hiran. And then again to another cave and to a resting place beneath a great slanting rock overlooking the valley of Khushaou. And yet again in a village at night beside a fountain in the garden of a mosque where we said good-bye. The period of my visit covered ten days and many subjects and many moods.

Mullah Mustafa got used to me and at last talked freely and easily. I got to know him as a man who maintained dignity and calm in all circumstances. He might be angered. But he never raged. He laughed, but not uproariously. He made a point of eating with his men or at least eating the same as they. Much of the time he also walked the same distances they walked instead of using the horses or mules that were always available to him.

Although he assumed these democratic attitudes, Barzani always maintained what I regard as an aristocratic reserve. He might joke with a visitor but he never became intimate and, so far as I could discover, had no intimate associates. The men around him changed constantly so that no one could claim to have the master's ear or to influence him exclusively. There was no "right-hand" man, no "ever present aide." His practice of constantly changing the circle of men around him, like his practice of moving from place to place, was probably partly security precaution and partly his political technique for maintaining contact with the widest possible number of his people, building his political fences with many individuals and many tribes. While he could be extremely charming and affable, he could also at times verge on rudeness. His remarks often had a cryptic, delphic quality that made the visitor wonder whether he had perhaps an insight that the visitor was unable to share or whether he had not understood the question. Possibly it was a bit of both. He lacked the kind of experience and education that would have enabled him to analyze questions in a manner a Westerner would regard as logical. But at the same time he had undoubtedly also a highly developed political intuition that enabled him often to penetrate to the heart and final conclusion of a matter while others were still immersed in the details.

Always his movements were secret. Although we were presumably quite closely attached to him we would awaken day after day to find that Barzani had "disappeared" during the night, moved on to some new camping place, the exact location of which was known only to a few intimates such as the men in his personal guard and those responsible for his personal welfare. The latter were the men I called "the specialists." There was Jamil whose job was to make his tea. Taha looked after his mule. Yunis took care of his field glasses and saw to his water. And Selim carried a special instrument of iron with which to prepare his place for sleeping or sitting. And there was Said Abdullah who cooked his food.

Ali Shaban and Hajik Mohammed were the leaders of the General's guard, numbering about twelve men. In addition there were always about a hundred scattered at outposts in the countryside surrounding him.

Although it was difficult to pin Mullah Mustafa down in direct reply to direct questions, I soon learned that he liked to convey his ideas by telling stories. One that seemed to be his favorite, for he referred to it again and again, concerned a family, a husband and wife, their child, and a visitor. The husband and wife could be regarded as representing Turkey and Iran where most Kurds live, or possibly Iraq. The child represented the Kurds. The visitor represented the United States or any one of the other great powers whose presence is felt in this region.

"One day the family had a visitor for dinner. During the meal the child farted. The parents were ashamed. Then the mother also farted. Even more embarrassed, the woman began to beat the child. A moment later the visitor also farted. And he began to beat the child, too. Then the woman turned to the visitor and asked him why he beat the child. 'Well,' replied the visitor, 'I see that it is the custom in this house that if one does such a thing one must beat the child.' "

"You see," said Barzani with a smile, "the Kurds want their rights so they must be beaten."

And he told another story. "There is a legend," he said, "about a country whose ruler was very cruel. This ruler fell ill. His doctor said that he must eat the brain of a child. The appearance of the child and his age must be thus and so. So the ruler called for this medicine.

"His officials found a child of the right appearance and age, but first they went to a judge to ask him if it were all right to kill a child and give its brains to the ruler. 'Would God approve?' they asked. The judge ruled that it would be all right to sacrifice the child because it would be a bad thing for all the people if the ruler died. The child's parents agreed to give him up so as to meet the needs of the ruler.

"Then the child was brought before the ruler. And the child laughed. 'Why do you laugh?' asked the ruler. 'Because,' the child replied, 'if I live in a country whose ruler wants my death so that he can live, and if I am born into a family with a father and mother who are willing to give me up to such a ruler, then it is better that I should die and not live in such a family and such a country. I am happy to die.'"

Again the child represents the Kurds, the parents are those Kurdish leaders and tribes willing to serve the governments of the Middle East in which they live and the ruler represents the government of any one of those countries which are willing to sacrifice the rights and welfare of the Kurds in the interests of their own survival.

Mullah Mustafa had yet another story which I got secondhand. The story was apropos of stupidity. "A man trained an elephant to fan him while he slept and keep the flies off him. One day while the man slept some particularly persistent flies settled on the man's head and would not be fanned away. I will fix those flies, thought the elephant. He picked up a rock and lifting it high with his trunk brought it down with a crash upon the flies on the head of his master."

But his favorite theme was: Justice.

"The poets and the philosophers and the governments of the earth speak of justice," he said. "They speak of kindness and goodwill. But in the lives of nations it is only strength that counts."

He gave me to understand that this principle had governed his life as a leader among Kurds. The Kurds had been beaten over and over again because they were disunited and weak. Because they were weak they had not been able to assert their rights. When the president of the Mehabad republic, Qazi Mohammed, had decided to surrender and throw himself upon the justice of the Iranian monarchy and of the world, he had been hanged. When his brother Sheikh Ahmed had obtained an amnesty from the Iraqi government and had returned to Iraq he had been thrown into prison. But he, Mullah Mustafa, had decided that he must fight, and so he had escaped. Since September of 1961 his brother Ahmed had chosen the road of submission to the government and neutrality. But he, Mullah Mustafa, knew that he and his people must be made to unite and to fight if they were ever to obtain the rights they dreamed about.

It was not that he did not believe in altruism and justice in relations among men, he explained. But in relations among nations it was strength and self-interest alone that counted.

I tried to get Mustafa Barzani to make a positive statement of what the Kurds were fighting for but from him personally I was never able to get much more than generalities. Perhaps he felt that what his people were fighting for was so obvious that it hardly needed to be spelled out. "We are fighting for autonomy, as you know," he said. "It is known in the world that all people have rights. We, too, have our rights, like other people in the world." I interjected that I presumed that if the Kurds were autonomous foreign affairs and military affairs would remain in the hands of the joint government, meaning joint Iraqi-Kurdish. He acknowledged the point, adding that "other matters would be in our hands."

In General Barzani's conception of the world there are two great powers only, the United States and Russia. If the Kurds have been denied their rights as a nation it is these two powers that must be blamed. "The East and West in their struggle for power think only of themselves," he said. "The small nations are crushed between them. They have no rights."

I observed that it was the General's habit to blame the United States and the Soviet Union evenhandedly for the misfortunes of the Kurds. I pointed out that the cases of the United States and the Soviet Union were surely very different. The Soviet Union had intervened actively in support of Premier Kassem and had supplied the Iraqi government with its arms, and in particular with the aircraft and the bombs with which it was attacking the Kurdish villages. The United States, on the other hand, could at worst be taxed with indifference. "We have done nothing against the Kurds," I declared.

In reply he laughed. "But you would supply Kassem with weapons if he would accept them," he said. And he recalled that Kassem's Iraq could have preserved the Baghdad Pact with itself a member had Kassem been willing to do so.

Barzani returned frequently to the possibility of the Kurds obtaining some kind of help from the United States. Once he asked me point-blank: "Do you think that it is possible for us to get help from the United States?" I replied that I did not really think so. As long as we were allied with the Turks and the Iranians in CENTO I did not see how we could help the Kurds. The Turks and the Iranians would consider it an act of betrayal if we did anything to help the Kurdish national cause. But General Barzani would not accept this contention. Over a period of several days he developed a web of arguments as to why the United States should and could help the Kurds.

Aid to the Kurds could be secret, he contended. "Are your training missions and supply missions not in Iran, just across the border, at Khane?" he asked. "Would it not be easy for you to provide us with ammunition, arms, or even clothes?" he asked. If these things were not possible could the United States not at least provide money?

"Help us now," he said, "and we will help you when you need us. Help us with arms, supplies, or even just money, openly or secretly. Help us to overthrow Kassem and we will make Iraq your soundest ally in the Middle East."

Barzani contended that the Kurds would be worth more to the United States than either Turks or Iranians. He said they were better fighters. Indeed they were the best soldiers in the Middle East and they were situated on the flank of any possible Soviet advance in the Middle East through the Caucasus. "In time of war you will need us. You cannot afford to ignore us."

He argued that the Kurds were winning already; United States aid would determine the extent of Kurdish victory and the speed thereof.

"We would be willing to offer all possible guarantees," he said. "If the United States were to set as condition of its aid that the Kurds refrain from interfering in Turkey and Iran we would be willing to accept. We would give our word not to agitate among the Kurds of Turkey or Iran."

He pointed out that in Iraq there is a Communist Party. "This party is a partisan of the Soviet Union," he observed. "If you help us we would be partisans of the United States. We would be useful to the United States."

These arguments General Barzani coupled with a warning that if the Americans did not find a way to help the Kurds the consequences could be "nefarious."

"If the Americans go on thinking only of the interests of Turkey and Iran, if the Americans never consider our interests, never ask how many of our people are in prison, how our crops are burned, how much we need medical aid, then there is a danger. The danger is that we will be obliged by necessity to accept aid from the Communists. Then it will not be our fault."

He implied that accepting aid from the Communists would be extremely distasteful to him and that he would do everything to avoid it. But he also left me without any doubt that he might be driven to it. Also, that his personal control of the insurgent Kurds could not be expected to continue forever and that there were other Kurds less wary of receiving aid from the Soviet Union. To Mullah Mustafa's completely realistic mind it was self-evident that there is no such thing as aid from one nation to another "without strings." He knew that if the Russians ever got arms to his hard-pressed guerrillas there would be some kind of political conditions, pressures, persuasions, brutal or subtle according to the circumstances.

I turned from the question of aid to the role of the Kurdish Democratic Party. "What was its part in the struggle?" I asked. The question seemed to agitate him somewhat. We were sitting with at least twenty-five men gathered around within earshot. "Well," he replied, "what it can do it does." And then he raised his voice for all to hear: "But according to me, there is no party, only the Kurdish people. Those who will win will be the Kurdish people."

Behind this somewhat enigmatic remark lay a long, involved and painful relationship between Barzani and the KDP. Although technically he is president of the party and

of its central committee, Barzani has little use for the generally leftist urban intellectuals who predominate in the party
leadership. He contends that the presidency of the party was
"forced upon me," without ever explaining who did the forc-
ing. Nor do the party leaders have much use for the tribal
chiefs, with their feudalistic attitudes and prerogatives, who
surround Barzani.

At every opportunity Barzani cast aspersions upon the
party. He declared that units under party command did not
start fighting "till they saw the red and white of our Barzani
turbans." He alluded to "certain people who think the party
is made for them."

There was something paradoxical about Barzani's own
sense of his role as a leader of the Kurds. At one point he
interrupted my political questions to explain: "You ask me
questions. But I have no right to answer. What we need is
a plebiscite." I observed that he surely could speak for the
Kurdish people. But this he stoutly denied. "No," he said, "I
do not represent the general will. I cannot say that I speak
for the Kurdish people." Unconsciously he compared himself
with George Washington by observing that he could do nothing without the Kurdish people, any more than such a man
as George Washington could have saved the United States by
himself. "He succeeded thanks to the people."

"I don't want to say that I did this or I did that," he continued. "But I can say that I have the confidence of the Kurdish people. I see that they have confidence in me."

I asked him whether he had any system, any organized
means of ascertaining the will of the Kurdish people. He
replied that there were around him a good many people
whom he could gather together and whose opinions he could
consult. "These can speak for the people," he said. "As for
organizations, have you not seen all these organizations that
are fighting? Do they not represent the people?"

Barzani maintained that the revolution in Iraq was
unique, that it had no relationship to any other part of Kurdistan in Turkey or Iran. "Those other Kurds," he maintained,
"have no means of helping us. Sometimes an individual

comes to us from Turkey or Iran. Some of them are outlaws in their own countries and come to fight with us. Then we keep them here. But in general we have no contact with them. We seek no help from them. They will be better off if they settle their problems with the governments of the countries in which they live. We are not fighting against the Iranian and the Turkish governments. We are fighting Kassem." In a related quotation, supplied to me by Richard Anderegg, who also visited General Barzani, he said: "We aren't fighting the Arabs, either. The Arabs are our brothers. We have lived with them for centuries and shall go on living with them. We can live with them. They have been exploited by Kassem just as we have."

"But do you not think in terms of a Greater Kurdistan?" I asked. He replied that all his efforts now were devoted to winning autonomy for the Iraqi part of Kurdistan. "This idea of a Greater Kurdistan," he said, "I do not even dream about it. Without the consent of the United States and Britain such a thing is chimerical. I do not concern myself with it."

Barzani's allusion to the United States and Britain implied that anything concerning a Greater Kurdistan would have to be approved by CENTO, which embraces Turkey, Iran, Pakistan, Britain and the United States. The United States, although in fact the most powerful and influential participant, is technically not a full member and merely sits on some of CENTO's committees.

Of course, as I continued to press him on this subject, I knew that in his heart there could be no difference between the Kurds of Iraq, Iran or Turkey. He turned to me appealingly and said: "Why do you press me on this subject? You know it is difficult."

Although Mullah Mustafa said that he had studied economics in Moscow he did not often let the conversation turn to economics. Asked whether he thought Kurdistan could become a viable state, his reply was that no state lived alone. "We, too, must live in relation to our neighbors. In some sectors we can be independent. In others we must live in contact with our neighbors. Like any family." He did not make it clear whether he was thinking in terms of Greater Kurdistan or Iraqi Kurdistan.

I tried to find out whether he believed in the separation of church and state, as is usual in modem secular states. I asked whether he believed that the Koran provided a sufficient legal foundation for a modem state. In the Middle East this is an important point. Thus one of the characteristics of Saudi Arabia's backwardness is that its rulers, insisting that the Koran is a sufficient basic law, have avoided endowing their country with a constitution. Egypt has meanwhile followed an opposite course. Apart from its constitution, which is strictly secular, it has supplemented traditional religious laws on personal status—marriage, divorce, inheritance—with a new body of secular law.

Somewhat to my surprise Mullah Mustafa replied that the Koran could supply the basic law of the state. Then, sensing my surprise and perhaps not wishing to give me the impression that he was "reactionary," Mullah Mustafa absolutely shut off any further discussion along this line. He said that this was not the time to worry about such things. This was a time for fighting.

Barzani talked readily about Abdul Karim Kassem. He said: "His vanity knew no bounds. One day, just for a joke, I told Kassem that I had been looking at the moon through a telescope and that I had seen his portrait in the moon. He took it quite seriously.

"You know," he declared, "if that man were to fart every time he tells a lie it would sound like a machine gun."

I asked Barzani whether Kassem had made any attempts to make peace with the Kurds. He said there had been a number of contacts initiated by Kassem. "But," he said, "they were all tricks. None were sincere. The first came in late summer of 1961. Premier Kassem sent me a message at Mergasor asking me to return to the government. If I did so all would be forgiven. But I replied that it was not for him to forgive me. 'You,' I told him, 'are the guilty one.'"

The next contact came at Sarsang on December 17, 1961. "An officer named Hassan Aboud came to me with other officers," Barzani recalled. "He carried this message: 'Tell Barzani that we are brothers. If he does not fight us we are willing to come to terms with him.' Aboud wanted to declare an amnesty during which all rebels might be forgiven. But Aboud's purpose was revealed by the fact that he had with him in a car a walkie-talkie with which his people hoped to be able to direct aerial attacks against me. I answered Aboud as I had answered before: 'I have not committed any crime. I am not the evildoer. You are the evildoer. It is I who cannot forgive you. So how can it be that you are offering to forgive us? No, we do not want your amnesty.'

"On June 23, 1962," Barzani continued, "the commander of troops in Kirkuk sent an officer named Ali Agha to discuss terms for a ceasefire. He said he was prepared to throw leaflets from airplanes to announce the ceasefire. He appointed a place for me to meet him but I did not go because I knew it was a trap, and in fact the place where we were to meet was bombed from morning until night. Meanwhile I sent back my answer with three conditions:

1. Withdraw all military forces from Kurdistan.
2. Release all political prisoners.
3. Disarm all the *josh*.

Then I will be ready to negotiate."

One day when General Barzani was quite relaxed, and for once we were alone except for our interpreter, our faithful Apo, I told General Barzani that some of his people's misfortunes might be attributed to the fact that they were so little known in the world. "Your greatest weakness," I told him, "particularly as far as the United States is concerned, is that the public hardly knows who the Kurds are. It knows nothing of their problems, their national cause."

From this I went on to argue that it was hardly fair to blame the United States for having done nothing on behalf of the Kurds. "Your real problem," I told him, "is a problem of public opinion. If you can reach the organs that influence American public opinion you might conceivably influence American foreign policy." I tried to explain to him that American foreign policy in the most basic sense is not made in the

State Department but on Capitol Hill, by Congress, more particularly by the Senate Foreign Relations Committee. I tried to make him understand the way the views of Congress and its committees reflected the views of the American public and the ways in which the views of the American public were formed by organs of mass communication such as the *New York Times*.

The reports sent in by embassy officials, I told him, are studied by State Department specialists, sometimes even by specialists of the Central Intelligence Agency. But even the best of these reports are readily filed away and forgotten, I told him. "There is no substitute in our system," I explained, "for reports made publicly to the public in general by independent reporters such as myself. The State Department is bound to take note in its policy formulation, sooner or later, of whatever views take hold in the newspapers and other journals and media of communication, in short, in what we call 'public opinion.'"

But I don't think that Barzani followed very much of what I said. He rejected my distinction between the American government and the American people. It was simply beyond his experience. He has, after all, never traveled in the West. He maintained that the American government *is* informed of the true situation in Kurdistan. The responsibility of the government, he insisted, is to see to it that American public opinion is correctly informed. If the American government did not do so it could only be because the American government did not want to help the Kurds. He asserted that both the American government and the Soviet government had ample means of knowing the truth about the nature of the battle in Kurdistan, about its rights and its wrongs and who was winning where and when. "And yet there are Americans who go on alleging that we get help from the Russians. And there are Russians who go on alleging that we get help from the Americans." These observations brought him full circle back to the point he had made when we had started our discussions some days before. "How can I admit that there is justice among nations?" he declared.

13

Last Days with the Kurds

Toward the end of my conversations with Barzani he urged me to see a little more of Iraqi Kurdistan. I agreed to several side trips, one of which took me to the village of Kula, a community of long, low concrete houses which the government had put up for persons displaced by the lake behind the Dukhan Dam. To reach it we waded for about three hours in the blackest night I could remember through marshland with the water sometimes halfway up to my knees as I sat astride my mule. The uncertain footing, the splashing sounds, the sense that the mule might slip and submerge rider, baggage and all made the night uncanny. Kula itself was ghostly when at last we reached it. We sat on the ground outside those long concrete buildings surrounded by gigantic sheep dogs and a Saluki and a wolf puppy. The baby wolf was tied up in the yard. But the dogs moved about freely, crouching ten or twelve feet away, watching for a chance to snatch some food. In the center of the circle our host placed a very bright pressure lantern. This was the only lantern of the kind I saw among the Kurds. It cast huge shadows, against the concrete walls, of the men sitting around it and the circling dogs.

Here we were right out in the open without any shelter from possible aerial attack. And so after a few hours' rest we started off again by moonlight and kept going across the open plain. When the sun came up we had not yet got back into the mountains. We pressed on as fast as we could, trotting and even galloping. We were all mounted.

About eight o'clock in the morning we sighted two MIG's and a helicopter, apparently moving in our direction. After watching them very briefly we dived under the bank of a dry riverbed to the right of the path on which we were moving. The aircraft circled, as though searching. Then the helicopter flapped away and the two MIG's came back again, straight at us it seemed, but without firing. This was really frightening. I heard the engines throb, the rush of air close overhead. They acted as though they were looking for something, and it might be us.

Fortunately I had pulled a light gray sweat shirt over my Kurdish costume during the cold of the night. Now I pulled it down far over the bright yellow sash I had around my waist. I also tucked the red-and-white checked Barzani headdress underneath me. A young Kurdish soldier who had taken cover next to me motioned me to cover up my camera, whose bright chromium parts he apparently thought might attract attention.

The planes came back a third time, and this time they fired. Right overhead I heard the deliberate rat-tat-tat, so merciless. I glued myself to the bank and pushed my head under a projecting rock.

Just as I was beginning to relax, the planes came around a fourth time and fired once more from the same position. Maybe they were after us. Maybe they were after our mules and horses, which were wandering aimlessly on the bank above us. But maybe their intention was to start a fire. For that is what happened in the field of dry stubble to the left of our path.

When the planes had gone, we scrambled on for an hour watching that fire spread slowly across and up a great mountainside. We rested with a shepherd and his family in their summer shelter, whose construction of boards made natural camouflage. As the fire crept up and over and down the other side of the mountain, I could see the shapes of two men, and perhaps also of a woman, flailing at the fire. Then those shapes disappeared. I wondered whether they had been overcome by the flames or had escaped.

Half an hour after we had started on our way again there was another alarm. I plunged down a steep bank through thistles and, sliding faster than I had expected, barely managed to stop myself at the end of a ledge. I looked over it into the entrance of a cave, where I could see a dozen faces. As I climbed around and down into the cave I heard them calling to me, *"Wera, wera."* As I learned later, this meant "Come here, come here." But as I did not know the meaning of the words at the time, and the entrance to the cave seemed blocked with branches, and the crowd of faces peering through the branches suggested that there was no room inside, I felt as confused as Alice in Wonderland when all the creatures at the Dormouse's tea party shouted, "No room! No room!" So I crouched near the entrance for a few moments, gazing at the faces which gazed questioningly back at me, and then I clambered back up the bank to find my companions.

That afternoon we ate and rested in a cave with the family of one of Abbas Mamand Agha's brothers. This was a cave deluxe, large and airy, its inhabitants bright and smiling, the children clean and friendly and unafraid. They made a comfortable place for me and I, exhausted by the morning's excitement, fell asleep almost immediately. Later I was introduced to the family's pet, an exquisite fawn. After I had admired it, it was all I could do to restrain them from giving it to me.

Refreshed by our rest we pushed on to the village of Plingo. At supper there we heard the dogs barking hysterically. Our host went outside and found them driving off a bear. Next morning as we walked along a ridge above the village of Warta, where the Kurdish forces maintain a hospital, we saw bear tracks six or eight inches across on our path. On the open slopes of the high mountains here we came upon horses being driven to new grazing grounds—a herd of perhaps thirty animals gamboling gracefully, easily, magnificently. It pleased me to reflect that there were still tribes who found it worthwhile to devote themselves entirely to raising horses.

That night we spent in a shepherd's tent of black

goatskin divided into two parts by hanging blankets and sacks containing I know not what. The women and children were on one side, except for a boy about ten who sat up late listening to the men and fell asleep on our side.

On the earth were felt mats and one good rug laid out as usual in a U-shape with bolsters for us to lean on, as in every proper Kurdish parlor.

The most important of the side trips we made from Barzani's headquarters was to Betwata, one of the insurgents' few permanent bases.

The night before our departure, which was set for 4 A.M., Ahmed said that if I wanted to write a story he would try to send it out by courier. That is, it would be taken out secretly from the area controlled by Barzani's men to one of the surrounding countries and mailed or telegraphed if, as and when censorship permitted. So I sat up and worked until two o'clock in the morning by the light of an oil lamp, with my typewriter balanced on a couple of boxes. The lamp, suspended from a nail in a post above my head, swayed and flickered. The paper in my typewriter blew back and forth in the breeze. My notes fluttered. All round me were sleeping men rolled up in blankets, either slumbering too deeply to be bothered by my light and noise, or bearing it with good grace. I was tired from the day's exertions and I longed for sleep. But the opportunity to get a story out was not to be missed. That story, if it had gotten through, would have been the first one filed from Barzani's headquarters. But I must sadly report, without revealing how my Kurdish friends tried to do it, that they failed. My story never reached its destination. Only one copy, which had been sent by several different routes, eventually reached my Beirut address, but it arrived ten days after I myself returned home.

Two short hours after I had finished my story Ahmed woke us with the unwelcome news that we must get started, although no tea or other food had been prepared. He said we would get food in one of the villages on our way. I was nonetheless in good spirits because I was cool and comfortable. Barzani had asked me the day before whether I really enjoyed wearing my Kurdish costume, and I had admitted apologetically that I found it pretty hot. "Then why do you wear it?" he replied. I explained why Ahmed had thought it wise for me to do so. "Oh, never mind that," he declared. "You can wear anything you like while you are with us." So that day I was wearing a cool pair of cotton pants and a white cotton shirt.

My good humor was soon dissipated, however, when I discovered that not only had the little mule with which I had become so familiar been sent back to its village of origin, but that the saddle upon its back had gone with it. I knew very well that in these mountains no other saddle could be found on short notice, and that a long day's travel on one of the Kurdish pack saddles would certainly not agree with my anatomy. Those saddles were five or six inches thick, the lower sides thicker than the top, so that there was an approximately flat surface on top of the mule. While this might be convenient for loading baggage, it required a rider to assume a position approximating the splits. The Kurds, of course, would curl their feet up under them, or swing around sideways, and jump on and off. But I knew that I would be condemned to hours in one agonizing position.

I was angry. With adrenalin pouring into my blood I declared that if I didn't have a proper saddle I would walk. If my Kurdish friends could walk all day so could I. No one tried to argue with me. I was in no mood to be reasoned with. And so walk I did, from five o'clock in the morning until noon, when at last we stopped to rest and eat around a little pool near the public fountain of a mountainside village. Many villages have these little pools arranged as small public meeting places, with room to recline all around them. We flopped down on the mats around the pool, and I was pleased to see that I was not the only one who was worn out. This was a time when the bowl of really cold *doh*, quickly passed around to weary travelers, seemed the most delicious drink in the world. One of the villagers brought tea while rice and mutton were being prepared. And Jamil, always trying to find some way to make me more comfortable, rolled a cigarette of native tobacco and offered it to me. Although I rarely smoke I had discovered by now that these home-rolled cigarettes were pleasant, especially at the end of a hard trek.

My companions washed in the little pool. They did not mind that the water looked dirty, and that all kinds of debris was in fact constantly being swept into it and accumulating in the corners where it could not be reached by the gentle current. Then villagers brought pitchers of ice-cold spring water from which we drank. What was left we, myself included, poured over our heads. Nothing on earth could be more refreshing.

Thus stimulated I was all for a quick snack and pushing on. But of course no "snack" can ever be had in the Kurdish mountains. We had to wait for water to be boiled and food to be cooked, and after it had been prepared and eaten, we would rest a while. It was four o'clock in the afternoon before we were ready to move on. Again I insisted on walking, though with less fervor than in the morning. The going had been over flat ground and rather smooth and easy. I was wearing tennis shoes. But by the time the sun was setting the trail began to get very steep. Sharp stones cut my feet and ankles and I began to look longingly at those mules.

It was Mustafa who came to the rescue. He removed one of the pack saddles from a mule's back, devised a thinner saddle of blankets, and rigged up stirrups of rope. This proved a most admirable contrivance, and I declared that it was Mustafa who should be called Kak Farzanda. To effect these improvements the pack saddle on one of the mules had to be loaded on another, so that the second mule had two saddles on his back. To this it objected. It began bucking like a bronco, broke away and began racing across the mountainside. Ahmed headed it off, grabbed the rope it was trailing and stopped the mule, but in so doing badly burned the palms of his hands on the rope.

After dark, more dead than alive, we arrived at Betwata.

In the morning we discovered that we were in the midst of a busy base—a supply depot with a small arsenal for repairing and handing out arms, a tailor shop with three Singer sewing machines, a small clinic, a radio-monitoring station, and a prison camp for prisoners of war and political prisoners.

At the armorer's shop in a spacious cave the head armorer, Osman Yusef, boasted that when he came across to the Kurdish national forces from the Iraqi army he brought with him 100 rifles, 20 pistols, 3 machine guns, 2 mortars of two-inch caliber, and 10,000 cartridges. He and his assistants carried an assortment of his weapons out in front of the cave, and I photographed a staged scene showing a Kurd handing in a battered, old hunting rifle and receiving in return a shiny, new Russian-made automatic.

A few yards away, the Singer sewing machines were singing away and a crowd of former policemen were handing in their Iraqi police uniforms and receiving in return a khak-colored, Kurdish-style uniform.

And then we went to see the prisoners. Very high up on the slope the rocks opened in a giant cave to which the Kurdish army had consigned ninety-one political prisoners, mostly former policemen, "informers," suspected *josh,* and officials of one kind or another who were accused of having mistreated the Kurds.

The prisoners were so crowded that they sat tightly against one another along the sides of the cave. It was hard to imagine that there could be room enough for them to stretch out and sleep at night. Four times a day and sometimes more often, they were taken out of the cave in single file, to climb down a steep path to a brook where they could wash and relieve themselves.

Observing that I hardly condoned the conditions under which these men were being held, my hosts told me atrocity stories about wounded men who were killed in Iraqi government hospitals, allegedly by the injection of air into their veins or by beating. But I told them that no matter what their enemy might have done it reflected no credit upon the Kurds to hold prisoners, no matter how detestable, under such conditions. My hosts told me they were already at work enlarging the cave, which was L-shaped, with two entrances, one of which had been blocked. The enlarging, I took it, was to be done at the elbow of the L.

From the political prisoners' cave we went to the opposite extreme of a small camp for specially privileged prisoners, all men considered especially friendly to the Kurdish people. They included three civil governors, one police officer, one police warrant officer, and an army officer. The army officer, who had studied radar at Forth Worth, begged me urgently not to publish his name. I think he hoped to be released soon, but feared that if the privileged status he had acquired among the Kurds became known to the Iraqi army it would cause him trouble upon his return. This group said they were given meat almost daily and really ate "better than the Kurds do."

Then we visited a group of ordinary prisoners, most of them regular officers of the army. There were about fifteen of them who seemed reasonably comfortable. I had visited another regular prisoner of war camp near Assad Hoshewi's headquarters in the western part of the Kurdish area, where I found seventeen men and was told there were nineteen others in a camp nearby. Most of the men were officers; a few were high-ranking civilian officials. One was a noncommissioned officer. At that time and until late in the summer the Kurds did not keep ordinary soldiers as prisoners, partly because it was too costly to feed them, partly because the knowledge that they could expect freedom encouraged easy surrender among the Iraqi soldiers and police.

The senior prisoner, a Captain Ata Jaj, a police commander with thirty years of service, conceded that he was being well taken care of, that the food was all right and his sleeping quarters comfortable. In addition to what they had on when captured, they had been given some new clothes, he said. Ata Jaj's only complaint was that he had never seen a doctor in the camp. He said he suffered from "high tension" and feared he had heart trouble.

These men slept and read all day. They were allowed to bathe in a little stream along the bank on which we sat.

One of them was the former *mudir*—a kind of district officer—of Upper Barwari, who had been stationed at Kane Mans. He had been in a group of one hundred and fifty Iraqi civilian officials and police who tried to escape to Turkey when they realized that the Kurdish insurgents had taken control of their area. They climbed to the top of a formidable mountain ridge to the Turkish border post, but the Turks would not let them cross and they had to surrender to the insurgents.

The names of all these prisoners had been reported by the Kurdish forces to the International Red Cross. They had sent letters to their families through the International Red Cross, and three of them had received letters from home by the same route. Kurdish couriers had smuggled this correspondence in and out of Iraq.

Our last visits at Betwata were to the monitoring station where we found Ahmed Ihsa, a Barzani who had worked at the government radio station at Arbil while he was a sergeant in the army, and to the clinic where we found three boys and a man who had been injured in an air raid four days previously. The radio monitors in a large airy cave kept close watch over everything the government and army said by radio. The wounded were stretched out on blankets spread on the ground below a ledge on which the clinic's few medical supplies had been arranged. I was told that there had been a great many more injured, all from the village of Gerawan, which had been heavily bombed while Barzani was sleeping nearby.

The man temporarily in charge of the entire camp at Betwata was Omar Mustafa, who had the nickname of "Kebaba," or "The Tank." Omar was usually attached to General Barzani's headquarters, and it was he who had, a few days previously, ordered my mule with its saddle back to its village of origin. Now, perhaps to make up for his mistake, he showed us special attention. When we were ready to leave he appeared with gifts. For me he had a fine Kurdish *hanjar,* a garish flowered sash, and a cap with "Long Live the Kurds of Kurdistan" written on it in English and Kurdish. Most important, he had waiting horses and saddles for Apo and for me. Apo's steed had a bit of a limp, but it was a great deal better than a saddleless mule.

We moved along until the moon set, and tried to continue even thereafter. But in the narrow and thickly wooded valley the darkness was so dense that we decided to wait in one of the villages until dawn. Then we pressed on again to a deserted village. In fear of air attack its inhabitants had fled and we could get no food there. But we rested on a rooftop, made tea and discussed what should be our next step. We were at the edge of a considerable plain, wide open and almost treeless. This we must cross to the mountains on the other side, where we hoped to find Barzani. Ahmed and some of the others felt that we should spend the day resting where we were and cross the plain by night. The sun was now quite high and crossing so large an exposed area would be dangerous. But I was impatient. I could not bear the thought of lying around all day while the precious hours slipped by. Now it was late in August, and I had been away from home since July 4. Tania probably had no news of me. She must be desperately worried and upset by now. I simply must finish my job in Kurdistan. And so I insisted that we go on. Since it was unusual for me to say anything at all about when or how we should travel—I made a point of leaving these things to my guides—Ahmed was startled at my sudden insistence; however, he agreed immediately. We split up into groups of two or three to cross the plain at intervals of about a quarter of a mile. In deference to everybody's nervousness about possible air attack in this exposed place, I wrapped a large gray shawl around my shoulders to cover my white shirt (and I decided that next day I would revert to my Kurdish costume, which provided natural camouflage). The sun burned down mercilessly and we were grateful to find in the middle of the plain several very small springs or seepages of water. Our men lay on the ground and drank avidly. A stork took flight from a clump of reeds nearby. On the other side of the plain at last, we came to a cool grove of poplar trees which, we suddenly realized, was alive with Kurds.

In this grove we found Mahmoud Kawani, one of the Kurds' greatest military leaders, lying in the shade of two blankets, with a soldier fanning him. He was in a coma and was dying. He had been wounded in the back of the head two days previously by machine-gun fire from an airplane. Everyone spoke in hushed voices. A man who had once been a hospital orderly came over to us, shook his head, and shrugged his shoulders. He said that he had done everything he knew for Kawani. No real doctor was to be found anywhere in the area. It would take five or six days to carry him to the Kurds' hospital at Warta, the only place where, at that time, the Kurds had a real doctor of medicine, and Kawani could not possibly be moved that far.

Mahmoud Kawani had been at Akubar village near Shaqlawa. About 5 P.M. he left the village just as three Iraqi planes came over, but he went on with his five or six guards. They were moving along under some big chestnut trees where refugees were camped when the planes came over for the second time. But the planes did not fire. Kawani was preparing to move on when the planes came over for the third time. This time they fired at the chestnut trees, where they had probably observed movements, spraying them with machine-gun bullets. In addition to Kawani, three men were wounded, and two were killed.

Kawani's injury was a big shock to the Kurds. His was a big name, much honored and loved. He was famed for his courage, and it was said of him that he was always victorious.

We left the little grove quietly and wound our way up into the foothills on the other side of the plain. A peasant woman working in a field stood up and called to us: "How is Mahmoud Kawani?"

That night, encamped rather uncomfortably on a steep mountainside, I was with Barzani again. It was quite cold, and Barzani's men lit two large bonfires. But Barzani seemed oblivious to the cold and made no effort to sit close to the fire. Ahmed embarrassed me by repeating to Barzani the whole affair of the mule and saddle that had been sent back. I would have preferred to have had it forgotten, especially since Barzani seemed annoyed.

That night he sat with us during supper and for several hours afterward. He talked a good deal of politics, and I discovered that he had a firmly entrenched anti-British complex. He found British machinations at the bottom of most of the Kurds' misfortunes. Thus he believed the British had a secret agreement with the Soviet Union under which the Russians were to supply arms to Kassem, and an agreement with Kassem under which he would pretend to threaten Kuwait, in order to distract attention from the Iraqi government's offensive against the Kurds. He believed also that Ali Amini's government in Iran was pro-American and under American influence, because, while it was in office, he had succeeded in sending several men into Iran for hospital treatment. The ensuing government under Premier Alam was pro-British and under British influence, he believed, because, while it was in office he had not succeeded in sending any more men to Iran.

But Barzani had a soft spot for the Americans, at least when talking with me. In his speculations he was always willing to give the Americans the benefit of the doubt.

As often happened, we had only a few hours of sleep before we were awakened to move to the small town of Hiran in the Khushnaou valley, which had just been taken by the Kurdish forces. This proved an extraordinary military movement. Although I had not realized it, a large part of the hard core of Barzani's forces had been camped in the mountains around us. With hundreds of armed men and pack animals spread out ahead and behind and all around us, we moved through the night along the top of a broad and long ridge, from which we could see on our left the very high peaks of Iran and on our right the bright lights of Shaqlawa and other smaller localities in the valley below. By the light of the moon, as far as I could see, the Kurdish revolutionary army was on the move.

At dawn I was disappointed to learn that one of Barzani's aides had ordered us to camp all day in the village of Bindar at the head of a valley leading down to the plain, where we would find Hiran. It was thought safer for us to wait until dark before we moved on again. But this was a bad miscalculation, as it turned out. For reasons which I could never understand—because camping inside a village was contrary to all the Barzani principles—we bedded down in dry irrigation ditches shielded by thick shrubbery and a thick terrace wall only fifty or sixty feet from the village fountain.

I extracted my portable typewriter from our baggage and made myself comfortable in a ditch to do something exceptionally unnecessary and pleasant. Knowing that our days together would soon be ended, I was writing a little note to Apo Jomart, telling him what a great man he was and how much I esteemed him when the planes came over. First a British Fury, then two Soviet-built MIG's. The Fury dropped four bombs spaced evenly and harmlessly across the mountainside, each leaving a crater about fifteen feet wide and eight feet deep. Then the MIG's firing cannon. And the Fury again, spraying the village and its surroundings with 30 mm. machine-gun fire.

As I hugged the earth under the terrace wall I was aware of an instant of silence after the MIG's passed over and then screams of women and children and the sound of many people scrambling over rocks. And then abrupt silence, broken off by the rattle of the machine gun when the Fury returned. And renewed screaming and scrambling. I looked up and saw a soldier standing a few feet away from me, blood streaming down his face. Dazed, he sat down on the ground and I rose unhelpfully to my feet and took his picture.

Then I scrambled up through the irrigation channels to the village fountain, where another soldier had been stretched out, his face quite ghostly white, his throat making gurgling noises. He seemed to be dying. Ahmed Tofiq was already there, wiping the man's face and instructing a soldier to fan him with a leafy branch to keep off the flies. The village meanwhile had burst into mad activity. A fence of tangled branches near the fountain had started to burn and Ahmed shouted to some villagers to bring water. They ignored him.

All over this village of about fifteen houses distraught people were rushing about, carrying things. A man stood in the doorway of a house that had been hit by cannon fire with the body of a little girl about six years old in his arms. Behind him a woman was moaning in pain. Apparently unable to decide whether to carry the little girl away or go back to help the moaning woman the man just stood in the doorway.

The ever-resourceful Ahmed told him to put the child down and went into the house to see what he could do for the wounded woman. Her legs were bleeding. A jagged hole about six feet in diameter, apparently made by a cannon shell, let sunlight into the house.

Somebody said there was a "doctor" in a neighboring village. Ahmed told the man to take a mule and to get the doctor. But the man demurred. He said the child was dead and there was nothing the doctor could do for his wife. A female relative had bandaged her legs, and within minutes she was up and herding her surviving children toward the grassy mountainside along with the other women and children in the village.

Not many minutes after the attack the village was quite empty, except for a very old woman who remained in a doorway upbraiding an old man who appeared to be her husband. I photographed them. The man smiled inanely while the old woman muttered furiously. The dying soldier remained by the fountain with another soldier fanning him. Someone had put a piece of gauze over his face. Several mules splattered with blood were driven by. They had been injured by flying fragments of bombs or stones.

The results of this raid were one child dead, one soldier dead, two soldiers injured, and two or three villagers injured. This sort of thing was commonplace all over northern Iraq in the summer of 1962. The day we were bombed at Bindar eight other villages in parallel valleys leading down into the Khushnaou valley in northern Iraq were also attacked.

The Iraqis may have guessed that General Barzani might be coming that way, but one may be sure that many another village was raided that day for much less reason. So it was in the village of Krko, where a single bomb exploding on the ground floor of a two-story house one day during the summer killed over twenty-one people.

Toward dusk, while we were still anticipating the possibility of another raid, we spied General Barzani with two or three men walking down the other side of the valley. We followed soon thereafter in the gathering darkness. At times the trail was so steep that I had to slide off my mule, and in so doing apparently I lost forever the *hanjar* I had received from Omar a few days before.

From the dusty Khushnaou plain, we approached Hiran through a long and narrow road flanked by fig trees and walls of piled stones. Through a labyrinth of mud huts, the road led to a center of concrete and brick houses. A few shops were open. I stepped into one just to look around the shelves of mixed groceries and odds and ends, cheap billfolds and combs and flashlights and watchstraps, lighted up uncertainly by an oil lamp. In front of the big concrete police barracks, we stopped long enough to observe through the windows the movements inside of several hundred Iraqi policemen, prisoners now, and resolved to return in the morning to photograph them.

Here and there in the town a family crowded at a window or around a door to watch the Pej Merga, who swarmed everywhere. Most of the houses had already been abandoned. For this was a doomed town. Taken two days previously, the wonder was that it had not already been bombed. But come the bombers surely would, as they did to every locality in the hands of General Barzani's forces. This one, large and strategically placed, would be no exception.

Very late at night I resumed my conversations with Barzani in the garden of the mosque at Hiran. A lovely place it was, especially at night, with flickering oil lamps reflected in a little pond and comfortable chairs set out at one end. How unusual to find chairs. Barzani was sitting in the largest of them. Although he seemed deep in conversation with another Kurd and I tried to sit modestly some distance away, he motioned me to take a place next to him. Barzani was in good spirits. Everywhere his men were succeeding. They had nearly surrounded a force of 10,000 men in the Rewanduz area. The capture of Hiran closed one escape route. Other insurgent forces were closing other possible routes of escape. Barzani hinted that a battle of great importance might be impending, but I suspect that a little of this may have been inspired by his desire to keep me with him at headquarters. I told him firmly that I must leave within the next forty-eight hours, no matter what.

We slept that night on mats stretched beside the pool in the garden of the mosque of Hiran, and rose at dawn to get some pictures of the captured prisoners. As the sun was edging over the horizon, Ahmed routed the prisoners out onto the steps of the police barracks, and I did my photographic bit. There were two hundred of them, more or less, all the Iraqi policemen from a considerable region round about Hiran. The Iraqi police captain who was in command said, in reply to my question, that he had surrendered his men "because we were in contact with the Barzanis and we had it on the honor of the Barzanis that we would be released."

I have never liked talking to prisoners. I find it embarrassing. And I know that prisoners, being under pressure, are unlikely to tell the truth about anything. So I turned my attention as soon as possible to the stream of householders leaving the city, mostly on foot with a mule to carry the family's most essential possessions. They hurried along, anxious to be away before the sun was high.

I, too, could not help thinking that this was a good idea, and so did the others in our group. Our departure from Hiran turned out to be a rather slapstick scramble. General Barzani had, as usual, disappeared before anyone else was up, and no one seemed to know exactly where he had gone. Our party somehow got divided. Jamil had gone on with Apo while Ahmed remained in the town to interview the Iraqi policeman, and I was left to the dubious care of Anwar.

Anwar and I, on horseback, joined the flow of townspeople out into the hills. They made a pathetic parade, the

crying children, the harassed old men, and the women loaded
with pots and bundles, the mules piled high with bedding.
Very few young men were among them, for they were away in
the service of Barzani, or of the Iraqi army and police. Except
in the case of the hated *josh,* whom the Iraqi government used
for the meanest tasks of reprisal and incendiarism, service in
the Iraqi armed forces reflected no discredit upon the Kurd.
After all, military or police service had for many years been
the refuge of the numerous young men for whom there was
no living to be had in the Iraqi mountains of the north. And
the Pej Merga considered their presence in those services now
a great advantage.

It was with their help, above all, that the Kurdish insurgents were able to maintain a constant movement of arms and
ammunition out of Iraqi supply depots and into the northern
mountains.

The refugees from Hiran seemed to me more pathetic
than those of the mountain villages because the people of this
little town are a little further removed than they from nomad-
ism. One of the things that makes it possible for mountain
villagers to stand up to heavy bombardment is that it comes
fairly easily to most of them to load their belongings on animals and their own shoulders and to move away, even if only
to a cave.

At the edge of the little town we came to a fork. I
thought we should turn right into the hills. Anwar was uncertain. So I said: "Let's wait for Ahmed." Anwar objected that
waiting was dangerous, so we headed off to the right. When
aircraft appeared overhead we took cover under some rocks
and stayed there until we heard Ahmed storming up the path
yelling for us, obviously annoyed. Indeed, he was furious with
Anwar, not so much because he had taken the wrong turn,
but because he had not left a sign on the path to show which
way he had gone, as a better-trained mountain Kurd would
have done.

To make up for lost time Ahmed decided to take a shortcut with me across a wide, stony field, while Anwar went back
toward the town to look for one of our horses that had strayed

while we were taking cover. I was on horseback again, but halfway across the field we heard aircraft and I dismounted hastily to take shelter.

Every time we thought all was clear and started across the field the aircraft would come back. And so we darted from rock to rock. When we were back on the trail and Anwar with his horse had caught up, Ahmed noticed immediately that one of the strayed horses' saddlebags was missing, and Anwar had to go back once more to look for it. (It was found.) Anwar had indeed become our "go-back-and-look-for-it" man, no doubt to make up for his other shortcomings.

Moments later we stumbled upon one of General Barzani's outer circle of guards and Anwar was able to persuade him to direct us toward Barzani's camp. We were lucky that morning. Sometimes his friends would spend half a day tracking him down.

Among the people clustered at a respectful distance from General Barzani's shelter on this morning was a young man named Bidjan Djindi, who was in charge of the captured policemen in Hiran. He was there to ask the General whether he should keep two of the men who could be regarded as political offenders, or whether he should release them along with the others. (General Barzani said to keep them.)

While we waited, Bidjan Djindi told me that he had gone to Russia with General Barzani, that he had succeeded in learning Russian well, and had brought back a Russian wife. Together he and his wife had taught Russian in Baghdad before the Kurdish revolution. After that, life had become too difficult for her in Baghdad, and she had returned to Russia while he went to the mountains. "After our revolution is over, we will be reunited. I hope it won't last more than another year," he said.

Barzani that day was particularly relaxed and talked about his family and childhood. Cross-legged on a mat on the ground, he leaned up against a slanting rock and calmly watched an airplane on the horizon. While some others, at the mere sight or sound of an aircraft, would rush to take cover, he had developed a sure sense for the direction a plane was taking. He posed indulgently for pictures, by himself and with his personal guard. I told the General then that I was determined to leave the next morning. He reminded me humorously that early in my visit he had said: "Consider yourself the commander of this army. You may do as you please in all respects except one, and that is that you may not leave until I let you." Now he held out the bait of at least one more conversation if I would remain one more day, and the prospect of lots more military action. But I knew that my departure was long overdue and I insisted. Then the General, turning to Ahmed, ordered that everything be arranged for me to go.

I saw General Barzani once more that night, back in the garden of the Hiran mosque. We said goodbye simply and warmly. He thanked me for coming and hoped I would have no trouble on the way out. I thanked him for his help and hospitality. Both of us hoped we would meet again soon. It was late, and I lay down for a few hours' sleep before departure at moonrise. Moments later, so it seemed, I was roused, and it was time to say goodbye to the others, and first of all to Ahmed, who had done more for me than any other single person. Indefatigable Ahmed at last looked really exhausted. He had been up while I slept, arranging my travel—those who would go with me, their supplies, their animals; writing letters to the various persons along the way whom I would have to meet or who should know about me. Now at the end of our adventure, Ahmed, our great speechmaker, whom we had sometimes called "Mr. Propaganda Minister," didn't make any speech at all. Perhaps I had kidded him too often about his speechmaking, or perhaps we had become such good friends that speechmaking to each other would have become too silly. I really liked and admired that fellow and I wish him all the best. So devoted, so competent, so relentlessly persevering.

Ahmed's speechlessness didn't stop the others. Everyone had his piece to say, especially those who had accompanied us from the start—Apo, of course, our faithful, incredible, indispensable interpreter; Jamil, Mustafa, Anwar, and one or two others—we had grown truly fond of each other on our

long journey and I made little speeches of gratitude to each
of them.

Then we were on horseback, or some of us were, and
heading out of town into the darkness, leaving behind
the swinging oil lamps outside the old mosque of Hiran.
As leader we had Paik Amin, a rather cadaverous-looking
young man who then served as General Barzani's secretary;
and we also had with us Ibrahim Mamand Agha, brother of
Abbas Mamand Agha, the great chief of the Ako tribe; and
three or four young fellows, including one named Kassem.
Young Kassem delighted in the fact that he had the same
name as Iraq's dictator. He laughed uproariously when we
called him Abdul Karim (Premier Kassem's first names). He
was one of the handsomest Kurds I have ever seen and was
of extraordinary endurance. On that march he sometimes
walked twelve hours and at the end of it was ready for circus
tricks on the back of a pack mule. It was reassuring to have
him along. He had more sense about when to take cover
from aircraft—and where—and when to ignore the planes
than any of the others. And that was the kind of sense that
we needed. For I had insisted so much on the urgency of my
getting out of Kurdistan and getting home that it had been
decided that we would travel during the daylight hours. This
reversed our usual but slower practice of taking cover by day
and traveling at night.

By midmorning we reached the village called Sitkan. We
breakfasted on figs and grapes and tea. As we were about to
take off aircraft came over. The depressing dull cadence of
bombs dropping far down the valley sent us scurrying to cover
under large stone ledges outside the village. Unfortunately
the planes came back again and again, and it was midafter-
noon before we were ready to move on. Before we left the
villagers brought us rice and tomato soup.

Then—appeared a courier on a mule, both covered with
sweat and dust. He had traveled fast and hard all day regard-
less of aircraft, bringing a carpet, a big one, a gift from Barzani for me.

Now I understood one of the reasons why the General,

and Ahmed too, had urged me so strongly to remain "just one more day." As the sweating messenger explained, General Barzani had sent "south" for this carpet to one of the towns still under the control of the Iraqi government. Secret couriers had carried it through.

The carpet was an old one, from Persia, with figures depicting scenes from the early days of Islam.

I sat down and wrote a note of thanks to General Barzani, and another to Ahmed thanking him for all he had done for me.

The carpet was folded and slung across the back of one of the mules where it remained, except at night, for the next few days, until I left my friends. Where and how I left them I will not say, any more than I described the route by which I entered the Kurdish-controlled area. These routes might have to be used again by me or by others.

Leaving was difficult. For me these forty-six days with my Kurdish friends had been a high point in twenty-five years of newspaper work. I think the Kurds liked having me around. For them I was a link with the world from which they hoped for recognition, a link with the America from which they hoped for help, a live American newspaper correspondent accredited to them as correspondents are accredited to regular armies. Someone, above all, who would tell the truth about them. I did not know if I would ever see any of them again. As it turned out, it was just six months later that our paths crossed once more.

14

Conversations with Barzani,
February 1963

In mid-February in Baghdad, where I was covering the aftermath of the Ba'athist coup d'etat, I determined to visit Barzani again. A group of Free Officers, predominantly members of the Ba'athist party, had on February 8 led a daring insurrection against Kassem. The Ba'athist party, whose ideals are similar to Nasser's and which had permitted some Nasserites to participate in its movement, was at first friendly to the Cairo government. It also seemed friendly at first with the Kurds, with whom its leaders had been in secret contact. The Ba'athist authorities seemed willing to overlook my previous visit to Barzani, of which they were uneasily aware. But they made it quite clear that they did not want Western journalists going from Baghdad to visit him now. They were unimpressed by arguments that he was now at peace and negotiating, and ought to have access to the world press equal to that of the government. To reach Barzani, therefore, a little legerdemain was required.

Jean Pierre Chauvel of *Figaro* and Jacques Sauer of *Match* magazine teamed up with me. On the pretext of making a "tour of the North" during the Moslem Id el-Fitr holiday, we obtained military permits to visit Kirkuk, Arbil and Mosul— but not Suleimaniya, which, as the military governor undoubtedly realized, would have been more convenient for a visit to Barzani.

Our permits authorized visits to the three towns only, and not to their surroundings. "Don't try to go farther," the military governor in Baghdad remarked as he signed our permits. "You might get killed."

In spite of this warning we decided to try to reach the Kurdish leader via Kirkuk. We were accompanied by a Kurdish student who had been assigned to us by Saleh Yussefi, head of the Kurdish delegation in Baghdad. In Kirkuk, while we waited discreetly in an obscure Kurdish hotel, our student—who must remain nameless—made contact with the local branch of the KDP. At six o'clock next morning a bright-eyed, nervous fellow from the party—also nameless—picked us up at our hotel in a Jeep station wagon of incredible dirtiness. The sides and windows were coated with mud—a help in obscuring the identity of the persons inside, and getting us out of town without being stopped at any checkpoint.

We loaded quickly, and, we hoped, unobtrusively, and set off with a jerk and a rush, whipping around corners, jamming on brakes, down back streets and up side streets, through all kinds of obscure alleys until suddenly I realized that we were out of town and into the oil fields.

I could see the tense lines, the taut muscles, the set jaws of our driver's neck and jaw as we sped out of the town. From time to time he stuck his head out of the window and looked back to see whether we were being followed. He and the Kurdish student were particularly nervous when we passed a crowd of about twenty-five IPC workers, who were apparently waiting for transportation. But the crowd did not pay any attention to us. We sped on past oil derricks, through rolling hills, always at top speed. Gradually I saw our driver and our student relaxing. They pulled out cigarettes. A few more oil derricks, hills ever steeper, and then we were out of the oil fields and into a wild, rocky, arid, open but still rolling country which our escorts joyously declared to be "Kurdistan." Here the authority was the Pej Merga—"the devoted ones," the army of Kurdish partisans.

Off to the right we passed a village which our guide

declared was "Communist." He said that the village had been "occupied" by Barzani's men after the ceasefire because its leaders had tried to respond to the Communist demands for a rising against the new regime. We stopped at a crowded subheadquarters of the Pej Merga, and here a Communist "prisoner" was pointed out to me. He was walking around, presumably under surveillance. One of the men recognized me from my visit of August 1962, and we shook hands with enthusiasm.

The first touches of spring brightened the foothills here. In every sheltered nook spring flowers had appeared, and I wished that somehow there could be a parallel between the hopeful feeling of rebirth in these hills and the negotiations that had been begun between Kurds and Arabs in Baghdad.

At a Pej Merga repair station a little farther on, all vehicles had written on them in white paint the words "Kurdistan Naman," meaning "Kurdistan or death." I saw a Jeep from the Ministry of Industries, a Jeep from the Ministry of Defense, a sedan from the Kirkuk Municipality and a taxi. Soon thereafter the road ended and we found one horse awaiting the three of us. I should have had a picture of three journalists on a horse, riding into Kurdistan. But we took turns riding and walking. The rolling flower-specked hills gradually became steeper, more barren and deeply clefted—a broken, ravaged landscape.

At dusk we came up over a long ridge, and before us stretched suddenly a great canyon, and beyond it the snow-capped Zagros mountains. This was as far as one could go on horseback. Now a footpath plunged down into the canyon. As dusk faded into darkness and we inched our way down the steep trail, our path turned sharply around a mass of boulders and we were surprised by a burst of artificial light shining from the bottom of a ravine. The lights were strung out over a distance of several hundred yards.

This was Chem y Razan, Jelal Talabani's headquarters for the southern sector. Welcoming hands led us to a warm cave, where a man identified as the "Responsible Officer" explained that most of the men from this headquarters were away on leave. A stove in the middle of the cave exuded welcome heat. A pipe driven through the ceiling of the cave kept the smoke out.

Our "Responsible Officer" was named Salar. That, at least, was his *nom de guerre*. He proved an affable and articulate companion. That night by flashlight and early the next morning Salar led the way, scrambling up and down narrow, steep paths through the various parts of the headquarters— immense caves filled with supplies of every kind—a kitchen and a bakery, a repair shop, a clinic with ten beds and a real doctor of medicine in charge, and a small prisoner of war camp. At the very bottom of the ravine were the generators that lighted the camp. At other times and places Kurdish guerrillas have sought security high up at the tops of mountains; here was a case of security deep down, at the bottom of a canyon. With particular pride Salar showed us "Kurdish artillery," a gun improvised out of pipes. I took it that these were water pipes, although Salar would not say for sure. Nor would he tell me how far the gun could shoot or what kind of ammunition it used or how many had been made. This was the first and only time that I found the Kurds using improvised firearms.

As we struggled up the steep sides of the ravine the next morning to where horses were awaiting us, Salar told me that he had sent two radio messages ahead, one to a subheadquarters at Koisinjak ordering a vehicle to meet us, the other to Barzani himself informing him that visitors were on their way to his headquarters, including "an old friend." He said that he did not mention my name lest the Iraqis pick up the uncoded message and make trouble for us.

Our trail led along the edge of the ravine at the bottom of which flowed the Zarzi river. We passed a place called Kora, where the Kurdish princes of the Middle Ages had built a castle on an island in the river. The trail dipped down near this island almost to the river and then steeply upward through a chaos of boulders. As we climbed upward, my horse somehow got himself wedged into an ungainly position with his front feet upon a rock and his hind feet stuck in a ditch four or five

feet lower. He could not move. I clung to his back and urged
him forward. Suddenly the strap holding my saddle and a
great quantity of baggage broke, and saddle, baggage and I
all slid off over the horse's tail into the rocks below. I went
down on my back in a confusion of rocks, saddlebags and
horse's hooves. The back brace I was wearing in deference
to my slipped disk probably saved me from any real damage.

After a short night in a farmhouse we found the vehicle
Salar had ordered, drove through Koisinjak, over a rather
barren mountain range into a broad, flooded valley where
we got stuck in a river. With the help of a dozen Kurds whose
Jeep was also stuck, we barely struggled out. Then we helped
them out. One of our riverside acquaintances—all Kurds in
national dress—gave me a photograph of the famed Kurdish
girl soldier, Margaret George. He was carrying it in his wallet
along with pictures of Barzani and other Kurdish leaders.

As night fell a steady, cold rain began. We stopped at
a village called Chwar Koma, a place of about five hundred
houses, to rest and warm up in the teahouse, and arrange
for a tractor to accompany us through the marshes we would
have to cross to get around the town of Ranieh. We had to
go around Ranieh because there was still a government garrison in the town. On the wall of the teahouse was a photograph of Fatima Khan, the famed Kurdish woman who in the
1920's and early '30's administered a group of eight villages
near Rewanduz. Also one of Sheikh Mahmoud, "the King of
Kurdistan" in the 1920's and early '30's. Sheikh Mahmoud's
family are religious leaders. The Kurds in this region swear by
Sheikh Ahmed, the grandfather of Sheikh Mahmoud, that is,
by "Kak Ahmed bin Sheikh." Escorted by a farm tractor with
huge wheels, we plunged into the marsh. Three times we got
stuck and three times the tractor pulled us out. We were more
fortunate than George Weller of the *Chicago Daily News* who a
week ahead of us had spent a whole night stuck in one of the
marshes on the way to Barzani's headquarters. In the distance,
to our left, we passed the lights of Ranieh glittering beyond
the dripping trees.

After ten o'clock that night we drove into Kala Diza, a

small Kurdish town near the Iranian border. Except for kerosene lamps it was without light. Supplies of fuel for the local electric power plant were exhausted. In the pouring rain and the dark we had some difficulty finding the house of the man whose name Saleh Yussefi had given me in Baghdad as the "contact" who would lead us to Barzani. At last, leaping from stone to stone across the flooded road, we reached our destination, a warm, dimly lighted house that seemed to be seething with wet Kurds. It is a commentary on the secrecy with which all matters concerning the Kurdish war and particularly Barzani's whereabouts must be handled that neither our Kurdish student nor the local Kurds who had guided us from Koisinjak to Kala Diza had any idea whom to see in Kala Diza in order to find Barzani. I alone had brought that vital link with me from Baghdad. I knew the name that we should ask for.

No sooner had we settled down in the home of our Kala Diza host, taken off wet and muddy clothing and begun to inquire about food, than a messenger arrived. His message was that Barzani was nearby and would be leaving again in the morning, and if we wished to see him we had better come now. This news produced from the three of us a gasp of momentary dismay. Since noon we had not rested or eaten, except for a stop to drink tea.

Of course we dressed immediately and plunged again into the chilling rain and darkness. "Only ten minutes," one of our escorts said reassuringly, but I knew by then that when a Kurd tells you ten minutes he uses Kurdish standards; for ordinary people it is more likely to be half an hour. We crossed a bridge over a river much swollen by the heavy February rain, scrambled up a steep bank and then headed across a plain, or rather a sea of mud that squished up over our shoes to the ankles. Lights on the other side of the mud beckoned. Barzani was there. Outposts halted us, waved us on to a group of large farmhouses. Except for guards and Barzani's own quarters this was a sleeping camp. Barzani likes to work at night.

We stepped into an outer room crowded with men. As

is the custom, they had all taken off their shoes, and I hastened to do likewise. Which is easier said than done, because whereas the Kurds have a technique of slipping shoes off with their toes in a jiffy, to get mine off I had to sit on the floor, there being no chairs, and wrestle with muddy shoelaces. I was still wrestling when the door opened into a more brightly lighted room, and I could see Mustafa Barzani standing in the middle. He could see me, too, and I spontaneously struggled to my feet and stepped forward to greet him, realizing too late that my hands were covered with mud. As I was about to clasp his hand someone stepped between us with a towel. I wiped my hand and, slightly abashed, completed the greeting.

Barzani seemed quite genuinely delighted to see me again. Rarely, I think, has a foreign visitor been to see him twice. He treated me like an old and long lost friend, bidding me sit beside him and favoring me with smiles and personal questions. How had I been since we parted? How had I managed to return? Altogether he was ebullient, very different from the difficult and elusive character I had interviewed in August of the previous year. Now he evidently felt on top of the world, on the threshold of victory. But when he spoke of the Iraqi government his demeanor assumed a ferocity that was new to me. He was angry, for reasons that will become apparent later.

As always he was dressed in his gray and white Kurdish national costume, over a black shirt. He toyed with his wooden cigarette holder.

"Where is Ahmed?" I asked—Ahmed Tofiq who had escorted me through Kurdistan the previous year. Barzani nodded, and gave an order to one of his men. Within a few minutes Ahmed appeared, and, grinning broadly, sat down next to me. This was a sentimental reunion.

Tea and cigarettes were placed before us, and my French colleagues and I, tired but elated, partook of both in great quantities. Barzani kept handing me cigarettes which he rolled himself. We were in a large, well-carpeted room, the walls hung with cheap tapestries, all of us cross-legged on cushions on the floor around the walls in the traditional Oriental manner. I sat on Barzani's right hand and Ahmed next to me while the two Frenchmen sat in front of him. A dozen other men sat around the other walls of the room, listening avidly.

Amused by the persistent activity of Jacques Sauer, who never ceased taking pictures, now with one camera, now with another, now in color, now in black and white, Barzani jokingly seized one of the cameras, and, pointing it at Sauer, declared that he was going to take as many pictures as had been taken of him.

It was well past midnight, but every time we began to bring the conversation to a close Barzani started it up again. He obviously was enjoying himself. He urged us to stay with him for a few days. But I explained that this visit to him was a news story that must be told immediately, and that we could not possibly linger. The best possible arrangement would be for us to fly back to Baghdad in the helicopter.

Barzani offered to arrange a helicopter the next day. But when the time came, the Iraqi district officer who was still in Kala Diza, a semi-prisoner of the Kurds, and who had to order the helicopter from the army at Kirkuk, asked so many questions about how we had got to Kala Diza that we decided to drive back.

Returning to Kala Diza, Barzani's men proposed a shortcut, which meant fording a river. One of Barzani's men demonstrated. On horseback he plunged into the raging torrent, his horse leaning far over against the current, struggling forward. It was a feat worthy of a circus performer and we declared that we were not up to it. The alternative was scrambling and clawing on all fours perilously from the riverside up a bank that seemed greased with mud and tramping through more mud to find the bridge.

In the morning with the rain ended and the sun out again we took a look around Kala Diza before returning to Barzani. A true Kurdish town, this. Everyone in the streets for the Id el-Fitr holiday. An improvised amusement park just off the main street with swings for the children. A mingling of colorful Kurdish national dress and black "Sunday best" suits crowding the main street and its teahouses and lounging at tables set out on the sidewalk. Most of the women were in marvelously gaudy Kurdish dress. A few, I noted with regret, had covered their bright colors with an outer robe of black, in the manner of the Arabs. The few Iraqi policemen and soldiers stationed in the town were fraternizing with the Kurds, and we photographed them, arm in arm, grinning.

After further meetings with Barzani, mostly for purposes of picture-taking, we bade him a final goodbye that afternoon on the road outside Kala Diza. Mounted upon a white stallion, he was moving along, very slowly, at the head of a score of other horsemen, westward across the plain—a lonely figure of great dignity. In the distance, just visible here, the snowy peaks of the Zagros, the ancestral home of the Kurds.

In an effort to avoid the horseback riding and walking we had experienced on the way in, we drove all that night on the only negotiable road. It led to Arbil where, in the dawn with a great show of good humor and confidence and waving of press passes, we got past the National Guard post. We were strictly on our own now; our student and escort stayed behind. By a stroke of luck we fell into the hands of a French-speaking Iraqi army captain who had been to Paris and was tickled to meet correspondents of *Match* and *Figaro*. He helped us past police and army controls in Arbil and authorized us to drive on to Kirkuk and Baghdad. Thus we were reestablished as law-abiding visitors to the Republic of Iraq.

The important thing that Barzani had to convey during our visit was a threat, a threat to go to war again if the Iraqi government did not by March 1 issue a declaration recognizing the Kurds' right to autonomy. That was within four days.

Barzani did not in fact go to war on March 1. On the night of the first the government issued a statement recognizing "Kurdish rights" which, while avoiding the question of autonomy, seems to have sufficed to head off his threat. But his words revealed to me for the first time that he believed that under certain circumstances he should seek independence and separation from the state of Iraq. This is what he said: "After the revolution in Baghdad I put a time limit of one week on our ceasefire. Then they sent Talabani to Cairo and Algiers, so we extended the ceasefire.

"We will wait until the end of this month, for four more days, until March the first. If there is no declaration of autonomy by March the first we will go to war again, and we may declare our independence."

I asked him to define what he meant by autonomy. "What does it mean to you?" I asked. "All over the world there is such a thing as autonomy," he replied. "It means that the Kurdish people should be safe. That we will not be in danger that someone will come and hit us at the last minute."

"Does it mean that the Kurds should have their own armed force?" I asked. "I already said that we would want to be safe," he replied. "How can we be safe without an armed force?" He was alluding to the Kurdish demand for a Kurdish state police and formation of a "Kurdish legion" within the Iraqi army.

He said that the fuller meaning of autonomy must be worked out gradually in negotiation. "But first they must recognize that the Kurdish people have the right of self-determination. If they declare that, it will be good. If they do not, the situation will remain as before. The Kurdish people are not begging for it. If they don't declare our autonomy the Kurdish people will fight for it to the death and maybe we will ask for separation. If they don't declare our autonomy within the Iraqi unity then we will fight and maybe we will have to declare our independence."

This was the first time that Barzani had publicly threatened to declare the independence of the Kurds in Iraq. He went on to explain that he had that day ordered his men to "return to their positions," to be ready to fight again if necessary. Many of the Kurdish forces had gone on leave since Barzani ordered a ceasefire on February 9.

He was indignant that his representative Talabani should have got himself mixed up with questions which, according to Barzani, were none of his concern. Asked whether he approved the trip to Cairo and Algiers he replied flatly: "No. He did not tell me that he was going to Cairo. I did not like him to go to

Cairo and Algiers. These visits to Cairo and Algiers have nothing to do with us." He gave the impression that he was angered not only because his representative had agreed to make the trip but because he felt that the trip indicated that the Iraqi government was not dealing seriously with the main question it faced—namely, the Kurdish demand for autonomy.

Chauvel told Barzani that Michel Aflak, the ideologist of the Ba'ath Party, had told him in Baghdad that it might be easier to recognize Kurdish autonomy if there were a union of Arab peoples. Barzani replied acidly that "Aflak has no right to decide this. The government of Iraq will decide. I did not ask for Michel Aflak's comment. If the government of Iraq agrees, all right. If not—I will fight. No, the Kurds have nothing to do with this problem of Arab unity."

Barzani was apparently unable, or unwilling, to recognize that in fact the Kurds have a great deal to do with the problem of Arab unity. Their best hope of obtaining political support or at least toleration in the Arab world was and is Nasser, the symbol of Arab unity. This was a point which Talabani obviously understood very well.

Asked whether he thought the Kurds' war for autonomy could become a war against the Arab people Barzani replied hotly: "I am not against the Arab nation. I am only asking for my people's rights. I am not asking for their land."

Barzani insisted that the Kurdish rebellion had been the main factor in bringing down Kassem's regime. To illustrate his point he told a story. "Once there were two hunters stalking a stag. One of them from a position high on the mountain fired and mortally wounded the animal. The other, close by in the valley, rushed up and finished off the animal. Then he claimed that the prize was his."

Barzani made no secret of his very low opinion of the new rulers in Baghdad. He observed that some of the Iraqi government garrisons had been withdrawn from the north "not for our sake, of course, but because they were weak in Baghdad." He went on to ridicule officers who at such a time as this promoted themselves to the ranks of general and marshal, as some of the leaders of the Ba'ath in Baghdad had done.

Was it a good thing to have two Kurds in the new government formed in Baghdad, he was asked. "No," he replied flatly, and took the occasion to return to the question of autonomy or independence: "If they don't give us our autonomy then we will declare our independence, and then we will announce our government with two Arab ministers." The idea seemed to amuse him and his eyes sparkled mischievously. His point was that Kurdish representation in the government should have been much larger. At another point he excluded himself as a possible vice-president or minister in future Baghdad governments.

Barzani insisted that his revolution concerned only the Kurds in Iraq. Informed there were reports that the governments of Iran and Turkey were treating Kurds a little better than in the past, he observed: "I have no relations with Iran or Turkey. I am in *this* situation, and I want to make *this* situation better. I am not concerned with people living outside this country. I am living in Iraq and dealing with problems in Iraq."

I pointed out to Barzani that since the new Ba'athist regime in Iraq was actively anti-Communist, the Communists seemed now to be fighting on the same side with Barzani. "What is your relationship to the Communists?" I asked.

"I have no relations whatsoever with the Communist Party," he replied. "Up to the time of this revolution they were with Kassem. Why should they come to my side? They were against me. I have no connection with them."

I asked what would be the status of the Communist Party in an autonomous Kurdistan. "It is not my right to decide this," he replied. "The government will decide this, the central government."

I asked him whether he had any special message for the American people at this critical moment in the history of the Kurds. "I have already spoken to the American people," he replied, alluding to the statements he had made in our interview of August 1962. "I asked the American people to help us, because the Kurdish people were in great need, to help us out of this bad situation." I asked him just what role he thought the United States could now play in helping the Kurds. Again he alluded to his previous appeals to the United States, which went unheard, and expressed pessimism as to the usefulness of further appeals. He said: "If a person could not see anything in his whole life, how could you expect him to see now?"

"Well," I persisted, "if you get your autonomy what do you expect from the United States? What is the greatest need right now?" I asked. His reply was general: "Anything you can see or think of, we are in need of it."

"Do you think the American government could do anything to intervene in the current negotiations with the Iraqi government?" I asked. "Of course," he replied, "the American government can do so if it wants to."

Chauvel asked Barzani whether he had invited the International Red Cross to come into Kurdistan. He said he had, but they had not come. "We only heard that some of them went to Baghdad but that the government prevented them from contacting us. I personally don't believe in this. There are more ways than one to come if they really want to do so. I personally believe they intended it that way." In reply to my further questions he agreed that what he meant was that if the Red Cross had wanted to, it could have reached him through Iran or Turkey.

Chauvel asked whether he had a special message to the world, and he replied: "I am asking every honorable man, every man who would help another man in need, to come to our aid. I have already told Mr. Schmidt during our last meeting that I asked help from every country, even from Luxembourg. I asked help from everyone who believed in justice."

15

The Great Double Cross

At the beginning of June 1963 the Kurdish delegation in
Baghdad was in despair. With the approval of General
Mustafa Barzani and of the Kurdish Democratic Party they
had long since submitted the Kurdish demands for autonomy,
spelled out in detail, as a basis for negotiating a settlement of
the Kurdish problem in Iraq. But on one pretext or another
the government had, ever since the coup d'etat of February
8, avoided real negotiations with the Kurds. The government
had responded to the Kurdish demands only with a general statement on Kurdish rights and a proposal for general
administrative decentralization that bore no relationship to
what the Kurds were asking.

Now in these first days of June the Kurdish delegation
found itself under such close police surveillance that they
felt they were under house arrest. Indeed they felt the Iraqi
government might at any moment end the talks by arresting
their delegation. They had sent a secret message to Jelal Talabani, their chief, who was in Beirut, warning him not to return
because he would probably be arrested as he alighted from the
plane. On Sunday, June 2, plainclothesmen swarmed into the
Semiramis hotel where the delegation was staying, and two
police cars were permanently stationed in front of the hotel.
On Monday the delegation sent a protest to Premier el-Baqr
and part of the surveillance was withdrawn. But all these were
relatively minor matters. More important was the delegation's

growing fear that the government was preparing not for a settlement but for war. Since May the government had been reinforcing its garrisons throughout the Kurdish area. Troops were being moved provocatively. At a number of points incidents had occurred that seemed to have been deliberately fomented. Most dramatic of all, Kurdish intelligence obtained a printer's proof of a leaflet (which was actually distributed after June 10) offering 100,000 dinars for the capture of Barzani.

The Kurdish delegation got word of a meeting in Baghdad, during the first days of June, of top officers of the Iraqi and Syrian air forces to discuss collaboration in general and, the Kurds suspected, against the Kurds in particular. On Friday, June 7, the Syrian officers visited air bases at Habbaniya and Kirkuk. Michel Aflak, the ideologist of the Ba'ath Party, was in Baghdad on party business at the same time; the Kurds assumed that he was aware of what was going on and that he was consulted.

On Wednesday and Thursday, June 5 and 6, the Iraqi army demonstrated at Kirkuk and Suleimaniya by driving through the streets with tanks which then moved off into the mountains. Thursday night at Suleimaniya, artillery inside the fortified camp of the twentieth brigade opened fire on Kurdish positions on Mount Azmer southeast of the town, and an Iraqi battalion followed up with an unsuccessful attempt to take the Kurdish positions by assault.

Alarmed by these developments, suspecting a double cross, the Kurdish delegates demanded and were granted a meeting with Premier Ahmed Hassan el-Baqr late on Thursday, June 6. The Premier denied everything. The proof of the leaflet offering a reward for Barzani's capture was a forgery devised by Communists to make bad blood between Kurds and Arabs, he said. "O God, O Koran," he cried. "Blind me and kill me along with my children if the government has any bad intentions toward the Kurds."

At this meeting the government also handed the Kurds a new version of its "decentralization plan." Saleh Yussefi, the acting chief of the Kurdish delegation, found this version to be "nothing but the old decentralization plan which we had already rejected." He said there were alterations from the original plan, "but on such minor points that they weren't worth mentioning."

The government delegation which was with the Premier insisted that the Kurds should submit the new government proposal to the heads of the KDP and to Mullah Mustafa. But Yussefi replied that this would be pointless since the delegation was already authorized to reject the old proposal and the government was offering nothing new. Some members of the government group told the Kurds privately as the meeting was ending that they should be patient as "we might have something better to offer you soon." They planned a further meeting between Kurdish and government representatives for Saturday, June 8, at 5 P.M.

From this meeting the Kurdish delegation returned about 9 P.M. in a state of some excitement. Saleh Yussefi thought he perceived a glimmer of hope. He thought he had found evidence that some elements in the government were still undecided about resuming the fighting, for he had received a new set of proposals so promising that he thought he must immediately submit them to his superiors.

The new proposals had the peculiarity—which made them somewhat suspect—that they were submitted not in the name of the government but in the name of Ali Haidar Suleiman, former Iraqi ambassador to the United States, who had been playing an important role as government representative at talks with the Kurds. Nor were the proposals by any means all that the Kurds wanted. Yet they seemed to be the first attempt by the government to deal in detail with the Kurds' specific demands. For the first time the government seemed to be offering a basis for negotiation. Yussefi therefore asked and received permission to fly with this document to the north to consult Barzani. That night Major General Taher Yahyia, the commander in chief, in a deliberate show of friendliness came to the Semiramis hotel with Fuad Aref, the minister of state for Kurdish affairs, to talk to the Kurdish delegates. He assured them that a plane would be awaiting them on the airstrip at Camp Rashid in the morning.

A sigh of relief meanwhile went around the Kurdish community in Baghdad. The government's offer seemed to have proven their worst fears to be groundless. That day some Kurds who had gone into hiding reappeared in public.

The morning of Sunday, June 9, Kurdish delegates sat with their bags packed in the riverside lounge of the Semiramis hotel. Fuad Aref and Baba Ali, the two Kurdish ministers, joined them as did a colonel of the military police, Said Suleimi. The Kurdish delegation present were Massoud Mohammed, lawyer and former Kurdish-Iraqi member of parliament from Koisinjak; Husain Khanaqa, former member of parliament from Kirkuk; Babakir Mahmoud Agha of the Pijdar tribe; Agid Sadiq of Amadiya; and Saleh Yussefi.

At ten o'clock an officer reported to Colonel Suleimi that transport was ready, and the Kurds drove off to Camp Rashid. But instead of being flown to the north, the Kurdish delegation was driven to prison in Camp Rashid.

While the Kurdish delegation was being imprisoned, the Iraqi police and National Guard were busy arresting Kurds all over Baghdad. According to one estimate, seven hundred persons were taken. Beginning that day Kurdish soldiers were separated from their units and sent south. Kurdish officials were removed from all government departments. That day also the head of the Ba'ath Party in Iraq, Ali Saleh Saadi, held a press conference that was in effect a declaration of war against the Kurds. He gave Barzani and his followers twenty-four hours in which to surrender—or else. The night before, on Saturday, while the Iraqi government was submitting Ali Haidar Suleiman's new and seemingly hopeful proposals to the Kurdish delegation, the army had surrounded the towns of Kirkuk, Arbil and Suleimaniya, had imposed a twenty-four-hours-a-day curfew in those towns, and had begun massive arrests (3000 in Suleimaniya) and massive deportations (most of the Kurdish population of 150,000 in Kirkuk). Bulldozers had begun to flatten the Kurdish suburbs of Kirkuk.

To appreciate the full impact of the Ba'athist government's sudden blow, to get the real flavor of the double cross, one must know what went before—one must go back to the secret negotiations between the Kurds and the Free Officers and Ba'ath Party while both were still fighting Kassem, to the commitments given the Kurds by the Free Officers and by the Ba'ath Party, to the long period of negotiation in Baghdad after the coup d'etat during which the leaders of the new regime over and over again gave the Kurds fervent pledges of good intention, hot assurances that they believed in the Kurds' right not only to autonomy, but to self-determination.

I have the story of the first contacts between the Kurds and the Free Officers from Jelal Talabani. These took place on February 8, 1962, when Ibrahim Ahmed, the secretary-general of the Kurdish Democratic Party, on a secret visit to the town of Suleimaniya went to the house of a Major Kerim Karani. Karani was a Kurdish officer in the Iraqi army whom the Kurds trusted. He had for several years served as personal bodyguard to Taher Yahyia while Yahyia was director general of police in the Kassem regime. Yahyia was dismissed from his post after the Shawaf rising in Mosul in 1959, and soon thereafter got in touch with the Free Officers plotting Kassem's overthrow. Karani became his contact with the Kurdish revolutionaries. He carried a message from Yahyia to Ibrahim Ahmed proposing collaboration. Ibrahim Ahmed replied, in a letter dated April 18, that the Kurds wanted to live with the Arabs in peace and fraternity, that he was ready to cooperate with the Free Officers if they would agree with two basic aims: firstly, a democratic system for Iraq; secondly, autonomy for Kurdistan. He wrote as follows: "The Kurdish people possess the inalienable right to separate from the Kurdish state, but do not desire to exercise this right. To avoid any misunderstanding in all future problems, it is indispensable that you should recognize in advance the internal autonomy of the province of Kurdistan and that this should be publicly announced in one of the first proclamations of the government of the revolution."

Taher Yahyia sent back a message in August agreeing to the Kurdish conditions and including the cryptic phrase: "The date is set." He asked the Kurds to propose six names to be included in the revolutionary government. Talabani recalled that he went with Ibrahim Ahmed, Nuri Shawes and Ali Askari, all leading members of the Kurdish Democratic Party, to discuss this matter with Barzani while Barzani was surrounding the town of Rayat in early July. They agreed on these names: Baba Ali, Fuad Aref, Bakr Karim, Omar Mustafa, Jelal Talabani and Ali Askari. They sent these names to Yahyia, adding that their first two choices would be Baba Ali and Fuad Aref.

This exchange created a semblance of confidence between the Kurdish leadership and the Free Officers, and some specific cooperation took place between Kurds and the Arab Free Officers. Thus the Kurds supported the students' strike in Baghdad, which immediately preceded the overthrow of Kassem. (The Communists took no part in this strike.) Shawkat Akrawi, who handled many of the undercover contacts, makes the point that private reservations nonetheless continued, especially between Kurds and Ba'ath Party members who were prominent among the Free Officers. The Ba'athists maintained that they could overthrow Kassem without help, but that they feared the Kurds. In Akrawi's opinion real confidence between the KDP and the Ba'ath was nil from the start. Attempts by the KDP since the beginning of the Kurdish revolution in September 1961 to contact individual Arab parties, with the exception of the Communists, ran into obstacles raised by the Ba'ath. Although the Istiqlal, a rightwing nationalist party, and Kamil Chaderji's wing of the more liberal National Democratic Party showed interest in cooperating with the Kurds, the Ba'ath apparently regarded the KDP as a branch of the Communist Party, or at best as fellow travelers. The KDP, for its part, regarded the Ba'ath as semi-Fascist and incapable of real understanding of the Kurdish question.

Some weeks before the revolution took place, Saleh Yussefi arranged a meeting with "the responsible man of the Ba'ath Party." This was Ali Saleh Saadi. At this meeting, according to Akrawi, the two parties "agreed on recognition of autonomy for the Kurdish people and agreed to conduct a joint coup d'etat to overthrow Kassem's regime." Saadi embellished the occasion, Akrawi recalls, by declaring that the Ba'ath Party was thinking not merely in terms of autonomy but of self-determination and the possibility of complete independence. He said that the Ba'athists could not be good nationalists if they did not think in these terms. He even said that the Ba'ath Party would help the Kurds to achieve their Greater Kurdistan.

This was February 4. At this time the plotters anticipated carrying out their coup between the end of February and mid-March. They decided to bring a tape recorder to a further meeting on Saturday, February 9, to make a record of the commitments entered into. But the arrest a few days later of Saadi himself and the disclosure that the government was planning to retire or transfer fifty-eight officers, many of whom were connected with the plot, obliged the plotters to move the date forward to February 8. Therefore, the meeting with the tape recorder never took place.

Discussing these contacts in February 1963, a few weeks after the coup took place, Mullah Mustafa admitted with what seemed to me a touch of regret that the agreement was not put in writing. He put it this way: "The Ba'ath has given its promise to give us our autonomy, but it is not a written promise. It is not on paper or signed. I cannot tell you the names of the persons and the times and places offhand, but I have it all written down in my personal records."

The coup d'etat was carried out on the morning of Friday, February 8, the fourteenth day of Ramadan. The Kurds were not informed in advance and did not play any part in the coup. But within a few hours after the coup three men, Fuad Aref, Saleh Yussefi and Shawkat Akrawi, went to the National Council of the Revolution command at the radio station, congratulated them, expressed admiration for their action and regret that the Kurds had not been given a chance to participate. They told the members of the revolutionary command that they would have the full support of the Kurdish people if they fulfilled their promises to the Kurds. After much shaking of hands and kissing, as is the custom in this part of the world, members of the revolutionary command explained events had moved too fast to bring the Kurds into the coup. They asked the Kurds to speak on the radio to mobilize the Kurdish people against Kassem. But the Kurdish group declined on the grounds that it was up to Barzani to do this. Instead they sent a telegram in the name of the Kurdish Democratic Party to the National Council of the Revolution including this phrase: "Your movement has welded itself to the great revolution of the Kurdish people against Kassem's tyranny." It described Kassem as a murderer and the greatest enemy the Kurds ever had. It went on to say that the Kurds admired the movement that had overthrown Kassem and were waiting for positive steps by this movement toward solving the Kurdish question on the basis of self-government, which would insure everlasting brotherhood.

This telegram was read over the radio repeatedly that day and the next, and as a result Kurdish officers and men everywhere began to cooperate with the revolutionaries. The same day Mullah Mustafa, who had been planning a major attack all over Kurdistan, ordered a ceasefire on all fronts.

Jelal Talabani, who commanded the Kurdish southern sector between Kirkuk and Suleimaniya, came down from the mountains and walked into Iraqi army headquarters at Kala Diza to announce Barzani's ceasefire order. At the same time, he asked the government to send a helicopter to the mountains of the north to bring representatives of Mullah Mustafa Barzani to Baghdad for peace negotiations.

In response to Barzani's request, the government sent a plane from Baghdad to Suleimaniya, where it was to pick up a helicopter that would fly to a designated rendezvous with Barzani's representatives in the mountains. Among the passengers on the plane that flew north were Abdallah Saleh Yussefi, head of the Kurdish Democratic Party in Baghdad, and Barzani's second oldest son, Lochman, who, together with a number of other Kurds, had succeeded on the day of the coup in breaking out of Camp Rashid, where he had been held a prisoner for several years.

In the end, because of weather conditions, Barzani's

representatives traveled south overland. Meanwhile Yussefi and Akrawi centered their efforts in Baghdad on getting the release of Kurdish prisoners, whom they estimated at 4712 on February 8. They got plenty of promised and about 2700 actual releases, but in the ensuing weeks about 1500 more Kurds were arrested so that there were about 3500 in prison when the second phase of the war began on June 10.

Jelal Talabani, as Barzani's personal representative, reached Baghdad on February 19, eleven days after the coup d'etat. Here is Talabani's own account of the event: "When I reached Baghdad, Yahyia (now promoted to the rank of major general and commander in chief of the army) came to see me with Fuad Aref, who had been appointed one of two Kurdish ministers in the government. Yahyia said in effect, 'All right, we agreed. We will announce Kurdish autonomy tomorrow.' The next day I went to the Presidency and was received by Premier el-Baqr, Minister of Defense Ammash, and Fuad Aref. They all welcomed me warmly. They were using new words. They said the Kurds would get all their rights. At noon we moved on to the headquarters of the National Revolutionary Council for a meeting with Ali Saleh Saadi, Ammash, Minister of State Hazim Jawad, and Air Force Commander Takriti. The two Kurdish members of the government, Fuad Aref and Baba Ali, were also there.

"We spoke frankly. They agreed again and again that the Kurds would have all their rights. To prove his sincerity Ammash said: 'I will explain some things. Like all other peoples the Kurds will get their rights sooner or later. It would not be good for us to be against the Kurds. If we suppress them they will rise again in two years. And again in three years. It would be very bad to create such an enemy on our right when we have Israel on our left. Economically it would also be disastrous, and politically. Furthermore, the Kurds are now raising their voice outside the country. How would our position be if we tried to destroy a free people?'

"The Kurds present all congratulated him on his speech and I said: 'Thank you for your good words; I will be happy if even half of them are realized.' Then they broached the idea that there ought to be a larger, more representative conference to deal with such an important matter as the Kurdish question. They said that all political elements ought to be represented, the Istiqlal and the others. Ammash proposed February 22 for this meeting, at which all Iraqi and all Kurdish political elements were to be represented, but it never took place.

"That same evening I was called to the Prime Minister's office. I was told that a delegation had been formed to go to Cairo to present congratulations on the anniversary of 'Unity Day' celebrating formation in 1958 of the Union of Egypt and Syria and that they wanted me to go along. I protested that Barzani had sent me to Baghdad, not to Cairo. I told them that I did not have permission from Barzani to make any such trip. But the two Kurds in the government, Aref and Baba Ali, insisted that I should go. There was no time to consult Barzani. I went, and I think I was right to do so."

In the end Talabani went not only to Cairo, but to Algiers, and the contacts he made in both places were of great importance to the Kurds. In Cairo he spent two hours with Nasser, Ali Sabri, and Abdel-Latif Baghdadi.

The substance of Nasser's observations, according to a diplomatic informant, was as follows: "No one can deny that the Kurdish people exist. Consequently, they have their rights and one of these is to seek autonomy. I don't see why the word autonomy should frighten you [meaning the Iraqi officials present]. Many European countries have adopted a system of technical decentralization without in any way imperiling their national unity." He went on to observe that Arab nationalism would be strengthened by securing the support of the Kurds against the enemies of the Arabs. Presumably he had in mind Turkey and Iran, with both of which countries Egypt has broken off diplomatic relations. In other conversations Nasser is reported to have developed the further thought that in the long run the Kurds could serve as a buffer between the Arab nations and the Turks and Iranians, and for that reason it was of great importance to the Arabs to win the friendship of the Kurds. Ben Bella was reported to have been equally outspoken in drawing a parallel between the Kurdish and the Algerian insurrections. He cautioned the Iraqis not to make the same mistake that the French had made.

Meanwhile in the mountains northeast of Kirkuk, where I visited him in late February 1963, Mullah Mustafa Barzani was fuming. As Talabani had anticipated, he took the attitude that he had sent his representative to Baghdad and not on a tour of Arab capitals. He was quite unwilling to entertain any idea that Talabani's trip could be useful. He demanded that the Iraqi government issue a statement by March 1 recognizing in principle the Kurds' right to autonomy, and declared that if it did not do so he would go to war again. He said he might even declare the independence of Kurdistan, its separation from Iraq. And to back up his threats he recalled his men from leave and ordered them to be ready for renewed combat.

I returned from my interview with Barzani to Baghdad just in time to meet Talabani upon his return from Algiers. As I described Barzani's anger to him, he blanched, quite literally. He was very upset. He was upset also by what I told him about Barzani's threats.

Brushing aside Iraqi government attempts to keep him in Baghdad, Jelal Talabani rushed back to the mountains to see Barzani. He saw to it that General Barzani did not carry out his threats. But the Kurdish leader's tough talk did, apparently, have some effect. For late on the night of March 1, in time to meet Barzani's deadline, Iraq's revolutionary council announced that it would guarantee "the rights of the Kurds." The statement did not really touch upon Barzani's central demand for recognition of the right of autonomy, but with its statement of Kurdish-Arab fraternity, it was a step in the right direction and it reduced tension. Textually it said: "In recognition of the ties of brotherhood and friendship between Arabs and Kurds, the Revolution of February the eighth is determined to eliminate all ill effects of the defunct Kassemite regime by guaranteeing the rights of Kurds."

Three days later, on March 4, the government followed up its words by sending to Barzani the two Kurdish members of cabinet, Minister of Agriculture Mohammed Baba Ali and Minister of State Fuad Aref, Major General Taher Yahyia and ex-Ambassador Ali Haidar Suleiman, also of Kurdish origin. The government proposed that the meeting take place at Kala Diza but Barzani, somewhat churlishly and with all the suspiciousness born of past experience of treachery, sent the following reply: "Mullah Mustafa does not intend to go to Kala Diza and he has no intention of changing his previously made plan of movements." At Mullah Mustafa's insistence the meeting took place at Karmi Maran ("the spring of serpents") where he evidently felt safer.

At this meeting Barzani restated the central Kurdish demands, which had already been set forth by Talabani at his meetings in Baghdad. As a first stage and point of departure he insisted on recognition in principle of the Kurds' right to autonomy, then, in a second stage, the more detailed Kurdish demands could be negotiated. The main points in these demands were:

1. Formation of a Kurdish provincial executive and legislative council; Kurds to elect a vice-president to sit with the president of the republic in Baghdad;

2. Creation of Kurdish security forces in the form of a Kurdish division or "legion" to be stationed in Kurdistan, although under Baghdad command; also, some form of Kurdish provincial police, whose status would be similar to that of a state police in the United States;

3. Withdrawal of non-Kurdish units of the Iraqi army from Kurdish territory except as agreed with a Kurdish provincial executive and legislative council still to be established; non-Kurdish units to keep out of Kurdistan except in time of war or danger of war;

4. A fair share of state revenues (mainly oil royalties) to be spent in Kurdistan;

5. Appointment of Kurds to all official posts in Kurdistan; Kurdish to be recognized as an official language, in addition to Arabic, in Kurdistan.

In effect, Barzani was asking for self-government in all respects except that of overall defense and foreign affairs, which would remain in the hands of the Baghdad government. Kurds were to be represented in the central government, but Barzani made it clear that he personally did not intend to participate.

On the government's side, in spite of all the warm words before and immediately after the coup, and Nasser's and Ben Bella's observations notwithstanding, Ba'athist reticence was evident. The Ba'athists did not like the idea of dealing with Barzani on a basis of equality, as though he represented something like a sovereign power. They were nervous also that they might be accused by their own followers and by the Nasserites of giving away the territory of the sacred Arab homeland, even though only under the title of autonomy. The latter concern explained their eagerness to take Talabani along for consultations with Nasser and Ben Bella, the two top leaders of the Arab nationalist cause. In spite of the understanding of the Kurdish cause shown by these two leaders the Ba'ath remained hesitant.

At one session Ammash, holding a finger to his neck, declared: "By God, Gamal Abdel Nasser would break our neck if we agreed to your demands." When Talabani insisted that Nasser had agreed to the principle of self-rule and would approve of any solution on which the two parties agreed, Ammash and Saadi replied that Nasser "talked one thing with you and another with us."

Anxiously searching for means of preventing Barzani from resuming warfare, the Ba'athist regime followed up its governmental delegation with a "popular delegation"—that is, a group of representative public figures who were not necessarily government officials—which flew to meet Barzani at Chawar Kurnah, near Ranieh, on March 7. This delegation had no official governmental status. It was nonetheless warmly received in view of the prominence of the members participating. They were Dr. Abdel Aziz el-Douri, the president of Baghdad university; Hussein Jamil, a former minister in the governments of Nuri Said and Kassem and a former ambassador to India; Sheikh Mohammed Rida el-Shabibi, a former minister in the government of Nuri Said and a former senator; Fayek Sammarrai, a well-known lawyer and former Iraqi ambassador to Cairo; Zayed el-Osman, a lawyer of Kurdish origin and a former member of parliament in the short-lived Iraqi-Jordanian Federation; and Faisal el-Khaizaran, a former ambassador to Moscow and former secretary-general of the Ba'ath Party.

This group achieved some of the very few gains made by negotiation. It succeeded in persuading Barzani to drop his insistence on the word "autonomy." He agreed that so long as the Kurds got the substance of autonomy the word "decentralization" would do. For its part, the popular delegation agreed to seek immediate approval by the central government of a series of Kurdish demands calculated to improve the atmosphere for negotiation. After that a joint committee would be formed by the two sides to draw up the broad lines of "decentralized" government.

The series of demands were the following:

1. Lift the economic blockade.

2. Revoke all orders confiscating Kurdish property.

3. Withdraw the army to its former regular positions. In effect, this would mean that only the second division of the Iraqi army, which is regularly stationed in the north, would remain in Kurdish territory.

4. Replace certain administrative officials in Kurdistan where these are considered offensive by the Kurdish people.

5. Issue a general amnesty for all persons convicted or under prosecution for their contributions to the Kurdish revolution; release all prisoners.

An amnesty order was in fact issued a few days later and published in the official gazette. But some of the Kurdish leaders believe the order was secretly countermanded. In fact the effect was spotty, as indicated by the figures given earlier. The Kurds agreed at the same time to release Arab prisoners in their hands, and in fact released about three hundred men. The economic blockade was partly lifted, although at no time was there completely free communication between the Kurdish and Arab areas of Iraq. The other points remained a dead letter.

On March 9 the government issued a statement

recognizing the Kurdish people's "national rights on the basis of decentralization." Although later it proved hollow, the statement was sincerely welcomed by the Kurds. The text of the statement was as follows: "Since one of the main aims of the Revolution of Ramadan 14 [February 8] is to establish a modern system based on the best administrative and governmental methods, and since the method of decentralization has proved to be beneficial, therefore, the Revolution, acting on the basis of the revolutionary principles announced in its first communiqué providing for strengthening of Arab-Kurdish brotherhood and for respect of the rights of Kurds and other minorities, approves the national rights of the Kurdish people on the basis of decentralization. This should be entered in the provisional and the permanent constitutions when they are enacted. A committee will be formed to lay down the broad lines of decentralization."

At this point General Barzani felt that the Kurds needed a widely representative conference, something more than himself and the Kurdish Democratic Party—a gathering that would be a true expression of public opinion on a national scale. The conference was above all Mullah Mustafa's idea. He nominated some delegates himself and sent his associates to all parts of Kurdish territory to recruit others—Shem Akrawi to Mosul, Ahmed Hamid Amin to Arbil, Jelal Talabani to Suleimaniya and Saleh Yussefi to Baghdad.

Preparations for this conference provoked among the Kurds some remarkable popular demonstrations which Talabani has described to me. He said that he got permission from the commander of the second division to travel with two Jeeps (one of them a station wagon) and fourteen men to Kirkuk and Suleimaniya. At Kirkuk, according to Talabani, his appearance in the town caused a demonstration by about ten thousand persons; at Suleimaniya, where he arrived the next morning, he estimated the crowd at thirty thousand. It took him one and a half hours to move two hundred meters through this crowd, he said. Finally he addressed the crowd for half an hour, praising Barzani and the party.

The Kurdish national conference was held at Koisinjak

from March 18 to 22. About two thousand Kurds gathered from all parts of Kurdistan, almost all of them in Kurdish national costume. Of these, 168 were official delegates who met at the secondary school every evening from seven until midnight. They met at night because they were still afraid that in the daytime they might be bombed by the Iraqi air force. And indeed during the conference there were several nasty incidents in other parts of Kurdistan. On March 21 an Iraqi army unit burned the village of Omar Baq near Shwan in the vicinity of Kirkuk. About the same time a unit of the National Guard was reported to have attacked the village of Alkosh. In the two clashes the Kurds riposted successfully, killing seven men and taking fourteen prisoners.

The delegates to the conference included representatives of most of the tribes, the politburo and central committee of the Kurdish Democratic Party, a number of intellectuals, some representatives of the Kurdish Youth Federation and the Kurdish Womens' Federation and the Kurdish Students' Federation. Also personalities such as Sheikh Tahsin Beq, chief leader of the Yezidis, some other religious personalities and six women. The commanders of the larger units of partisans were also represented.

Mullah Mustafa declared that he did not want to be chairman and nominated Jelal Talabani in his place. Talabani gave the conference a report on the military and political situation. He explained the problem of autonomy and the decision to try to come to terms on the substance of it rather than the word.

A committee of thirty-five was formed to prepare proposals. The committee included representatives of the party, the tribes, intellectuals and professional groups. This committee worked all night to prepare its proposals so that the general meeting on the second night could discuss them, and the meeting on the third night could vote them article by article. On the fourth night the conference decided that Barzani should send a telegram thanking the government for its March 9 recognition of Kurdish national rights. The conference elected fourteen delegates with Talabani as president.

Seven, including Talabani, formed the negotiating team; the other seven were designated advisers.

The real significance of this conference was that it brought together so many Kurds who had had little contact with one another for several years during their struggle against Kassem, and that it gave the Kurds a renewed sense of national solidarity. Simultaneously Barzani arranged an inner-circle conference to try to overcome differences between the tribes and the Kurdish Democratic Party.

The party representatives were the following: Ibrahim Ahmed, secretary-general of the Kurdish Democratic Party and a member of the politburo; Nuri Shawes, a member of the politburo and probably number two in the party; Jelal Talabani, Ali Abdullah and Saleh Yussefi, all members of the politburo. The only one of the six-man politburo not present was Omar Mustafa.

The tribal representatives were Abbas Mamand Agha, the great leader of the Ako tribe; Bapi Agha Babakir Agha, of the Pijdar tribe; Mohammed Ziad Agha, a former deputy from Koisinjak; and Hossein Boskeni, a famous religious as well as military figure of the Barzindji family, whose members included Sheikh Mahmoud of Suleimaniya.

At this restricted meeting, as well as in the general meeting, the party representatives criticized Barzani for denying the vanguard role of the party, namely the necessity for having a party to mobilize intellectuals, merchants, professional people and other urban categories. The party people argued that if the Kurdish revolution were only a tribal affair the world would laugh at it. They would call it a narrow feudalistic movement.

The tribal representatives, and Abbas Mamand Agha in particular, apparently feared that the party would organize the tribesmen in such a way as to undermine the authority of the traditional tribal leaders. Some of the young men of the Pijdar and other tribes had joined the party.

In the end the tribal representatives agreed that the party had its own importance and was necessary to victory. All agreed that future differences should be overcome by consultation. Also that the party must contribute to the needs of the tribal forces. And that all must work to win for the Kurdish national cause those aghas who were still with the central government, such as Mahmoud Zibari, Sheikh Nakshbandi, and Sheikh Brivkani.

The conference showed that a number of tribes that had formerly worked with the government were now working with the Kurdish nationalists, including the Harkis, the Khushnaou and the Bradost. One of the sons of Sheikh Lolan, one of Barzani's oldest enemies, had rallied to Barzani's side.

On March 30, Jelal Talabani, at the head of a delegation of fourteen Kurds, arrived in Baghdad to negotiate with the government. But the new rulers of Iraq seemed increasingly reluctant to negotiate with them. The Kurds were met in Baghdad not by an official government delegation, but by members of the popular delegation who had visited them in Kurdistan some weeks earlier. After a few days of discussion with this group, Jelal Talabani submitted to them a formal question: "Can you speak for the government?" he asked. The members of the so-called popular delegation had to admit that they could not. Talabani decided therefore to see Prime Minister el-Baqr. The Prime Minister sent word apologizing for the long delay in opening official negotiations and promised that beginning on Saturday, April 6, he would devote full time to negotiations with the Kurdish delegation. Just two hours after they had received this message from the Premier the Kurdish delegation heard an announcement on Baghdad radio that Premier el-Baqr would leave on Saturday for Cairo to begin discussions with the Egyptian government. Five days later the Iraqi delegation returned from Cairo and a high-level meeting was at last held including Minister of Interior Saadi, Minister of Defense Ammash and Air Force Commander Takriti. At the request of this group the Kurdish delegation prepared a formal memorandum setting forth its demands, which were essentially what they had always been. The memorandum was submitted on April 24.

A document similar in importance was the Kurdish note to the Iraqi delegation to the Cairo union talks that ended on April 17. Its three main points were: firstly, if Iraq were to remain in its present form without structural change the Kurds would accept decentralization as proposed in the March 9 announcement of the Iraqi government. Secondly, if Iraq were to become linked with other Arab countries in a federation, then the Kurds would claim autonomy in its widest meaning. Thirdly, if Iraq were to be dissolved in a complete Arab unity the Kurds would demand that they form a separate region.

Although some Arab critics have interpreted these demands as constituting in effect demands for secession, the Kurds explicitly denied any such intention. They asserted their desire to continue to live as part of the Iraqi republic, an autonomous area within the state.

The Premier had agreed to meet the Kurdish delegation at 11 A.M. on Wednesday, April 24, to receive the memorandum setting forth their demands. The Kurds were especially anxious to see him for several reasons: firstly, although they had originally welcomed the government's statement recognizing their "national rights on the basis of decentralization," they had found in talks with Iraqi officials that this plan had little bearing on the rights they were demanding. It had turned out to be a general decentralization scheme applicable to all parts of Iraq. It would not treat the Kurds as a unified group within the country nor accord them any special recognition or institutions. Secondly, the Kurds were upset by reports they were getting from Kurdistan that the government was reimposing the economic blockade, by blocking roads leading to Kurdish areas. Also that the government was concentrating troops and deploying aircraft, artillery and tanks against the Kurds.

The delegates presented themselves at 10:45. The lieutenant in charge at the Premier's residence said that he was asleep. Indignant, the Kurdish delegates deposited the document setting forth their demands and declared that they would leave and return to Kurdistan. They went to see Fuad Aref, the minister of state for Kurdish affairs, who telephoned to Taher Yahyia, the commander in chief, and urgently, all within the hour, arranged for a meeting with the Kurdish delegates.

Still burning with indignation, the Kurds went to Yahyia's office and announced that they had come to say goodbye, that they were returning to Kurdistan. Talabani declared that he was now convinced that the Iraqi government did not intend to negotiate seriously.

General Yahyia showed great dismay. If the Kurds went back the appearance would be given that the negotiations were finished, he declared. This would be most unfortunate.

"Are there any negotiations?" Talabani asked hotly. "Oh, yes," General Yahyia reassured him, "we are giving a great deal of thought to your proposals." But Talabani insisted that he had reason to believe that the government did not wish to solve this question seriously.

General Yahyia rushed to his desk, took out a Koran and swore upon the Koran that if the government had any ill intentions toward the Kurds God should strike him blind. "Please don't go," he said. "Stay over the Id el-Fitr holiday and after the Id we will have serious talks." Meanwhile, he said, the Kurdish proposals would be sent to Nasser and to the Syrian government to get their points of view.

Reluctantly the Kurds agreed to stay until after the holiday, and on May 1 Premier el-Baqr at last received them. Talabani frankly expressed his resentment over the delay in negotiations and the preparations for resumption of fighting. Thereupon the Premier raised the Holy Koran above his head and said: "By this Koran I swear that I have no ill intentions toward you." He said the Kurdish demands had been sent on to the governments in Cairo and Damascus to get their opinions.

Talabani replied bitterly: "By this Koran you may have no ill intentions—but the intentions of all the leaders of the Ba'ath are bad as far as we are concerned."

Then he asked el-Baqr for authorization to fly to Cairo in order to explain the Kurdish demands to Nasser. He had in mind private statements of the Premier, Saadi and Yahyia that the best way, perhaps the only way, to get negotiations between Kurds and Iraqis moving would be to get Nasser to take a clear-cut stand. The Premier said he would put the question to the National Revolutionary Council. Later the same day he sent word through Yahyia that the permission was granted, and the Ministry of Interior opened its offices, in spite of the fact that it was the Id holiday, to renew Talabani's passport. That the Council should have granted this permission and allowed one of the most effective of Kurdish spokesmen to leave the country and reach places where he could speak freely amazed the Kurds. They have never been able to explain it.

Next day Talabani flew to Beirut. Shawkat Akrawi had preceded him to Beirut by a few days. Together they flew to Cairo and saw Nasser on May 25.

Publicly Nasser said nothing, and his people said nothing. But they let it be known indirectly that they had shown Talabani, the Kurdish representative, every courtesy and a good deal of sympathy; that they regarded the Kurdish demands as reasonable; that they would regard any attempt to solve the question by force as folly; that they disapproved of secession but did not believe that the Kurds were secessionist. This was Talabani's second meeting with Nasser; they had met before when Talabani accompanied the Iraqi delegates to Cairo in February.

The moral effect of Nasser's meeting with Talabani was immense. For the first time the Kurds were getting a hearing in the Arab world. For the first time sections of the Arab press showed the Kurds some sympathy.

Talabani did not return to Baghdad after his meeting with Nasser. Although he clung to the idea that Nasser's support might make it psychologically easier for the Ba'ath to come to terms with the Kurds, he also got word from Baghdad that it would not be safe for him to go back. He decided instead to meet the press in Beirut and then to go on with Akrawi to Europe to try to meet the friends and influence the foes of the Kurds.

Sometime in October, by means and routes which must remain secret, Talabani returned to Kurdish territory in northern Iraq. In November he was back in command of his men at Chem y Rezan, in time to receive two Iraqi army officers who under a flag of truce came to inquire whether the

Kurds were ready to resume negotiations. Talabani replied contemptuously that the Kurds had a negotiating team in Baghdad—the team he himself had headed until late in May—and that in order to negotiate this team need only be released from prison. He was undoubtedly thinking especially of Saleh Yussefi, the gentle, quiet man whom he had left in charge of the talks and who, the Kurdish leaders believe, has been cruelly tortured in captivity.

In his sector Talabani has encouraged the Kurdish Democratic Party to establish a Kurdish civil administration. In villages and towns, councils have been elected. The Kurds have taken the first steps toward creating a de facto autonomous state.

While Talabani is undoubtedly one of the best Kurdish military leaders, as he has proven again since his return from Europe, the Kurds will miss him on the international political and propaganda front. Young, trained as lawyer and journalist, articulate, with a brilliant record as guerrilla leader, Talabani is an excellent spokesman.*

---

* For details of the events immediately preceding June 10, I am much indebted to Richard Anderegg of the Swiss Broadcasting Network, who was in Baghdad until the afternoon of June 9.

16

Evaluation

The struggle of the Kurds of Iraq is epic; it is also tragic: a whole people in a life and death struggle for the right to exist.

We have seen in the preceding chapters the past and present of the Kurdish people, their struggles, their gains and their losses. In conclusion I will try to look a little into the future by asking what it is that Barzani and the KDP want, what it is that their foes want, how their conflict relates to the worldwide East-West struggle, what is the most likely outcome of the war, and what American policy should be.

Barzani and the KDP are of course fighting for the autonomy of the Kurds within the Iraqi state. Barzani and his tribal followers agreed with the Kurdish Democratic Party at the Koisinjak conference in March 1963 on a set of demands which were formally presented to the Iraqi government on April 24.

To appreciate fully the meaning of these demands, to get an idea of the character they would give to an autonomous state of their own, one must evaluate Barzani and the KDP.

Barzani is basically a tribal leader; he has shown a certain capacity for growth and he has shown distinct limitations. He has developed around himself the mystique of "The Leader" even though he will not let anyone call him "Leader." Very much in the manner described by De Gaulle in his *Le Fil de l'Epée* he has shrouded himself in mystery, allowed a legend to be woven around his name.

While he sees a great many people he also spends a good deal of time alone; those he sees are of a wide variety, but if he can be said to have personal friends they are the traditional leaders—sheikhs, aghas, landlords. He depends on no one, neither a particular secretary nor an adviser. He worships independence and strength.

You sense the aloofness of the man when you see him on his daily walk (when he has a chance to engage in such activities). Very erect, a cherrywood shepherd's crook in his right hand, he steps slowly, deep in thought, looking neither to left nor to right. Apparently unaware of the persons he is passing, he makes no attempt to greet them.

Barzani's prestige among the Kurds is now immense. I believe it extends like a myth, or legend, beyond the borders of Iraq to the Kurds of Turkey and Iran. If there were peace today he could undoubtedly be president, or prime minister, in Iraqi Kurdistan, or in all of Kurdistan as the occasion offered itself.

In his conversations with me he showed both the breadth and the limitations of his outlook. At times I was appalled at his seeming inability to grasp what I or others were telling him; at other times I suspected he merely pretended not to understand so as to reinforce his own point of view.

Thus he seemed unable to grasp the value of Talabani's trip to Cairo and Algiers; yet I suspected he was assuming this attitude in order to insist on the urgency of action by the Iraqi government, to show that he could not be put off by fine words, no matter where they came from.

Then again he seemed unable to grasp my points about the power of public opinion in the United States. But it occurred to me later that he did not want to understand, that he deliberately acted obtuse because I was arguing the power of public opinion and the lack of information available to public opinion as an excuse for the callous and indifferent policies of the United States government, and because he wished to insist on what he regarded as the responsibility of the United States government.

His breadth and wisdom are intuitive. His limitations

are set by the tribal environment in which he has spent
his life, and by his education. Although he has had a good
deal of religious instruction he has had very little secular
education. During his twelve years in Russia, while ostensi-
bly studying history, geography and economics, he seems to
have successfully isolated himself not only from the ideological influences which he detested but also from more useful
knowledge which he might have acquired. In Russia he must
have known some Russians, for he did learn to speak the
Russian language fluently; apart from that he has known very
few Europeans.

His own sense of limitation was displayed in a little out-
burst reported by Eric Roulot during his meeting with Barzani
in March 1963. When asked about the economic and social
problems of the Kurds Mullah Mustafa replied: "They say I
am not perfectly educated to understand these difficult questions; so you had better ask the wise intellectuals, these cave
politicians whom you know." He meant Ibrahim Ahmed, who
in fact dwelt in a cave which Roulot had visited before he saw
Barzani.

In Barzani's mind the traditional values of his tribe
undoubtedly stand first. One of these is the duty of the son to
his father and to his family. Thus, because his older brother
Ahmed wished it and because Ahmed was the head of the family, he allowed his own second oldest son, Lochman, to go on
a mission to Baghdad where he fell into Kassem's hands and
was imprisoned. Speaking of this event he did not criticize his
brother. "He is an old man who has been broken by twelve
years in prison," Mullah Mustafa observed. "He is the father
of us all; it is he who brought me up."

Barzani is able to play his role of leadership because he
has proven himself as a military technician and as practical
politician. No one else among the Kurds retains in his own
mind so much information and is able to use it with such
shrewdness whether in military or political matters. His habit
of constant movement restricts the amount of radio and
other equipment in his headquarters. But then he does not
try to maintain constant contact with all fronts. He leaves his

commanders wide discretion. When he gets an urgent radio message he is likely as not to put it aside to be answered "in the morning." And then he may send his answer in Arabic longhand, by courier. Yet it was he who in the course of 1962 developed these tactics into a well-planned grand strategy that left the Kurds in a dominant position at the end of the year.

Constant movement also serves Barzani as a practical politician. Instinctively he is forever building his political fences, forever reinforcing the Kurdish unity of which he is the most important architect. He has—and that is his greatest merit—united the Kurds of Iraq for the first time; by consent or by force he has coordinated tribal forces with the elements of the Kurdish Democratic Party and has thus made it possible for them to fight the Iraqi government.

Barzani and Ibrahim Ahmed, the leader of the Kurdish Democratic Party, are so different that they are hardly comparable. Whereas Barzani speaks in riddles and drives home his points with folktales and legends, Ibrahim Ahmed expresses himself with intellectual precision. If Barzani were to disappear it is hard to imagine that the Kurdish national movement could hold together; he is indispensable. But Ibrahim Ahmed could undoubtedly be replaced. Yet Ibrahim Ahmed has nonetheless put his mark on the Kurdish Democratic Party and has led it gradually out of the clutches of the Communist Party. Partly because of the cleavage that has developed between party and tribal elements in Iraq, the membership with which the party has had to work has been almost entirely urban and inclined to be "leftist." Although in Iran in the early days of the Komala the party attracted many tribal leaders, in Iraq it is composed predominantly of educated Kurds, graduates of secondary schools and universities, technicians and professional men. These "intellectuals" are almost automatically thrown into opposition to the traditional "feudalistic" tribal elite.

For the time being the old tribal structure is suffused with life, because the traditional elite is able to provide the best military leadership. But in the long run, as urbanization progresses, as roads creep into the mountains and schools are opened, as they surely must be, the tribal structure is bound to weaken; in the long run the Kurdish Democratic Party must supplant the tribal forces on which Barzani's leadership is based. For the party offers the Kurds an alternative to the dying tribal structure; an alternative also to the structure of the state to which they aspire and to the structure of the non-Kurdish states which have been imposed upon them. The significance to the Kurds of a political party may be appreciated if one considers that after the Turkish government had completely destroyed the traditional tribal structure a secret organization of the Kurdish Democratic Party offered the Kurds of Turkey the only hope of maintaining an organizational structure.

Because of the influence of the Communists, who had motives other than the welfare of the Kurds, the Kurdish Democratic Party was slow to put its heart into the war for autonomy. When they did fight the party forces were less successful than Barzani's; the party's foreign propaganda activities, its fund raising, its support of dependents, its recruiting activities, its information gathering, indeed, all its activities seemed inadequate.

Yet all were functions which only a party could perform; except marginally (especially in the propaganda field) these were things that Barzani could not do for himself.

On the positive side one may say that during the eighteen months of the first stage of the war for Kurdish autonomy the Kurdish Democratic Party escaped from the shadow of the Communist Party. Since then the KDP's hold on some of its followers has been threatened again because the Soviet Union and the Communist Party have overtly supported the Kurds against the Ba'ath, while one of the principal Western powers, Great Britain, has been supplying the Baghdad government with arms.

However, the KDP has stood firm. It is now fully committed to the war. It is fully independent of the Communist Party. It is also keenly aware of the necessity of cooperating with Barzani, more aware than Barzani, it seems, of the complementary nature of the two great elements in the Kurdish forces.

Indeed, the party leaders submit almost masochistically, it seemed to me, to Barzani's constant open insults, denigration and belittlement. They know that the party would not represent much of a force without the unique and irreplaceable mystique of Barzani's leadership and the military strength of the tribes.

The rivalry between party and tribal forces probably will come to a head when and if there is a real end to the fighting. Then the danger will become acute that Barzani and the party might each think they can do without the other.

Ranged against these Kurdish forces were, first Kassem, then from June 10 until the army coup of November 18, the Ba'athist-led government of Iraq. What did the Ba'ath want? The Ba'ath was committed to destroying Barzani, to "purging the mountains." Why it should have entered into such a commitment is somewhat puzzling. To find the answer I think that one must consider a variety of factors. The Ba'ath was a vital new force in the Middle East—a much more dangerous enemy to the Kurds than either Nuri Said or Kassem. The Ba'ath had gained power in Iraq as well as Syria and it meant to hold on to power. The Ba'ath was ambitious. One aspect of its strength was that it was the first non-Communist Arab party organized on a disciplined cell basis, the first party whose ideology could, with a little stretching, be called homegrown, that offered the intellectuals an alternative to Nasser. These were the characteristics that made it a vital new force.

But the Ba'ath also had its weaknesses. Firstly, its membership was thin; while it did appeal to many of the more educated Arabs, it had so little popular base that it found difficulty in staging street demonstrations. Secondly, by breaking with all other political elements and ruling virtually alone it isolated itself and imposed a party dictatorship.

Resuming the war against the Kurds was one way of mobilizing the force of the army for the purposes of the Ba'ath Party—a fairly easy thing to do, because the Kurds are not popular among the Arabs of Iraq. Fighting the Kurds enabled the Ba'ath to exploit the lowest racialist feeling of the Arab Iraqi.

It enabled the Ba'ath also to exploit the element among the army officers who believed that they had never really had a chance to lick Barzani, that Kassem had never really tried, that the army had been held back and that they could dispose of Barzani "in two weeks." If these officers were busy vindicating themselves in the mountains of Kurdistan at least they would not be plotting the overthrow of the Ba'athist regime in the streets of Baghdad.

A certain desperation in the attitude of the Ba'ath Party toward its campaign against the Kurds may explain the ferocity and the tendency to racialism with which the Iraqi army conducted the second phase of the war. What the army could not do to Barzani's men it did in some cases to civilians. It bombed and burned villages, deported thousands of men, women and children. It seemed as though the Ba'ath were following the example of the Turkish campaigns against the Kurds between 1925 and 1938, whose objectives were to destroy Kurdish society as it had existed.

But the Ba'athist campaign failed. Much as Kassem's reverses at the hands of the Kurds prepared the way for his overthrow, the Ba'ath's failure may have proved its undoing.

The intentions of the successor regime headed by President Abdel Salaam Aref were still uncertain at the beginning of 1964. Aref appealed to the Kurds as good Moslems to lay down their arms, but he said not a word about their rights. Meanwhile the army, weary and demoralized, refrained from attacking.

How this conflict relates to the East-West struggle becomes evident when one knows that the United States government worked hard (but not hard enough) to prevent the Iraqi-Kurdish war from resuming. Secretary of State Dean Rusk in his messages to the Ba'athist government urged a settlement; and in one message that was relayed verbally to Barzani he urged the Kurdish leader not to resume fighting but to try to settle his differences with the Baghdad authorities by negotiation. The message had some influence in that it encouraged the Kurds to believe that the United States was working for peace and that there was a chance of settlement.

The United States wanted a settlement with an autonomous Kurdistan fitting peacefully into the Iraqi republic because the resumption of the war could only serve Communist designs. It offered the Communists and the Soviet Union a just and dramatic cause which it could and eventually did exploit to the full—at least propagandistically. With an overtly anti-Communist Ba'athist government in Baghdad, Soviet propaganda struck out hard for the Kurds against Ba'athist Baghdad. (The Russians were restrained, no doubt, by the knowledge that if Baghdad were to switch to a pro-Communist, pro-Soviet line they would want to drop or tone down the Kurdish cause again, as they did in the days of the vacillating Kassem. After all, they have committed to the Kurdish cause only their word, whereas on the side of Baghdad they have committed many millions of rubles in economic and military aid.)

Although the Ba'ath was actively anti-Communist, its campaign against the Kurds was most unwelcome to Washington. For the reasons stated Washington considered the Ba'athist campaign foolish—an unjust war, a war the Iraqis could not win, a war that would in any case serve the enemies of the United States. But the United States felt and still feels restrained by its ties through the Central Treaty Organization to Turkey and Iran from saying or doing anything in support of the Kurds. If peace had been preserved and a settlement found the United States could have done much, by economic and technical aid, to help the Kurds develop their autonomous region. Furthermore, on the political side, a sensible, peaceful settlement of the problem in Iraq would surely have led in time to similar reforms in Turkey and in Iran. In bringing this about the United States could have legitimately and constructively used its influence through CENTO and as an ally of both Turkey and Iran. One could imagine in time the evolution of three autonomous Kurdish areas, in Iraq, Turkey and Iran, the three linked culturally with one another, and economically and politically with their Iraqi, Turkish and Iranian partners. In a further stage the three areas might develop special economic links. This would have been the path of reason, based upon the rational examples of bilingual Belgium and trilingual Switzerland or the economic union of the Common Market.

But the Ba'ath followed the opposite course, the path of repression, which raises immense dangers for the West. It raises the question whether the Kurds, denied the right of self-determination and the opportunity of free development in a Western-dominated Middle East, may not at last become the instrument of the Soviet Union. More precisely, the danger is that his foes will at some stage press Barzani so unmercifully that he in desperation will declare the independence of Iraqi Kurdistan and its separation from the Iraqi republic. Already some hotheads of the KDP and among Barzani's forces are demanding an end to the talk about autonomy and a forthright declaration of independence.

When and if that time comes, it will have inevitable repercussions in Iran and Turkey. The situation would then be ripe for physical Soviet intervention. By that time the rapprochement between Moscow and Washington that began with the 1963 atomic test ban may be over, and Moscow may be ready to strike a blow at the West where it will hurt. It might begin supplying arms and ammunition and all other kinds of supplies to the Kurds of Iran, Turkey and Iraq—might in other words back a rising of the Kurds in these three nations— to "blow up" the Middle East as we know it. Then, indeed, the prediction made by W. H. Hay in his book *Two Years in Kurdistan* might come true. "The day when the national consciousness of the Kurds is awakened and when they unite, the Turkish, Iranian and Iraqi states will fall like dust before them." This is the hidden dynamite in the Kurdish problem.

This day may never come; it need not come. The very idea of active alliance with the Soviet Union is distasteful to the present leadership of the Kurds. Nor do Barzani or the party want to involve the Kurds of Iran and Turkey. Such an expansion of the Kurdish war would tragically transform Kurdish territory into a kind of Korea with the Russians backing the Kurds and the Western powers backing the Arabs, Turks and Iranians against them.

In this situation Britain seems to be playing an unfortunate role. When the Soviet Union cut its arms shipments to Iraq following the Ba'athist coup, British suppliers moved in to replace them.

Turkey and Iran, who are the Western Allies most affected by the ultimate implications of the new war in Iraq, are meanwhile maintaining relatively constructive attitudes. In the period before the Ba'athist campaign the Iranians had in fact improved the cultural regime of the Kurds, and the Turks had made the (for them) remarkable concession of allowing a publication in Kurdish in Istanbul (since suppressed). Nor is there any evidence, Kurdish suspicions notwithstanding, that the Central Treaty Organization is planning any repressive measures against the Kurds of Iran and Turkey in collaboration with Iraq.

Most encouraging to the Kurds is the attitude of President Nasser and Egypt. Although he has refrained from openly supporting the Kurdish cause, Nasser has expressed distinct disapproval of the Ba'athist war against the Kurds and has shown visiting Kurdish leaders, such as Jelal Talabani, every courtesy and sympathy. It is perhaps opportune to recall the wise words of another Egyptian, Abdul Rahman Azzam Pasha, who, as secretary-general of the Arab League, wrote in the periodical *Al-Hilal* of October 1943, as follows: "The Kurds . . . should not be given the impression that the realization of Arab unity might injure their interests. They are Moslems and, many times in history, they have thrown back invasions which threatened Islam. They know very well that Arab unity will raise the prestige of Islam since it will unite the best elements of this religion and of this family. The future and the ambition of Iraq do not lie in an extension to the detriment of the Kurds. The Arab nation gives them a choice. They may unite themselves with the Arab nation, if they so desire, but they may become autonomous when they like without any ill feeling. It is not permissible that a Kurdish question should arise in Iraq when one considers that the Kurds have given the Arab nation sovereigns and military chiefs at all times of history long before Saladin and long after him. These

Kurds were symbols of piety and partisans of Arabism. The Kurds should beware of foreign intrigue and the Iraqis should be on guard to show themselves patient and concerned not to alienate Kurdish sympathy, for the problem is easy and the protection of the interests of the Kurds should be assured."

A pity indeed if in a flash flood of hate the relations between Arabs and Kurds should be so much envenomed that the Kurdish-Iraqi war should become a racial conflict. In the past Kurds and Arabs have lived together peacefully in a wide variety of situations. In the past they shared a common opposition to Turkish central authority. Kurdish and Arab communities in many places merged together. Islands of Kurds, such as the Kurdish community of Damascus, lived fruitfully side by side with Arab communities for many generations. Distinguished families such as the Ayoubis, the family of Saladin, still play a prominent role in Arab public affairs. The Barazi family of Syria, for instance, has contributed a prime minister to Syria but remains proud of its Kurdish heritage. Indeed in some parts of the Arab world a certain snobbism attaches to Kurdish origins.

The possible results of this war can be grouped, I believe, under four headings:

1. A negotiated settlement, either by direct talks or through mediation;

2. Victory of the government;

3. Victory of Barzani;

4. Indefinite prolongation of the struggle as a war of attrition.

Several attempts to give the impression that it was still willing to negotiate a settlement were made by the Ba'athist government and the military regime that replaced it on November 18. These have been more in the nature of attempts to split away some tribal elements than serious efforts to reach an accord. The Ba'ath, after double-crossing the Kurdish negotiators in Baghdad in June 1963, was not really capable of attempting a settlement, nor has the successor regime seemed more sincere. Yet a new group of Free Officers like those who contacted the Kurds in April 1962 may even now be plotting yet another coup, may even now be negotiating with the Kurds.

A government victory on the field of battle is unlikely. The Kurdish guerrillas are most unlikely ever to expose themselves to a major battle in which their main forces could be annihilated. They might be defeated, however, if the pressure of attrition should cause a breakup of their unity, either by tribal defection or open split between party and tribal forces. If driven to desperate straits it is possible, as I have already suggested, that the Kurds might declare their independence and separation from Iraq, call upon their fellow tribesmen in Turkey and Iran for help, declare a Greater Kurdistan state and at the same time ask and receive material aid from the Soviet Union.

On the other hand, a Barzani victory in the field is also unlikely. A guerrilla army equipped only with rifles and mortars cannot defeat a fully equipped modern army. But the Kurds are sure to continue scoring many small tactical successes. They may at times even isolate and destroy a battalion. The effect on the Iraqi army and on Baghdad will be cumulative. I do not believe that any government in Baghdad can be stable until it comes to terms with the Kurds.

Which leads to the final alternative—indefinite prolongation of the war. I personally believe it will be long but not indefinite, that finally Barzani will prevail, by holding out longer than the Iraqi army and whatever government are able to maintain their pressure, and by participating in yet another overthrow of the Baghdad regime. This time they will no doubt seek commitments in writing from the Free Officers with whom they collaborate.

Although I anticipate ultimate Kurdish victory along the lines of the war as it is being fought today, unpredictable developments could prove me wrong. For instance, the death of Barzani and his replacement by a personality less wise and less friendly to the West could bring about the kind of disaster I have already envisaged. Close associates of Barzani have told me that during the summer of 1962 the Communist parties of Iraq and Iran each made three urgent secret approaches—making a total of six approaches—to Barzani with the following proposition: Barzani was to extend the Kurdish revolution to Iran, whereupon the Soviet government would send across the border into Iranian Kurdistan all the arms and other supplies and money the Kurdish revolutionaries could use.

Barzani rejected the offers—probably because he correctly identified them as a Communist Party maneuver meant to cause bad blood between himself and the West. Barzani wanted and still wants to confine the war to Iraq. He knows that in the Middle East as it is today the United States would have to support the Iranian (or Turkish) government against a Kurdish rising in their countries and he does not want to fight the United States. Far from fighting the United States I believe that he would welcome a "special relationship" with the United States; he seems to have in the back of his mind the idea that the United States could become the "protector of the Kurds" and the Kurds the faithful ally of the United States.

The United States will be taking a long chance if it does not safeguard itself against the devastating possibilities that could make the Kurds instruments of the Soviet Union—six, nine, possibly twelve million of the most warlike people in the Middle East located in three countries, or if one includes Syria, in four countries, of the Middle East; in the heart of the only part of the Middle East allied with the West.

What, then, should United States policy be?

United States policy must, of course, be shaped according to United States interests. I believe it is in the interest of the United States to support the Kurds.

The moral basis of United States policy—and it is in the interest of the United States that it should have a moral basis—is that the United States stands for the self-determination of peoples. By military effort, by their historical tradition, by their present culture, the Kurds have won the moral right to self-determination. Kurdish claims are just—as valid as any national claims in the world—worthy of United States support.

The Kurds will get their rights some day anyhow; it is better that they should get them with United States help. A positive policy supporting the Kurds' rights, judiciously backed by the President of the United States, would in the long run strengthen the moral position, and consequently the political position, of the United States in the Middle East and in the world.

At the same time the military value of the Kurdish nation must give pause to our policy makers from both positive and negative points of view. On the positive side they are a natural guerrilla force, always armed, always in place on the flank of the most likely Soviet invasion route into the Middle East. Negatively, they are a people who might be drawn into the service of the Soviet Union and against us. But this need not happen.

Put another way, the Kurds are one of the most important submerged peoples in the world, a people whose friendship could be useful to the United States and the West; on the other hand, a people who, in the hands of the Soviet Union, could do us great harm.

It is in the interest of the United States that the Kurdish problem should be solved within the framework of the Iraqi republic and not eventually in the framework of a Greater Kurdistan. When the Kurds feel obliged to proclaim a Greater Kurdistan they will also be proclaiming their alignment with the Soviet Union.

Therefore, it is important that the United States should do everything possible to bring about a settlement of the conflict in Iraq. By whatever means may be necessary—by diplomacy or by getting them military supplies—the United States should see that the Kurds get their rights.

The job of helping the Kurds must be handled with discretion. The Russians and the Chinese Communists have done this sort of thing in many situations—in Laos, in Viet Nam, in Greece. The United States can do it too.

The American aim should be to modify the structure of the Middle East in the way that we want it, before the Soviets modify it in the way they want it. We should encourage

Kurdish autonomous areas within the states of Iraq, Iran and Turkey.

Our policy should be gradualist, not abrupt. We should make the Iranians and the Turks understand that the United States remains their ally, working for their preservation. At the same time we should take the position that the United States, which has done so much to support them, which has assumed so much responsibility for their defense, has the right to take a hand in the solution of a problem which it considers vital to the defense of its interests.

There are times when a strong stand for a just cause is more important from the long-term point of view than short-term harmony; we don't have to help freeze an inequitable status quo, especially when we find it contrary to our interests; there is virtue sometimes in casting light upon and in attempting to correct the more outrageous practices of our allies. A less forthright policy would be unworthy of a great power.

An Iraqi officer once said to me with a snort: "The Kurds will never get their independence." I replied that it was hardly necessary to give them "independence," that it should be possible to find the kind of rational solution to the problem of national rights that has been found among some European nations, that it was surely unjust and foolish for the Iraqis to go on trying to turn Kurds into Arabs, while the Turks tried to turn Kurds into Turks and the Iranians tried to make Kurds into Iranians. He replied, "Well, perhaps in a hundred years." The task of the United States is to shorten that time, to shorten that hundred years to a few years, to use its great power to replace madness with compassion, intelligence, reason.

EPILOGUE

"One More Chance"

Since this book went to press the struggle between Kurds and Arabs within the state of Iraq has taken a new turn. A cease-fire, proclaimed by Mullah Mustafa Barzani and President Abdel Salaam Aref on February 10, 1964, has given the Kurds and Arabs one more chance to make peace. They have now another chance to let reason prevail, to avoid the great dangers to themselves and to the world implicit in a continuing and expanding conflict between them.

I had the good fortune to be able to establish some of the facts in this situation at first hand during a visit to Iraq at the end of February 1964. On this occasion I was cordially received, was granted an interview with President Aref in Baghdad on February 25, was invited to accompany a Ministry of Guidance tour of the north, including meetings with the governors of Suleimaniya and Kirkuk, the governor of the north and the commander of the second division, and was finally and incredibly flown in an Iraqi air force helicopter to a meeting with Mullah Mustafa Barzani at Ranieh.

This was my third visit to Barzani, and very different from the previous ones, when I entered northern Iraq clandestinely in the summer of 1962, and when I reached him by hoodwinking the Ba'athist authorities in February 1963. This time I went with the blessing of the Ministry of Guidance and in the company of nine correspondents representing United Press International, Reuters, Agence France Presse, TASS, Radio Moscow, Middle East News Agency, the Chinese Communist News Agency, and the East German News Agency.

For the Iraqi authorities to provide transportation for this cross section of the world's press from the army base at Kirkuk to the mountains of Kurdistan for a meeting with Barzani was indeed an extraordinary thing. Clearly, something very radical had happened to the Iraqi government's attitude toward the Kurdish leader. The government's gesture was a recognition of Mullah Mustafa, of his role as the representative leader of the Kurds, and of his return to legality.

What brought about the change? I think that, by way of answer, it will be worthwhile to examine the events that began with the coup d'etat of November 18, 1963, by which a group of officers headed by President Abdel Salaam Aref overthrew the Ba'athist regime.

This was not quite the coup I had anticipated. In contrast to the undercover negotiations between Kurds and Free Officers that preceded the Ba'athist coup against Kassem nine months earlier, on February 8, 1963, this time there were no advance contacts between the Kurds and the revolutionaries.

But it can be said that the failure of the Ba'athist-led campaign against the Kurds in the summer of 1963 had shaken the Ba'athist regime to its foundations and precipitated the internal dissension that led to the new coup.

The new regime, in which President Aref became not merely a figurehead, as before, but a real power, understood what the Ba'ath had never learned: that an Iraqi government cannot fight the Communists, and Nasser, and the Kurds, all at the same time. President Aref's right-of-center regime continued to fight the Communists, but it made a friend of Nasser and, after a period of tacit truce, has taken steps to come to terms with the Kurds.

The Aref regime's steps in this direction were almost certainly inspired in part by President Nasser during the summit meeting of Arab chiefs of state which ended in Cairo on January 17. President Aref, who has long been a personal admirer of Gamal Abdel Nasser, was undoubtedly on the one hand influenced by Nasser's disapproval of the Ba'athist campaign against the Kurds, on the other strengthened by

Nasser's personal assurances that he approved the grant of some "national rights" to the Kurds so long as this did not mean secession.

Earlier in the winter Shawkat Akrawi, who had been serving as emissary abroad for the Kurdish Democratic Party, and who had had a number of interviews with Nasser, had made his way secretly from Cairo with a letter from Nasser to Mullah Mustafa Barzani offering to mediate the dispute between the Kurds and the Iraqi government. Mullah Mustafa agreed, but before Akrawi, carrying Mullah Mustafa's reply, could get through the snow-clogged mountain passes on his way back to Cairo, the government in Baghdad established direct contact with Barzani.

The first steps seem to have been taken by General Naif Hamudi, governor of Kirkuk, who boasts that he personally wrote letters to certain officers formerly in the Iraqi army and now in the service of Mullah Mustafa, suggesting that the time had come for a cease-fire. Whether as a result of these letters or for other reasons, Mullah Mustafa's older brother, Sheikh Ahmed, who throughout the conflict has played a neutral role, traveled to Baghdad in late December or early January and met President Aref. Soon thereafter Mullah Mustafa received a letter from Baba Ali Sheikh Mahmoud, the former Minister of Agriculture. Baba Ali, the son of the great Sheikh Mahmoud of Suleimaniya, who was once called king of the Kurds, has frequently played the role of intermediary between the government and the fighting Kurds.

Baba Ali's letter was followed by a meeting at Ranieh on January 31 between Mullah Mustafa accompanied by the principal Kurdish leaders, and the governor of Suleimaniya, Brigadier Abdul Razzak Said Mahmoud, accompanied by Mullah Mustafa's brother Ahmed. Four meetings between Mullah Mustafa and the Governor resulted in a cease-fire agreement that was approved by President Aref and broadcast on the night of February 10.

The principal points in the cease-fire proclamation, apart from the commitment to stop fighting, were these:

1. The government endorsed "the national rights of the Kurds within one Iraqi national unity. This is to be included in the provisional constitution now being formulated."

2. The government promised to release political prisoners and to lift the economic blockade of the Kurdish areas of the north. It undertook to reconstruct demolished areas in the north.

3. The Kurds agreed to permit return of government administrators to the northern areas and to cooperate with government measures to restore "law and security in the northern areas."

When I interviewed President Aref in Baghdad fifteen days after the cease-fire I found him very relaxed, clearly pleased with the deal he had made with the Kurds. He leaned way back in his chair behind the big presidential desk and smiled broadly.

There had not really been an "agreement" with the Kurds, he explained, only a "return to normality" in relations between brothers. And I realized, upon reflection, that the February 10 cease-fire had in fact not been announced in the form of an "agreement" but as separate statements by Barzani and President Aref. All the terms had, furthermore, been contained in the President's statement except the order to cease fire, which was mentioned only in Barzani's statement.

I asked the President whether there would now be negotiations to define the national rights which, according to his statement, would be included in the provisional constitution, and he replied emphatically: "No, no negotiations, no discussions."

Would the President, in that case, please give me his definition of Kurdish national rights, I asked. He replied as though I had asked a general question about national rights rather than one about the Kurds, and as though national rights consisted only of the right to assert national origin. He said every Iraqi individual was free to assert his national origin. "Our Arabic nationalism does not believe in superiority of one nationality over another. Nor do we oblige any people to accept Arab nationality even though all are part of the same Iraqi community."

I was puzzled. Could Barzani, after twenty-nine months of intermittent fighting and suffering, have agreed to a deal like that? What about all the specific "rights" the Kurds had claimed in the memorandum which Jelal Talabani had submitted to the Ba'athist government on April 24, 1963? What about the Kurdish executive and legislative councils, what about the Kurdish claim to a fair share of state revenues, the Kurdish security force, the Kurdish division, the demand that Kurds be named to all official posts in Kurdistan, that Kurdish schools be taught in Kurdish, that the Kurdish language be recognized as an official language?

President Aref seemed to be playing the role of "Great White Father," generously dispensing justice in measured doses. Although there could be no doubt about his desire to end the fighting, he could apparently not bear the idea of dealing with the Kurds as equals, as would be implied by the words "agreement" and "negotiations." And yet the real situation resulting from the failure of the Iraqi army to subdue Barzani's forces, from the Kurds' numerous military successes and from the resistance put up by the Kurdish civil population, required negotiations and agreements.

Eight months previously, during a tour of army positions in the north, President Aref had exhorted Iraqi troops to "clear the area of criminals and traitors." In a speech at the officers' club at Kirkuk he had called for a "complete purge" of the "traitors." The insurgents, he had said, "must be destroyed."

It so happened that for the day after my interview the Ministry of Guidance had organized a trip for foreign correspondents "to the north," with a chance that it might lead to a meeting with Barzani.

A day and a half of interviews with the leading officials of the "north" increased my puzzlement. Like the President, these men clearly wanted to end the fighting. The governor of Suleimaniya, Brigadier Abdul Razzak Said Mahmoud, was full of admiration for Barzani, as "the man who can be trusted," "the best of them all," who is acting "very wisely." He noted the general acceptance of Barzani's leadership, the way in which other leaders accepted his judgment, the respect with which they treated him. He was proud of his own role as chief negotiator with Mullah Mustafa, proud to have presented to the Kurdish leader, after they had signed the February 10 statements, his own Parker 51 fountain pen.

The governor of Kirkuk, General Naif Hamudi, was proud too of his role in writing the letters that seem to have brought about the first moves toward ending the shooting.

The commander of the second division, General Ibrahim Faisal al Ansari, declined an invitation to review the military events of the previous year with the remark that, "It is important to forget the past."

But, as in the case of the President, these men's desire to end the fighting seemed subordinate to their desire to have their own way. General Hamudi astonished us with the information that the Kurds had agreed to hand over their arms to the Iraqi army, and that fifty per cent of them had already done so. These weapons, he said, would be replaced with shotguns, "for use against animals." Informed that there was no mention of handing over arms in the published terms of the cease-fire, he said that it was taking place under a "gentleman's agreement."

The commander of the second division asserted that Barzani was "gradually dissolving his fighting forces," and he added:

"You have an idea that there are two equal forces in the north. This is not true. Barzani is liquidating his forces. And there is no more Barzani movement. The Iraqi army is in control of all Iraq."

The contrast between these statements and what I heard on February 24 and 25 from Jelal Talabani and Mullah Mustafa Barzani was something out of *Alice in Wonderland*.

Jelal Talabani, the Kurds' commander in the south, with whom we spent a full day while awaiting Barzani's return from a boar-shooting expedition, confirmed what I suspected, that there was more to the deal between Kurds and government than the cease-fire proclamations of February 10. Also, that the Kurds were still very much under arms, that they had not handed over any weapons.

Talabani said that in addition to the published terms there were eleven unpublished, secret articles which were the "most important." These articles were not signed. The governor of Kirkuk probably had them in mind when he mentioned a "gentleman's agreement."

Precisely what was in the unpublished agreements neither Barzani nor Talabani said, but I believe the main points were these:

1. In addition to and simultaneously with the conditions listed, the Iraqi army was to withdraw from the Kurdish area. Talabani told me he expected this in March.

2. All units of the Iraqi army except those "normally" stationed there, that is, the second division, were to withdraw from the Kurdish areas of the north.

3. A definition of Kurdish rights, economic, political and cultural, was to be worked out. But how it was to be worked out was apparently not specified.

4. When the government had met these conditions as well as those attached to the cease-fire—release of prisoners and reconstruction, or a beginning of reconstruction, in the north—the Kurds would make the biggest sacrifice of all: they were to dissolve their armed forces. Kurds who had deserted from the Iraqi army with their arms were to return to the army with their arms. Others were to go home.

The main difference between the Kurds' and the government's interpretation of these points was that the government's leading officials talked about the ultimate and conditional Kurdish sacrifice—dissolution of their armed forces—as though it were already a reality. From this they went on to treat the entire complex of agreements as a Kurdish surrender.

In denying the existence of secret agreements with the Kurds as they did in a statement on Baghdad radio the night we returned from our trip to the north, the officials had the technical justification that the agreements were not signed (much as President Aref may have felt that because the original cease-fire was in the form of two statements rather than a single agreement he was correct in denying to me that there was any "agreement" at all, much less negotiations to modify it).

Here surely were flagrant demonstrations of the Arab proclivity for substituting not only words but wishes for reality.

Among the Kurds there were also important differences, between Mullah Mustafa's and Jelal Talabani's views of the cease-fire and the possibilities of a larger settlement.

I felt it was just possible that Barzani sincerely believed this was the historical moment for a real settlement. One could argue that the position was favorable, that the Kurds were in a strong position militarily, that Kurdish leadership furthermore stood intact and strong in contrast to all other political elements within the borders of Iraq which had been ravaged by a succession of fierce purges: First the Kassem revolution had purged the royalists, and after a while the Nasserites; then the Ba'ath revolution had purged the Kassemites and what remained of the Nasserites, and the Communists; finally Aref's revolution had purged the Ba'athists.

But I also felt it possible that behind Mullah Mustafa's words lay a canny conviction that the terms of the cease-fire would not work, that the dissolution of the Kurdish forces would never come about, that he could not trust President Aref or the other officers with whom he was dealing, that he would soon have to fight again, and that his real object in the whole exercise was merely to give his people a rest, to get their supplies, military and civil, replenished.

It is also possible that Mullah Mustafa was uncertain. I got the impression that in contrast to the ebullient, belligerent attitude he had assumed after the cease-fire with the Ba'ath in February 1963, he was deeply troubled, both weary and worried. Remembering the long history of treachery the Kurds have suffered at the hands of their neighbors, he must have wondered whether he was indeed doing the right thing at the right time or whether he was perhaps being maneuvered into a trap.

Mullah Mustafa is not easily read; I could not tell for sure what he had in his mind. The most revealing things he said were these: "We are going to give the government a chance to show what it is willing to do for the Kurds by way of granting national rights. If they don't live up to their promise we will be forced to fight again. . . . We have not yet reached the end of negotiations. When the time comes I will balance the good and the evil and we will decide how to act."

Also revealingly, he made much of the suspicion with which he had treated the government's negotiators. He had at one point proposed that an international commission composed of the American, Soviet and Egyptian ambassadors in Baghdad be invited to witness the agreements reached between himself and the government; he had declined an invitation to go to Baghdad and had instead invited the military governor, General Rashid Musleh, and the prime minister, Major General Taher Yahyia, to come to Ranieh for further talks. Musleh, but not Yahyia, did in fact journey to Ranieh in mid-March.

I asked Barzani whether he was still insisting on the demands made in the memorandum of April 24, 1963. I mentioned the executive and legislative councils, the internal security force, the Kurdish division. He replied in each case that he was not making this demand now.

"Can I say that you have deferred these demands?" I asked. "Yes," he replied. "You may say that."

In sharp contrast to Mullah Mustafa's attitude was that of Jelal Talabani, commander of the southern front. Talabani said quite frankly that he had opposed the cease-fire, that he did not trust Aref or the other leaders of the present regime, and that he expected to fight again. Although he had submitted to Mullah Mustafa's authority, he did not believe it was in the best interests of the Kurds to stop fighting at this time. He believed the Kurds were not only in a strong position, stronger in men and in ground held than they had been in February 1963, but in a position now to make important further advances. He claimed the Kurdish Democratic Party was now organized for action in the towns of Iraq. He discoursed at length about the fourteen battalions—possibly 9000 men—he had helped organize into regular units. He said he had ordered these units to continue intensive, four-hours-a-day field exercises. He said these men would never give up their arms. If ordered to do so, he said, they would fade into the hills.

Talabani's influence is likely to grow. Mullah Mustafa is now sixty years old, right of center in inclination, basically a tribal leader, a man who dislikes party politics, whose mystique of leadership radiates better from a mountain cave in times of adversity than from a conference room in times of peace. Talabani, on the other hand, is only thirty, inclined to the left, a political party man; he is the dashing young man, who has distinguished himself in battle, in negotiation, as a propagandist. If there is any such thing, he is today Barzani's "number two." Some regard him as the crown prince.

My conclusions about the situation in the spring of 1964 are these:

I can see plenty of grounds for future conflict and misunderstanding between the Kurds and the government, in implementing the terms of the cease-fire and in carrying on further negotiations and agreements as provided in the unpublished and unsigned articles of the "gentleman's agreement" that accompanied the cease-fire. I can see plenty of grounds for future conflict between Mullah Mustafa and Jelal Talabani.

And yet, in Kurdistan in the spring of 1964, the really important thing is that there is a chance for peace.

LANDMARKS

2350 B.C. First mention of the kingdom of Gutium by Lugal-anni-Mundu, king of Sumerian city of Agab, on a foundation memorial tablet.

2264 B.C. First invasion of Babylon by Gutium.

1600 B.C. Invasion of Babylon by the Kassites (Lurs).

13th century B.C. Assyria defeats the Guti, Kassites, and Babylonians.

612 B.C. King Cyaxares, the Mede, of Gutium, allied with Babylon, destroys the Assyrian Empire.

550 B.C. Cyrus the Persian overthrows Astyages of Gutium, and the Achaemenian power with its capital at Persepolis replaces the Medes.

538 B.C. King Ugubaro's Guti cavalry helps Cyrus to occupy Babylon.

486–465 B.C. Xerxes reigns over the joint empire of the Medes and Persians.

331 B.C. Alexander defeats Darius III at Arbela, thereby destroying the Achaemenian Empire.

3rd century A.D. Organized Christian communities in Kurdistan.

640 Caliphs of Islam begin Arab invasions of the Persian Empire, including Kurdistan.

12th century First Seljuk invasions.

1138–1193 Life of Saladin.

1210–1500 Mongol and Tatar invasions.

1514 Sultan Selim I defeats Shah Ismail Safavid at Chalderan. Kurdish princes support the Sultan, who recognizes self-governing Kurdish principalities.

1596 Prince Sharafeddin writes book on Kurdish principalities.

1588–1638 Turkish-Persian wars.

1650–1706 Life of Ahmed Khane, author of *Mem u Zin,* Kurdish patriotic classic.

1834–1839⎱ Attempts by Ottoman Empire to impose its
1842–1847⎰ authority, collect taxes and recruit soldiers in semi-autonomous Kurdish areas; Kurdish rebellions.

1847 Kurdish Prince Badrikhan of Bitlis surrenders to General Osman Pasha.

1881–1885 Revolt of Sheikh Ubeidullah of Shamdinan.

1908 Young Turk Revolution; first Kurdish club and first Kurdish national school, Constantinople.

1914–1918 Kurdish and Armenian provinces devastated; Armenian massacres; mass deportation of Kurds.

1918, 1922 Sheikh Mahmoud Barzindji under British protection, quasi-autonomous at Suleimaniya.

1920 Treaty of Sèvres recognizes Kurds' rights to autonomy or independence, but not signed by the Turkish government and remains unimplemented.

1923 Treaty of Lausanne signed with Turks; ignores Kurdish problem but guarantees minority rights; leaves disposition of Mosul up to League of Nations.

1925 Sheikh Said leads Kurdish rebellion.

October 28, 1927 Declaration of Kurdish independence by the Hoyboun.

1925–1938 Repeated rebellions of Kurds in eastern Turkey; Kurds killed or dispersed on massive scale.

1931 Mullah Mustafa Barzani leads his first revolt in Iraq.

1943–1945 Barzani rebellion in Iraq.

1946 Kurdish republic at Mehabad in Iran; Barzani one of principal military leaders.

1947 Mullah Mustafa Barzani escapes to the Soviet Union.

1958 Mullah Mustafa Barzani returns from the Soviet Union to Baghdad.

September 10, 1961 Kurdish war for autonomy in Iraq begins.

February 8, 1963 Kassem regime in Iraq overthrown; Barzani supports new Ba'athist regime.

June 10, 1963 Ba'athist regime of Iraq attacks Kurds.

November 18, 1963 Army ousts Ba'athists.

INDEX